Youth, Identity, Power

Youth, Identity, Power

The Chicano Movement

◆

CARLOS MUÑOZ, JR.

Revised and Expanded Edition

VERSO
London • New York

First published by Verso 1989
© 1989, 2007 Carlos Muñoz, Jr.
All rights reserved.

The moral rights of the author have been asserted

3 5 7 9 10 8 6 4

Verso
UK: 6 Meard Street, London W1F 0EG
USA: 20 Jay Street, Suite 1010, Brooklyn, NY 11201
www.versobooks.com

Verso is the imprint of New Left Books

ISBN-13: 978-1-84467-134-2   (hbk)
ISBN-13: 978-1-84467-142-7   (pbk)

British Library Cataloguing in Publication Data
A catalogue record for this book is available from the British Library

Library of Congress Cataloging-in-Publication Data
A catalog record for this book is available from the Library of Congress

Printed in the USA

Contents

Para Chela, mi amorcito corazón y sueño realizado

Acknowledgements

It has been a long road from my birthplace in *el segundo barrio* in El Paso, Texas to the completion of this book. Ralph C. Guzmán nurtured my love for teaching. Ernesto Galarza was a constant source of inspiration as an activist and scholar and encouraged me to attempt the project. May they both rest in peace. I am eternally grateful for the comradeship of those I worked with in the building of UMAS and MEChA, especially Maria Baeza, Monte Perez, Carlos Jackson, Herlinda Quintero, Arturo 'Tudy' Sandoval, Oscar Martinez, Gloria and Richard Santillán, Gil Cárdenas, Raul Granados,Connie Arriaga, Pat Borjon, Carlos Navarro, Lillian Roybal, Juan Gómez-Quiñones, Raúl Ruiz, Luis Arroyo, José Joel Garcia, Ysidro Ramon Macias, Frank Hidalgo, Jesús Treviño, Moctezuma Esparza, Hank Lopez, Susan Racho, Castulo de la Rocha, Henry Gutiérrez, Anna Nieto-Gómez, Christina Vega and Jorge González. Felix Gutierrez, Maria Lopez, and Maria Diaz were key supporters while serving as staff in the California State University at Los Angeles administration.

I also am grateful for the comradeship of those I worked with in the building of La Raza Unida Party, especially Daniel Moreno, Armando Navarro, Richard Santillán, José Angel Gutiérrez, Mario Compeán and Raúl Ruiz; and those with whom I worked in building the National Association for Chicana and Chicano Studies, especially during its formative stages: Mario Barrera, Lea Ybarra, Daniel Moreno, Tomás Almaguer, Ray Burrola, José Cuellar,

Victor Nelson Cisneros, Ada Sosa Riddell, José Limón, Belinda Herrera and Reynaldo Macias.

Chapter 1 would not have been possible without the assistance of librarian Richard Chabran, who obtained a complete set of The Mexican Voice on microfilm for my use. I am grateful to Felix Gutiérrez, Jr., and René Cardona for allowing me access to unpublished documents and materials from the private papers of the 1930s Mexican-American Movement founders Félix Gutiérrez and Paul Coronel. I deeply appreciate the time taken by veterans of MAM and former officials of the YMCA who granted me interviews and answered my correspondence, especially Charles Van Winkle, Harold Wagner, Juan Acevedo, Manuel Ceja, Guadalberto Valdez, Steve Reyes, Taylor Reedy, Clifford Carey, Sam Frazier, Manuel Ruiz, Jr., and Bert Corona who, although not a member of MAM, was a participant in the Mexican Youth Conferences that gave birth to MAM.

Américo Paredes, Bert Corona, Ernesto Galarza, Edward Roybal, Octavio Romano-V. (may they all rest in peace), Luis Valdez, Chris Ruiz and Rudy Acuña provided much information essential to chapter 2.

Chapter 3 benefited from interviews with Reies Lopez Tijerina, Rudy Acuña, Sal Castro, Jorge Garcia, Katia Panas, Irma Castro, Juan González, Vicente Cabeza de Baca, Anna Nieto-Gómez, René Núñez, Christina Rodriguez, Castulo de La Rocha, Luis Nogales, Ron Lopez, Luis Valdez, Carlos Jackson, Juan Gómez-Quiñones, Ludy Tapia, Christina Vega, Armando Valdez, René Cardona, José Joel Garcia, Pablo Sanchez, Lea Ybarra, Jesús Chavarría, Alex Saragoza, Eliezer Risco-Lozada, Robert Carrillo, Luis Arroyo, and Ysidro Ramon Macias. Andres Jimenez assisted me with the interviews. Librarian Francisco Garcia-Ayvens facilitated the acquisition of FBI documents on organizations of the Chicano Movement through the Freedom of Information Act and compiled a bibliography of materials on the movement for my use.

Chapter 4 benefited from interviews with La Raza Unida Party activists, especially José Angel Gutiérrez, Mario Compeán, Raúl Ruiz, Armando Navarro, and Richard Santillán. Mario Barrera co-authored one of my early essays on the party, that contributed to the development of this chapter. Elena Flores and Mario Barrera assisted in the interviews of party activists.

I also appreciate the research assistance I received from Beatrice Pesquera and Patricia Zavella who were graduate students at the time and are now two of my distinguished colleagues.

The first edition underwent many revisions during the ten years it took to complete it. Early chapters were edited by Tomás González. The final draft was improved by the editorial work of Betita Martinez and Steven Hiatt. I was greatly helped at various stages of writing by the useful suggestions and insightful comments of my wife, Graciela Rios Muñoz, Ernesto Galarza, Carlos Cortez, Ron Takaki, Larry Trujillo, Alex Saragoza, Francisco Hernandez, Tomás Almaguer, Mario Barrera, Daniel Moreno, Clayborne Carson, Rudy Acuña, Peter Salomon, Margarita Melville, Mike Davis, Albert Camarillo, Armando Valdez, Octavio Romano-V., Jesús Martinez and Charles Henry.

Steven Hiatt did all the editing for this second edition. I appreciated his diligence and patience throughout the several drafts he worked on. I am grateful to my wife, Chela Rios Muñoz, Maria Baeza, Mario Barrera, Danny Moreno, and Norma Alarcón for graciously taking the time to critically read drafts of my preface and epilogue and providing me with helpful suggestions and comments. I am also grateful to Beatrice Pesquera, Lillian Castillo-Speed, Betita Martinez, Maria Elena Gaitan, and Jesús Treviño for their prompt responses to my requests for specific information essential to the revisions I made in this edition.

I remain grateful to Abel Amaya, who, when working for the Ford Foundation, helped me get a grant that enabled me to travel during a sabbatical in 1974 to collect information and interview movement activists throughout the US. I thank Armando Valdez, former director of La Causa Publications, for permission to use sections from *El Plan de Santa Barbara* and Raúl Ruiz for permission to use photos from *La Raza* magazine and *Chicano Student News*. I have received the enthusiastic support of the UC Berkeley Chicano Studies program and library staff of past years and the present; Myrna Flores, Rosa Johnson, Nelly Quiñonez, Dorothy Thomas, Gabrielle Schubert, Maria Hernandez, Magali Zuniga, Ana Cornonado, Chris Wuesthoff, Luis Reyna (may he rest in peace), Lillian Castillo-Speed and Carolyn Soto. My thanks also to all my activist students who throughout the years dedicated themselves to keeping alive the positive aspects of the legacy of the Chicano movement and the other civil rights movements of the 1960s.

My family has been the most important source of strength in my life. I regret that my parents, Carlos Garcia Muñoz and Clementina Contreras, did not live long enough to see the fruits of their labor. May they rest in peace. My children, by order of age, Carlos, Marina, Genaro, Daniel, and Marcelo have been and always will be an important part of my life. I did not have grand-

children when I wrote the first edition of this book. I now have seven. Their
names are, by order of age, Esperanza, Emany, Amaya, Chloe, Sydni, Joshua,
and Hailee. They are one of the major reasons why I have continued to march
for freedom, peace and justice in the world and to speak truth to power. My
wife, Chela Rios Muñoz, has been my constant source of encouragement and
support as lover, best friend, best critic, and compañera de la vida. I dedicate
this book to her.

Preface to the Second Edition:
Reframing the Chicano Movement

The second edition of *Youth, Identity, Power* commemorates the 40th anniversary of the two key events that sparked the emergence of the Chicano Civil Rights Movement, which came to be known simply as the Chicano Movement. The first took place during the first week of March 1968, on the streets of East Los Angeles when over ten thousand students walked out of four high schools. The student strike, called the 'walkouts' and 'blow-outs' by its organizers, lasted a week and a half. It disrupted the largest school district in the nation and captured front-page headlines and national attention. The second was the arrest three months later of thirteen civil rights activists who were identified as the organizers of the walkouts. It marked the first time that Mexican American activists had ever been imprisoned on charges of conspiracy. Within a year other student strikes occurred throughout the southwestern US, and new militant and radical youth organizations emerged to identify themselves as part of the Chicano Movement.

The major purpose of the Los Angeles walkouts was to protest racist teachers and school policies, the lack of freedom of speech, the lack of teachers of Mexican descent, the absence of classes on Mexican and Mexican American culture and history, and the inferior education provided to Mexican American students. In addition to its historical significance to Mexican Americans as their first large-scale protest in US history, the walkouts marked the entry by youth of Mexican descent into the history of the turbulent sixties as they

1

engaged for the first time in direct mass civil rights protest.

The walkouts and the arrests of the thirteen activists marks a personal historic life changing moment for me. I was one of the organizers of those high school student walkouts and one of the thirteen arrested. I was then a Vietnam War–era veteran, an activist in the anti-war movement, attending college on the G.I. Bill. I was a first-year graduate student in political science at California State University at Los Angeles where I was president of the United Mexican American Students (UMAS). I was arrested in the early morning hours by Los Angeles County sheriff's deputies who stormed into my apartment wearing riot gear and with guns drawn. I had been hard at work on a research paper due the next day in my graduate seminar on international communism. The seminar was taught by an anti-communist professor; I had taken the seminar because it was required for my master's degree and I was far from being a communist. But when one of the deputies found books by Karl Marx, V. I. Lenin, and Leon Trotsky on my kitchen table, he shouted, "We've got the goods on him!"

My arrest and that of the twelve other Mexican American students and community activists was orchestrated through the FBI's Counter Intelligence Program (COINTELPRO), which coordinated city, state, and military intelligence agencies throughout the nation. COINTELPRO's purpose was to undermine the civil rights, anti-war, and other protest movements of the 1960s. We were then indicted on 27 May 1968 by the Los Angeles County Grand Jury for conspiracy to "violate the Educational Code of California" and "disturb the peace and quiet of neighborhoods" in the City of Los Angeles. Normally, disrupting the peace is considered a misdemeanor. But *conspiring* to commit a misdemeanor was considered a felony – a manipulation of the legal system much favored by district attorneys at the time. Each one of us thus faced a total of sixty-six years in prison if found guilty on all the counts enumerated in the indictments. As defendants we became publicly known as the 'East Los Angeles 13' in the community and throughout the Chicano Movement. Our case marked the third time conspiracy charges were used against activists involved in protest activities. The first case, that of the Oakland 7, involved the leaders of 'Oakland Stop the Draft Week' in Oakland, California in the fall of 1967, and the second, student and faculty antiwar protestors at the University of Iowa. The fourth group of defendants was the famous Chicago 7, who were charged with conspiracy for the disturbances that occurred in August 1968 during the Democratic Party's presidential nominating convention.[1]

Two years after our arrest and imprisonment, a California appellate court ruled that we were not guilty by virtue of the First Amendment to the US Constitution, with our protests being protected as free exercise of speech. In the law books, this case is known as the *People v. Castro et al.*[2]

A year after the walkouts and the East L.A. 13 case, approximately a thousand representatives from movement organizations met in March 1969 in Denver, Colorado at the first National Chicano Youth Liberation Conference. It was hosted by the Crusade for Justice, a civil rights organization founded by Rodolfo 'Corky' Gonzalez. The conference adopted *El Plan Espiritual de Aztlán / The Spiritual Plan of Aztlán*, a manifesto advocating civil rights, social and economic justice, and self-determination in the context of a Chicano cultural nationalist framework. In a sense, *El Plan Espiritual de Aztlán* merged the ideas of nonviolence articulated by Dr. Martin Luther King, Jr., and later adopted by César Chávez, with the more militant revolutionary Black Nationalist ideology espoused by Malcolm X.

The following month, approximately 100 Mexican American student leaders, faculty, and staff, from throughout California held a conference on the campus of the University of California, Santa Barbara. I was one of the organizers of the conference. Our purpose was to produce a plan of action to institutionalize Chicano equal opportunity programs (EOP), Chicano Studies programs, and other programs to serve Chicano students on the state's college campuses and aimed at serving the educational needs of Mexican American youth. At the urging of student activists who had participated at the Denver Conference, the conference also became the site for the founding of El Movimiento Estudiantil Chicano de Aztlán (MEChA). MEChA became the largest of the student organizations that made up the Chicano student movement, spreading across college and university campuses throughout the southwestern United States and other areas of the nation where Mexican American student activism was emerging. MEChA, the Mexican American Youth Organization (MAYO) and other student organizations played a major role in the building of the Chicano Movement.[3]

Prior to my participation in the walkouts, I had been involved, along with other UMAS members, in an effort to develop a Mexican American Studies Department on our campus. Mexican American faculty with PhDs were practically invisible in academia at that time. As I document in Chapter 5, there were only a handful throughout the nation. That is why graduate students like me, as well as undergraduates, were the ones involved in the development of the initial Chicano Studies Programs in California and elsewhere. After my release from prison on bail, I was therefore asked by UMAS to serve as the chair of what turned out to be the first Mexican American Studies Department in the nation. It was renamed Chicano Studies after the Santa Barbara conference. We started teaching two courses in the fall semester of 1968. I taught the Chicano Politics course and Gilbert Gonzalez, another graduate student, taught the Chicano History course.

In 1970, I played a leadership role in the founding of La Raza Unida Party and was an organizer for the party in California until 1972. It was the first independent Mexican American political party in US history. In 1973, I became a cofounder and chair of the National Association for Chicano Studies, which later evolved into the National Association for Chicana and Chicano Studies.

This book is a direct product of my participation in these events and organizations that contributed to the making of the Chicano Movement. As I noted in the first edition, I did not offer it as the definitive study of the Chicano Movement. I viewed it as a first step toward a critical documentation of the movement and a more complete history of the sixties. I am pleased that other scholars have since produced books toward that end.[4] I placed my book in the context of the political and intellectual development of Mexican Americans. I did not rely entirely on my own participation and observation, but incorporated information from primary sources – unpublished movement documents, movement newspapers, and interviews with key movement leaders. My concern was not to write a romantic interpretation of the movement but rather to produce a critical study useful to understanding the history of the sixties and specifically to understanding the roots of the Chicano Movement, its contributions and the lessons to be learned from the past that can be useful in shaping future struggles.

I have not made major revisions in this second edition of *Youth, Identity, Power*. The revisions I have made are meant to underscore the fact that women were an important part of the Chicano Movement, as they have been throughout history in all Mexican American struggles prior to the movement's emergence.[5] I have included an analysis of gender issues as the women of the movement raised them, not as an expert on gender, but in the spirit of critical study and self-reflection. When I wrote the first edition, my main concern was to capture the historic moment of a movement that was focused on racial and ethnic inequality, not a struggle against other injustices, including gender inequality.

In my personal life, I had grown away from some of the negative male-centered attitudes and behavior associated with Mexican and US patriarchal cultures. My experience as a single parent had contributed toward my re-examination of family gender roles and patriarchy. My research on revolutions in Mexico and the Third World had opened my eyes to the historical reality that women played important roles in struggles for social change. I respected women and supported their efforts to overcome the patriarchal obstacles in their paths, especially in higher education. I took sides with women against domestic violence and confronted the men who victimized them. Despite my personal experiences, however, I did not feel I had an adequate critical understanding of gender issues to offer a more substantial analysis beyond the points I made in the first edition.

The men and women of the Chicano Movement were products of both a patriarchal and a homophobic culture. In contrast to gender issues, however, gay and lesbian issues did not emerge within the movement until after its decline.[6] We were therefore not confronted with those issues at the time of the Chicano Movement. However, since gays and lesbians have of course been part of Mexican American communities, there must have been movement activists who were gay or lesbian. My exposure to gay/lesbian issues after the movement and my interaction with gay/lesbian activists in social justice and anti-war movements since the 1960s contributed to my re-examination of my own homophobia. Unfortunately, there continues to be an absence of literature specifically focused on the gay/lesbian activist experience in the Chicano Movement, which remains one of the missing chapters of the movement's history to be researched and written. Over the years, I have encouraged my gay and lesbian graduate students to undertake the task of documenting that experience. It is my hope that a study will be published in the near future that will shed light on homophobia in the movement as experienced by activists.

The men and women of the Chicano Movement rejected the accommodationist and assimilationist politics of the Mexican-American generation of the 1930s. But we did not break away from the Mexican patriarchal and homophobic cultural traditions that historically had defined the gender roles of both men and women. As products of both Mexican and US cultures, both of which are marked by strong patriarchal and homophobic structures and practices, we did not question traditional gender roles and did not confront our homophobia at the time of the movement's emergence. The student and community organizations that initially became part of the Chicano Movement were, with rare exceptions, characterized by male leadership. Gender roles in the movement thus mirrored the traditional roles played out in Mexican American families. Men became the public leaders, duly elected or selected to fill those roles by the male and female constituencies of those organizations. One of the popular posters of the movement that underscored its patriarchal nature read 'La Familia de La Raza' and featured images of both parents and their children, but with the father as the dominant figure.

This explains in part why I became the president of UMAS at my college campus. I was one of two students nominated. The other was Maria Baeza. I was personally impressed with her leadership skills and told her that I would gladly be her vice president. Maria expressed two important reservations: As a green card holder and not yet an American citizen, she felt vulnerable and feared that she would not be protected under the country's equal rights laws. Additionally, she felt strongly that, not withstanding her demonstrated leadership skills, most male and some female members of UMAS were not ready to follow the lead of a female president. Maria was a political science major and, like many other young women in the movement, keenly aware of the national discussion on feminism. She engaged other students in discussions concerning the differentiation of gender roles expressed in Betty Friedan's *Feminine Mystique* and the ideas found in Simone de Beauvoir's *The Second Sex*. Although written by white feminists, those books compelled both male and female UMAS activists to begin to question and reevaluate their traditional roles, though initially with little apparent impact. Maria was elected vice-president of UMAS during my tenure as president. Had she been president, as I proposed, she might have been arrested and deported as an 'outside agitator'.[7] In addition, as a woman, she may have met more difficulties in leading the organization than I encountered. Indeed, the few young women who took on the challenge of serving as the heads of student and community organizations did not have an easy time dealing with the sexism that permeated the movement.

Reflecting the patriarchal nature of both Mexican and US cultures, it is no coincidence that those who became the major national leaders of the Chicano Movement were men. Rodolfo 'Corky' Gonzales led the Crusade for Justice, and José Angel Gutierrez led La Raza Unida Party. The leaders of two other Mexican American movements that achieved national visibility were also men: Reies Lopez Tijerina, leader of the land grants movement in New Mexico, and César Chávez, the leader of the farm worker movement in California.

The patriarchal nature of the student and Chicano movements as a whole did not mean that women did not play important and significant roles in the development of the movement from the time of the 1968 East Los Angeles walkouts.[8] They may not have been as visible as the (male) national or state leaders of the movement, but many were leading organizers, especially at the local community levels. Whereas men were the visible leaders, women for the most part were the 'behind the scenes' organizers responsible for effective mass mobilization, communications, and the day-to-day tasks of movement building, which included recruitment into the movement. In addition, they performed the duties of secretaries, cooks, and other tasks that women normally performed in their families.

In the epilogue to this second edition I critically analyze the changes that have taken place since *Youth, Identity, Power* was published. The Latino/a population has undergone profound demographic changes and the world is now very different than it was in the 1960s. When the Chicano Movement emerged, there were only three visible Latino/a groups in the nation, with Mexican Americans the overwhelming majority. The other two groups were the Puerto Ricans and Cubans. There are now seventeen distinct Latino/a groups as a result of globalization. US intervention and economic domination throughout the Americas has resulted in a much more complex Latino/a population. Latino/a immigration, legal and illegal, has been fueled by displacement in their homelands due to civil wars and economic upheavals brought about by neoliberal free market economic policies.

Globalization has also contributed to redefining the politics of these times. The revolutionary politics of the 1960s gave way to the conservative counter-revolution. The United States has become a global empire far beyond the dreams of the Founding Fathers. They had designs to expand the US empire throughout the Americas, but the Bush imperial presidency has far exceeded their dreams. The war in Iraq, although it has become another Vietnam War–style guerrilla conflict with no military victory in sight, has demonstrated the military superiority of the US empire throughout the world. Few nations dared to attempt to stop President Bush from declaring war on a sovereign nation that had nothing to do with the 9/11 terrorist acts. Indeed, no one in the US Congress, with the exception of Congresswoman Barbara Lee, spoke out against it.

The Bush administration created the Department of Homeland Security after 9/11 to fight terrorism at home – but as part of this initiative it declared war on undocumented Latino immigrants. The US–Mexico border is now a militarized zone. A massive wall dividing the two countries was built, ostensibly to stop the waves of poor men, women, and children who enter the US in search for work and a better life. Conservatives, as well as many liberals, perceive them as potential terrorists and as a serious threat to the dominant eurocentric culture of the United States.

Globalization has also had serious consequences for Latino/as and other people of color, especially the working class and the poor, with the poor becoming poorer while a small elite has profited enormously. The Democratic and Republican parties have both become more ever more devoted to the interests of the corporations and the military-industrial complex. During elections, the Democrats express concern for the welfare of the middle class but not for the poor or working class. Once known as the party of the working man during the presidency of Franklin D. Roosevelt, the Democratic Party has become as conservative as the Republicans on matters dealing with the economy. The conservative counter-revolution succeeded in turning back the clock on many of the positive contributions of the Chicano Movement and other movements of the 1960s. Conservatives have thus so far succeeded in preserving the structure of racial/ethnic/class/heterosexual patriarchal privilege that has characterized US society.

I conclude my epilogue with a call to forge a new radical politics based on the lessons of the Chicano Movement. I argue that this new movement must be based on the critical understanding that the struggle for social justice must be a struggle against all forms of oppression inclusive of gender, race, ethnicity, class, sexuality, and disability. It must be a politics that does not perpetuate the limited democracy of the present. It must instead be a politics framed with a new vision of an authentic multiracial and multiethnic democracy that will promote social justice and peace at home and throughout the world.

Notes

1 See Ian F. Haney López, *Racism on Trial: The Chicano Fight for Justice*, Cambridge, Mass. 2003, for the legal, racial, and political context of the case.

2 One of the thirteen was high school teacher Salvador Castro, whose name topped the alphabetized list of the East LA 13. In addition to Castro and me, the others were Carlos Montes, David Sánchez, Eliezer Risco, Patricio Sánchez, Moctezuma Esparza, Joe Razo, Ralph Ramirez, Fred López, Richard Vigil, Gilberto Cruz Olmeda, and Henry Gómez.

3 An excellent study of this student organization is Armando Navarro, *Mexican American Youth Organization: Avant-Garde of the Chicano Movement in Texas*, Austin 1995.
4 See, for example, George Mariscal, *Brown-Eyed Children of the Sun*, Albuquerque 2005; Alma M. Garcia, ed., *Chicana Feminist Thought: The Basic Historical Writings*, New York 1997; Ernesto Chavez, *Mi Raza Primero*, Berkeley 2002; Lorena Oropeza, *¡Raza Si! ¡Guerra No!: Chicano Protest and Patriotism During the Viet Nam War Era*, Berkeley 2005; Lorena Oropeza and Dionne Espinosa, eds, *Enriqueta Vazquez and the Chicano Movement*, Houston 2006; Armando Navarro, *La Raza Unida Party*, Philadelphia 2000; Ernesto B. Vigil, *The Crusade for Justice*, Madison, Wis. 1999; Dionne Espinosa, *Revolutionary Sisters: Chicana Activism, Cultural Nationalism, and Feminism in the Chicano Movement*, forthcoming 2008.
5 See Elizabeth 'Betita' Martinez, ed., *500 Years of Chicana Women's History* (forthcoming from Rutgers University Press in 2007).
6 The first book that critiqued homophobia in Mexican American culture as a whole was Cherríe Moraga and Gloria Anzaldúa, eds, *This Bridge Called My Back: Writings by Radical Women of Color*, Watertown, Mass. 1981.
7 Interview with Maria Baeza.
8 See Dolores Delgado Bernal, 'Grassroots Leadership Reconceptualized: Chicana Oral Histories and the 1968 East Los Angeles School Blowouts' in *Frontiers*, vol. 19, no. 2 (1998), pp. 113–42; Dionne Espinoza, '"Revolutionary Sisters": Women's Solidarity and Collective Identification among Chicana Brown Berets in East Los Angeles, 1967–1970', *Aztlán*, vol. 26, no. 1, Spring 2001, pp. 17–58.

Introduction

The Chicano Movement and the Sixties

The history of the United States has been marked by periods of mass protest and political struggle against class exploitation, unpopular wars, and racial and gender inequality. The decade of the 1960s was unique, however, because it marked the first time that youth *as* youth played a central role in the shaping of oppositional movements aimed at those in power. It was also unique because the politics of those times were characterized by mass protest specifically aimed at the resolution of policy debates traditionally limited to established institutions. Young people had never before taken to the streets by the thousands to dramatically challenge those institutions responsible for the perpetuation of racial inequality at home and military intervention abroad.

Youth protest led to the creation of student movements that helped to shape larger struggles for social and political equality. In the South, African American student protest gave birth to the Student Nonviolent Coordinating Committee (SNCC), which became a major force in the development of the civil rights movement.[1] From the ranks of SNCC came men and women who played key roles in the formation of the Black student unions (BSUs) and the larger Black Power Movement of which they were an integral part. Mexican American student protest in the Southwest led to the formation of El Movimiento Estudiantil Chicano de Aztlán. MEChA and other Mexican American student organizations contributed heavily to the development of the Chicano Power Movement. They also played a key role in the building

11

of a Chicano political party, La Raza Unida Party. In Chicago and New York, Puerto Rican student activists contributed to the formation of the Young Lords Party and the Puerto Rican nationalist movement.[2] Asian American and Native American student activists were perhaps less visible, but they were also participants in the formation of opposition movements in their communities. Students for a Democratic Society (SDS) and Berkeley's Free Speech Movement (FSM) contributed to the building of a national white student movement and the New Left.[3] They became the major force behind the development of the movement against the war in Vietnam.

The literature about the 1960s and in particular about student radicalism and protest has mushroomed in recent years. By 1968 twelve books and sixty-four articles had been published on the 1964 Berkeley student revolt and the Free Speech Movement alone. Now there are dozens more books about that tumultuous decade. Some recent works have limited their focus to a single year, 1968, as the most dramatic and significant of the decade. Nonwhite student radicalism and protest, however, is generally missing from the pages of the literature on the 1960s. The history of that decade has been largely presented as a history of white middle-class youth radicalism and protest.

Much has been published about the African American civil rights movement, but it is the SDS, the FSM, and the white New Left that have been perceived as the major youth protagonists of the 1960s. In addition, those who have written about the civil rights movement from a nonwhite perspective largely ignore the role of nonwhite youth and students in it. Their role has been overshadowed by the figure of Dr. Martin Luther King, Jr., and the role played by Black middle-class civil rights organizations like the National Association for the Advancement of Colored People (NACCP). Clayborne Carson's book on SNCC, *In Struggle*, is the only substantial work available on the role of students in the making of the Southern civil rights movement.

Various explanations have been offered by white scholars and former sixties radicals for their failure to incorporate nonwhite youth radicalism into their work. Sociologist Richard Flacks, a founder of SDS and one of the most quoted authorities on student protest, explained his focus on white youth in this way:

Given my experience, research and background, I have found it necessary to exclude some issues of great importance. In particular, I have been unable to write with any authority on the situation and actions of black and other third world youth. Similarly, I have failed to come to grips systematically with the problems of working-class white youth. Thus, what you will find here is woefully 'ethnocentric' (as is much of academic sociology and contemporary white radicalism). I could not bring myself to theorize about matters that were beyond my direct experience.[4]

Another scholar explained his exclusion of nonwhite youth from his research on the grounds that it was 'abnormally difficult' for him to 'discover' how they operated since, for example, membership in the Black student unions was 'exclusively reserved to blacks', their meetings were 'closed, and their communication with other black groups' was secret.[5]

Yet another expert gave a different explanation for his exclusion of non-white student radicalism. Seymour Martin Lipset believed that the Black student movement was not radical enough to merit serious consideration. In his mind, white student radicalism advocated potentially revolutionary changes in society, whereas Black student activists represented a reformist politics:

Their principal objectives are not to change the fundamental character of the society or to engage in expressive personal protest, but rather to improve the position of blacks within the larger society generally and inside the university in particular. Although to achieve their objectives they often find it necessary to engage in militant, sometimes violent forms of protest ... their goals are ... a better life, more money, a job with higher status, social dignity.[6]

Other scholars have followed Lipset's example. David Westby, for example, did not view Black student radicalism as worth 'independent analysis' because it was simply an 'extension or outreach of the ghetto revolts', and those revolts in his mind aimed only at opening up opportunities for African Americans:

This has given the campus politics of blacks-*qua*-blacks a very different cast from student protest generally ... it has been able to garner considerable faculty support, largely because, despite the rhetoric and confrontations, it has been a demand for social justice in harmony ... with American abstract values, if not practice.[7]

Without any critical examination of the Black student movement, Westby concludes that its leadership resisted attempts to align with white radicals because of the 'dangers' such an alliance would pose to the 'typically limited, reformist goals' of Black student protest.[8]

The work of New Left scholars in the 1980s continued to promote the false image that the history of the 1960s was a history centered on white radical middle-class youth. One example was a book by a collection of former sixties radicals, *The 60s Without Apology*. It was acclaimed as the 'most serious overall assessment of the 60s yet to appear' because it 'captures the diversity of the experience of the decade'.[9] Nevertheless, the book narrowly focuses on the white New Left. There are only two pieces on the Black experience and one on Native American students out of ten chapters and forty-six assorted personal statements by sixties radicals. The Mexican American and other nonwhite experiences were excluded. Another example is the highly praised *The Sixties: Years of Hope, Days of Rage* by another SDS founder, Todd Gitlin. Gitlin promotes the idea of the white New Left as the 'dynamic center of the decade'.[10] Athough he briefly acknowledges the importance of African Americans in the making of that history, Gitlin does not even footnote the contributions made by Mexican American or other nonwhite youth. George Katsiaficas is the only white New Left scholar who has produced a book, *The Imagination of the New Left*, that places the New Left and the 1960s into a global analytical framework that incorporates both white and nonwhite youth radicalism.[11]

Not surprisingly, Hollywood has yet to produce a film with a focus on nonwhite youth activism in the 1960s. Countless movies have appeared, ranging from *The Big Chill* to more recent ones like *1968* and *1969*, all with white middle-class youth as protagonists. Even the first major motion picture to be made about the civil rights movement, *Mississippi Burning* has a white hero in what was the struggle of a Southern Black community for civil rights. To add insult to injury, the unlikely hero of *Mississippi Burning* is an FBI agent. The record shows that the FBI did very little to protect the lives of Black people in the South. On the contrary, the FBI's counter-intelligence or COINTELPRO program attempted to destroy the civil rights movement and undermine the positions of Martin Luther King and other leaders.[12]

Commemorations of the 1960s in the mainstream print media have also followed the same pattern, promoting it as a decade of white political activists. *Time* magazine, for example, in its 11 January 1988 issue called 1968 'the year that shaped a generation'. Its headline story and dramatic photos capture many of the events and movements in the news of that year, but the focus is on white liberal and radical political figures and celebrities from Robert F. Kennedy to rock singer Janis Joplin to white student leaders like Mark Rudd. The assassination of Dr. King is mentioned, and the civil rights and Black Power movements receive scant attention. But the Chicano Movement is ignored, as are Mexican American political leaders. Interestingly, even César Chávez is not included in spite of the fact that he appeared on the cover of *Time* in 1968.

More political and intellectual public events commemorating the decade of the 1960s have for the most part also focused on the legacy of the white student movement and the New Left. Two examples come readily to mind. The first was the twentieth anniversary of the Free Speech Movement, held at the Berkeley campus of the University of California, in which I participated. Mario Savio, one of the former FSM leaders, once again spoke eloquently on the steps of Sproul Plaza to thousands of students surrounding and on the rooftops of buildings overlooking the 'free speech' plaza area. Later, hundreds more jammed into Wheeler Auditorium, the largest lecture hall on campus, to listen attentively to other ex-FSM leaders and their stories about how their struggle came to be. Nostalgically, they recounted how the whole world watched them making history.

One evening was devoted to a 'third world' panel of former sixties radicals from the Chicano, Black, Asian, and Native American movements. They had been invited to speak about their experiences and how they had contributed to the making of the history of the 1960s. They addressed a near empty hall. Most of the few in attendance were people of color. This panel did not get the local and national media coverage common to FSM events during that week. There were no reporters or television cameras. Even the left-leaning student newspaper, *The Daily Californian*, did not assign a reporter to cover the panel, nor did the paper mention the event in the next day's edition.

The second event commemorating the 1960s was a symposium held in 1987 in San Francisco. It was entitled 'The Sixties, Its Leaders and Its Legacy'. The featured speakers were white radical sixties celebrities, including Abbie Hoffman, drug guru Timothy Leary, and feminist writer Betty Friedan. When I asked if a Mexican American had been invited, I was told that none had because 'they were probably not involved in the struggles of the sixties'. Ironically, the symposium was organized by a professor of history at San Francisco State University, the site of the first major college student strike of the 1960s led by African American and Mexican American student activists.

The twentieth anniversary commemoration events for the 1968 San Francisco State strike and the 1969 Berkeley Third World strikes were completely ignored by the media. At Berkeley, for example, the commemorations were largely ignored by faculty and students as Third World strike veterans spoke to nearly empty auditoriums. A rally at Sproul Plaza, the free speech area, drew only two hundred students compared to the thousands who had overflowed the plaza in 1969.

Scholars in Chicano Studies have not done much to correct the ignorance about Mexican American student protest and radicalism during the 1960s. Mexican American historians, for example, have yet to produce a book on the sixties, and only two of them, Juan Gómez-Quiñones and Rodolfo Acuña, have touched on it, though they have different interpretations of the importance of Mexican American youth during that era. Gómez-Quiñones argues in his essay on the history of the Chicano student movement in Southern California that 'students were central to the political vortex of 1966 through 1970'.[13] Acuña, on the other hand, concludes that 'it is an error to characterize Chicano youth in the 1960s as rebellious or to attribute the Chicano movement to them'.[14] Of course, not all Mexican American youth in the 1960s were rebellious. But thousands were. It is also true that the Chicano Movement was not restricted to those under the age of thirty, but the fact is that the overwhelming majority of those who identified with it were. Mexican American youth and particularly students were central to the building of the Chicano Movement and especially to the shaping of its ideology.

The lack of a substantial and critical history of Mexican American struggles in the 1960s has resulted in the romanticization of the Chicano Movement. For the most part, the polemic by freelance journalist Armando Rendon, *Chicano Manifesto*, is a case in point.[15] The true nature of the Chicano Movement as a movement of working-class youth rooted in the politics of the 1960s has gone largely unacknowledged. The prevailing interpretation of the movement is that it was simply an extension of previous struggles. Acuña, for example, takes the position that those who place the birth of the movement 'during the second half of the 1960s' are wrong.[16] In his view, 'Mexicans in the United States have responded to injustice and oppression since the US wars of aggression that took Texas and the Southwest from Mexico.'[17]

Based on Acuña's analysis and that of others, the Chicano Movement was simply any political activity involving people of Mexican descent in the United States since the US–Mexico wars of 1836 and 1846–48. Most who have referred to the movement have viewed it in those terms. Mexican American leaders, regardless of ideology, have been referred to as leaders of the Chicano Movement. Organizations that predate the rise of the movement are referred to as part of the movement. The same has held true for organizations that arose long after the movement's decline. The League for Revolutionary Struggle (LRS), a multiracial communist party, is a case in point. It identifies itself as part, if not the vanguard, of the Chicano Movement. The more liberal leaders of the League of United Latin American Citizens (LULAC), a middle-class organization founded in 1929, have also considered that organization part of the Chicano Movement. But critical examination shows that neither the LRS nor LULAC promotes the ideology or the original goals of the Chicano Movement.

The term *Chicano* has been applied uncritically by both Mexican American scholars and political activists since it was popularized in the late 1960s. It has come to mean simply those who are of Mexican descent, whether born in the United States or in Mexico. The political and ideological significance attached to the term by the founders of the Chicano Movement has been largely lost or modified to fit contemporary political struggles.

The farmworker struggle led by César Chávez has been the most glaring example of misinterpretation. Chávez was consistently referred to as the leading Chicano Movement leader. According to Acuña, 'César Chávez gave the Chicano Movement a national leader'.[18] In fact, Chávez was the leader of a labor movement and later a union struggle that was never an integral part of the Chicano Movement. He made it clear, especially during the movement's formative years, that the farmworkers' union did not support Chicano nationalism or neo-separatism and that he did not consider himself to be a Chicano leader but the organizer of a union representing a multiracial constituency of rank-and-file workers. Luis Valdez and his Teatro Campesino left the farmworkers' movement precisely because Chávez did not agree with Valdez's efforts to locate the union in the framework of a Chicano nationalist ideology.[19] Chávez and the UFW represented a farmworker movement with a largely Mexican American rank and file, but they never evolved in the context of a quest for Chicano identity and power.

Chávez and UFW cofounder Dolores Huerta built the union by virtue of developing a multiracial and multiethnic coalition of diverse sectors of the farmworker community along with white liberal democrats, including progressive clergy. Filipinos were a key component from the inception of the

union – and in fact were the first to launch a strike against agribusiness without the participation of Chávez or the Mexican American rank and file. The
UFW also included representation of Arabs and Jews. The Kennedys were
key UFW supporters, and consequently the union built strong ties to the
Democratic Party. Chávez never supported La Raza Unida Party, since adopt-
ing the cultural nationalist ideology of the Chicano Movement would have
meant the end of the UFW.

It is nevertheless true that many Mexican American student activists, including this author, were inspired by Chávez and many rank-and-file union
members came to identify with the goals of the Chicano Movement. And
Chávez was certainly the first Mexican American leader to receive national
recognition and support for his cause.

Reies López Tijerina, another charismatic leader of Mexican descent, has
been referred to by Acuña and others as a leader of the Chicano Movement. It
is true that he was a source of early inspiration to many movement militants
and radicals as a direct consequence of the armed take-over of the county
courthouse in Tierra Amarilla, New Mexico by members of his Alianza de
Pueblos Libres (Alliance of Free Peoples). But Tijerina, like Chávez, never advocated Chicano nationalism. Tijerina's objectives were restricted to the land
grants issue, a struggle that he did not originally place in the context of a quest
for Chicano identity and political power. Although Tijerina himself was of
Mexican descent, his constituency was largely from the 'Hispano' rural class.
Some were direct descendants of the colonizers who were given title to land
by the king of Spain in the territory that became New Mexico.[20] Tijerina and
his followers referred to themselves as *indo-hispanos* and not as Chicanos. Like
New Mexicans in general, they de-emphasized their Mexican roots.

Nevertheless, activists with quite diverse ideologies have claimed their political projects to be part of the Chicano Movement. Similarly, Democratic
Party politicians of Mexican descent who never participated in the movement
and who in fact disagreed with its ideological objectives have placed their politics in the context of the Chicano Movement. Mexican American members
of communist and socialist parties have promoted their party lines as part
and parcel of the Chicano Movement. For a time, for example, the Socialist
Workers Party maintained a direct relationship with the Crusade for Justice
in Denver, Colorado and promoted La Raza Unida Party in the pages of the
party newspaper, *The Militant*.

Framework for Analysis: The Politics of Identity

The Chicano Movement needs to be placed in the context of what I call the politics of identity or the identity problematic. Mexican Americans, more than any other ethnic or racial group in the United States, have been given a multitude of identity labels.[21] In contrast to the experience of other nonwhite groups, the question of Mexican American identity has been rooted in regional cultural contexts. In a very real sense, diversity has marked Mexican American culture. This diversity has been further complicated by the fact that Mexican Americans are among the most racially mixed nonwhite people in US society. They are indeed a *rainbow people* difficult to define in traditional race and ethnic relations terms. The multicultural realities of the Mexican people in both the United States and Mexico thus need to be addressed critically.

In Mexico, the original *mestizaje* occurred between the colonizing Spanish conquistadores and the indigenous women from various tribes or nations. But over time other races and cultures have modified this original mixing. African slaves were brought to the eastern seaboard of Mexico, mostly in the area of Vera Cruz. Asians and other white Europeans followed. In the United States, this multicultural and multiracial mixture has been complicated by intermarriage between people of Mexican descent, African Americans, Asian Americans, and white Americans or 'Anglos' as they are commonly called by Mexican Americans.

Mexican Americans with names like Joe Kapp and Jim Plunkett, or Maria Smith and Elena O'Reilly, are becoming more commonplace as more Mexican American women marry non–Mexican American men. The result is that most drop their Spanish surname in favor of their husband's name.[22] In addition, men have anglicized their names in the past in order to obtain better jobs. Children who are products of such marriages find it difficult to identify as Mexican Americans.

Regional and subcultural realities are related to the fact that the integration of Mexican Americans into the political economy of the United States has historically been an uneven process. The result has been different levels of assimilation into both the class structure and dominant culture. In addition to class differences, there have been and continue to be internal cultural differences. Mexican Americans in south Texas have differed from those in other parts of the state; those in the Mexican border and rural areas differ from those in the large urban areas of central and northern Texas. The differences have been reflected in cultural forms, notably musical forms.[23] The same holds true for

Mexican Americans in California: those from Southern California have differed from those in the central and northern parts of the state. Those living in
Los Angeles have been more the product of a Mexican American urban culture, whereas those in Fresno have been products of a rural culture. Those in
the San Francisco Bay Area are products of a more mixed Latino culture that
reflects that area's diversity and the presence of large numbers of Nicaraguans,
Salvadorans, Chileans and other people of Latin American descent: in this
area, *salsa* and not Mexican *ranchero* music predominates.

In addition to local cultural differences, broader regional differences have
been important. The majority of Mexican Americans in New Mexico, especially those in the northern part of the state, cherish a Spanish legacy as opposed to Mexican traditions, although this changed a bit during the height of
the Chicano Movement.[24] They have accordingly identified as *Hispanos* long
before the term *Hispanic* was popularized in the late 1970s. The same has held
true for Mexican Americans in Colorado. *Spanish-American* has been equally
as common as *Hispano* in both states.

Mexican Americans in California and Texas have also evolved in dispa-
rate ways. The former have historically been 'less Mexican' than their counterparts in the Texas borderlands; there, Mexican identity has remained
strong because of proximity to northern Mexican *norteño* culture. In general,
California Mexican Americans have historically been more assimilated and
Americanized. Even when California was part of the Mexican nation, it was
divorced from the mainstream of Mexican culture and society, given its dis-
tance from the heart of Mexico. This partly explains why the Chicano student
movement in California emerged as a quest for identity and power, whereas
the student movement in Texas did not place as much emphasis on the politics of identity.

As a result, the multicultural, multiracial, regional, generational, and class
character of the Mexican American people has contributed to the uneven
development of political consciousness. Identity has therefore been a central
problem in political organizing. The leaders of middle-class organizations
have generally promoted a white ethnic identity for Mexican Americans in
the shaping of tactics and strategies for a politics of assimilation, integration,
and accommodation. The leaders of working-class organizations, on the other
hand, have largely forsaken the question of ethnic identity and promoted the
class interests of workers in the organization of strikes and unions.

In the mid-1970s Mexican Americans acquired yet another identity label.

The term *Hispanic* reflects a continued politics of white ethnic identity, which de-emphasizes, if it does not reject, the Mexican cultural base of the people.[25] The term *Hispanic* originated in the corridors of the federal bureaucracy and in the offices of the four Mexican American and one Puerto Rican member of Congress after the decline of the Chicano Movement. For bureaucrats it was a convenient term to apply to all Spanish-speaking people in the United States, especially in the context of health, education, and welfare programs. For the politicians, it was a convenient label with which to promote a coalition politics among their constituencies that would enable them to form an influential caucus in Congress. The Hispanic Caucus was subsequently the result this effort.

The major problem with the term *Hispanic* is that it ignores the complexities of a multitude of different cultural groups, each with its own unique history, class realities, and experience in the United States. Although they may all share the common denominator of the Spanish language, it cannot be said that they all suffer from the same degree of racial and class discrimination – or for that matter, the same prospects for upward class mobility. Mexican Americans are, after Native Americans, the oldest inhabitants of North America. They are products of imperialist wars waged by the United States against Mexico in 1836 and 1846–48, which resulted in the loss of half of Mexico's territory to the United States and in what was then northern Mexico becoming the southwestern United States. To complicate matters, they are also products of contemporary Mexican immigration into the US. Some can therefore trace their roots to the 1500s when the Spaniards colonized New Mexico, others to their ancestors' arrival during the Mexican revolution of 1910–20, while others are children of more recent arrivals from Mexico. Puerto Ricans, on the other hand, became colonial subjects and citizens after the United States waged an imperialist war against Spain in 1898. Puerto Rico remains a colony although it is officially classified as a US commonwealth. Puerto Ricans have 'emigrated' to the US mainland as a consequence of poverty in their homeland. Anti-Castro Cubans first arrived in the United States in significant numbers after fleeing the Cuban revolution in 1959. Central Americans, notably Salvadorans, are the more recent immigrants. Most are in the United States as a consequence of political repression and civil war in El Salvador.

The term *Hispanic* also complicates the question of identity for each of the groups it includes. It is a concept rooted in the old melting-pot theory of assimilation first applied to white European ethnics and, before the 1960s, also applied to people of color. It implicitly emphasizes the white European culture of Spain at the expense of the nonwhite cultures that have profoundly shaped the experiences of all Latin Americans. Hispania was the name the Romans gave to the Iberian peninsula, most of which became Spain. There is nothing in the term that relates to any of the nonwhite indigenous cultures of the Americas, Africa, and Asia, which historically have produced multicultural and multiracial peoples in Latin America and the United States. In an example of such blindness to the multiracial reality of Mexican Americans, a recent Census Bureau study by Frank Bean and Marta Tienda, *The Hispanic Population of the United States*, argues that most Hispanics are white.

The diversity of cultures represented by 'Hispanic' peoples makes it difficult, if not impossible, to effectively mobilize them according to one racial or ethnic political consciousness. Ideologically, for examples, Cuban Americans are far more conservative than Mexican Americans. The former are largely Republicans and members of the middle class, whereas the latter are primarily Democrats and working class.

The diversity of subcultural differences within the Mexican American population has historically reflected different levels of political consciousness. The fact that most have been Democrats has not meant that they have been unified ideologically. Among Mexican Americans, the selection of a particular identity and label for it has been a political choice related to location in a particular subculture and class. Also reflected in their choices is the fact that, like most other US citizens, Mexican Americans have been conditioned by the schools, the church, and other US institutions to believe in the myths of the American Dream.

The Chicano Movement was a historic first attempt to shape a politics of unification on the basis of a nonwhite identity and culture and on the interests of the Mexican American working class. The movement rejected all previous identities, and thus represented a counter-hegemonic political and cultural project.

Framework for Analysis: The 1960s

The Chicano student movement and the larger Chicano Power Movement which it generated also need to be placed in the context of the history of the 1960s. Mexican American youth were an integral part of the youth rebellion that emerged to become a political force during that period. I therefore place my book in the context of what I consider to be the two major – and conflicting – schools of thought that permeate much of the literature on youth radicalism and the 1960s.

The first is what I call the mainstream academic approach. It generally interprets student movements in largely negative terms. The paradigms of these scholars are rooted in the psycho-historical Freudian method, structural-functionalism, pluralist democratic theory or a combination thereof. Youth radicalism is seen as an expression of father–son, love–hate relationships and student movements as manifestations of irrational behavior that contribute to social and political instability. Lewis Feuer, a distinguished member of this school of thought, writes:

> With a melancholy uniformity, the historical record shows plainly how time and again the student's most idealistic movement has converted itself into a blind, irrational power hostile to liberal democratic values. ... For student movements have thus far been too largely an example of *projective politics* [Feuer's emphasis] in the sense that they have been largely dominated by unconscious drives; the will to revolt against the de-authorized father. ... A politics of the unconscious carries with it untold dangers for the future of civilization.[26]

Feuer's work, and that of others offering a Freudian analysis of youth movements, has political implications in that it reinforces existing power relationships. The problem posed by student movements, they argue, is a function of *individual* behavior and not of the nature or structure of political institutions in advanced capitalist society. Some, like Seymour Martin Lipset, acknowledge the positive nature of student movements in the Third World, at least in the initial stages of the overthrow of dictatorial and undemocratic governments. But Feuer, Lipset, and others believe that the United States has a political system that allows for the maximum degree of citizen participation at the local, state, and national levels. Their interpretations of student protest and radicalism as irrational and undemocratic in nature have therefore been colored by their values and commitment to the myth of a pluralistic, open democratic society.

The second major school of thought permeating the literature on the 1960s interprets student protest and radicalism in largely positive terms. In contrast to the establishment bias of the first group, scholars in this second school adhere to paradigms rooted in radical and neo-Marxist perspectives shaped

by those who were themselves students and youth activists in the 1960s or
those who identified with the goals of the New Left. Whereas the first school
is largely oriented to the psychological nature of student protest, the second
stresses its political/sociological aspects.

Collectively, works from this school of thought see student radicalism in
the 1960s as a product of a repressive or stagnant political system and a reflection of fundamental social and cultural conflict resulting from, for example,
the 'problem of discontinuity between' a humanistic 'family tradition and the
values of the larger society'.[27] Central to this approach is the concept of the
student movements as representing a youth counterculture that rejected the
materialist values of the dominant culture in favor of alternative values geared
toward humanistic goals.

The major problem with both schools of thought, as I suggested earlier,
is their narrow focus, which has led to their interpretation of student movements in the United States as basically a 'revolt of the advantaged' and a political phenomenon rooted in the white middle-class. The phenomenon, as described by Flacks, was a 'disaffection not of an underprivileged stratum of the
student population but of the most advantaged sectors of the students'.[28] This
was indeed true of SDS and the Free Speech Movement, but not true of the
Chicano and Black student movements.

Apart from the limited focus characterizing this literature, there are other
problems. With few exceptions, most works do not describe in detail how
student organizations actually emerged and how and why they declined.
Their attention is restricted to a more general analysis of student protest and
radicalism. With the exception of Feuer, most do not place the subject in any
substantive historical context conducive to comparing previous student movements with that of the 1960s. And although youth radicalism is analyzed as
a middle-class phenomenon, it is generally not placed in the context of class
conflict. Finally, the major figures in both schools have not placed the subject
in the context of the patriarchal nature of American politics and institutions.

While I disagree with Feuer's negative conclusions about student movements, I find his definition of student movements useful and consider it applicable to the Chicano student movement:

We may define a student movement as a combination of students inspired
by aims which they try to explicate in a political ideology, and moved by an
emotional rebellion in which there is always present a disillusionment with

and rejection of the values of the older generation; moreover, the members of a student movement have the conviction that their generation has a special historical mission to fulfill where the older generation, other elites, and other classes have failed.[29]

Feuer is also on target in making the point that student movements are primarily intellectual movements since 'students are above all intellectuals, persons with ideas.'[30]

Both schools of thought have a tendency to emphasize internal divisions and ideological discord as central factors in the decline of student movements. In my view, there were additional factors equally, if not more responsible for their decline. First, the role of dominant political institutions and ideological hegemony were critical. The movements were under political surveillance and were infiltrated by the FBI and other police intelligence units from the moment of their inception. Undercover agents and paid provocateurs effectively created internal divisions. Second, radical oppositional ideologies, as has been the case historically, were never able to take root in society outside their university centers. Student protest gave birth to student movements, which developed a counter-hegemonic process to challenge the dominant ideology and the institutions through which it permeates society. But this counter-hegemonic process was eventually undermined by the strategies of repression and cooptation on the part of those who ruled those institutions.

Other important factors contributing to the decline of student movements were their own success and changes in the environment that had given them birth. By the early 1970s, Congress had passed civil rights legislation, and many of the demands of the movements had become federal law. Freedom of speech and access to white universities for nonwhite youth had been gained, albeit not to the extent desired, and ethnic studies programs had been established. The war in Vietnam came to an end. The War on Poverty programs created by the Johnson administration had contributed to the radicalization of nonwhite youth and the growth of a liberal political climate, despite the repressive role of law-and-order institutions. The transfer of power from Johnson to Nixon signaled the end of those programs and the beginning of a shift to a more conservative era.

I place the development of youth radicalism as a whole in the context of a framework that acknowledges racial, class, and gender inequality as significant factors in the shaping of student movements. Student movements and youth radicalism are manifestations of both class and generational conflict. Student movements are also oppositional movements that directly confront the political institutions of those who rule. Included among those institutions in the 1960s were the Democratic Party, secondary schools, and institutions of higher education. I agree with the radical school that youth protest and the student movement they engendered were not irrational or antidemocratic in nature, but rather political forces aiming to make society more just and more democratic.

In this context, the Chicano student movement was very much an integral part of the overall youth rebellion of the 1960s. Thus it shared many of the objectives of the white student movement. But it also reflected other characteristics related to the nature of racial and class oppression experienced by the Mexican American working class. With rare exceptions, its leadership and rank and file came from that class. Whereas white youth radicalism contributed to the making of a counterculture stressing humanistic values, Chicano youth radicalism represented a return to the humanistic cultural values of the Mexican working class. This in turn led to the shaping of a nationalist ideology, which although antiracist in nature, stressed the nonwhite indigenous aspects of Mexican working-class culture. This nationalism defined Mexican Americans as *mestizos*, a mixed race people, and rejected identification with the white European/Hispanic roots of Mexican culture. It further called for the rejection of assimilation into the dominant, white Anglo-Saxon Protestant culture of the United States.

I define the Chicano student movement and the larger Chicano Power Movement as a quest for a new identity and for political power. The movement represented a new and radical departure from the politics of past generations of Mexican American activists. It called for new political institutions to make possible Chicano self-determination. As such it was a counterhegemonic struggle and held certain of the characteristics of the New Left as defined by George Katsiaficas: it opposed racial, political and patriarchal domination and economic exploitation; it called for freedom from material deprivation and the freedom to create *La Nueva Raza*, a new people proud of their Mexican working-class culture; it called for the expansion of the democratic process and individual rights for Mexican Americans; and it emphasized direct political action.[31]

The uniqueness of the Chicano Movement and the generation of activists it produced cannot be understood without first appreciating the political devel-

opment of previous generations of activists. In chapter 1, I trace the origin of
Mexican American student activism to 1929 when Ernesto Galarza, a student
at Stanford University, spoke out in defense of Mexican immigrant workers.
I then describe the political development of youth in the context of the shaping of the Mexican-American Generation during the 1930s and 1940s. The
response of that generation to the segregation and the racist, anti-Mexican attitudes permeating US society was the development of organizations promoting a politics of assimilation and accommodation.

In describing these movements, I make a subtle but significant distinction in my use of the term *Mexican American*. When I use it with a hyphen,
Mexican-American, it refers to the generation of the 1930s and 1940s or the
political ideology shaped by that generation. Unhyphenated, the term is ge-
neric, referring to the people as a whole – specifically, Mexican Americans as
a people of Mexican descent born and raised in the United States.[32] I limit the terms *Chicano* and *Chicana* to specific references to the Chicano and
Chicana generation and the Chicano Movement, thus keeping my usage consistent with my analysis of the Chicano Generation and Chicano Movement
as products of the 1960s. The term *Chicano/a* refers to both Chicanos and
Chicanas. Although these distinctions may at times complicate the narrative,
I hope that they will allow the reader to easily grasp the distinctions between
the Mexican-American, Chicano, and Hispanic generations.

I use the term *Latino* to refer to all peoples of Latin American descent in
the US, including Mexican Americans. *Latino* and/or *Latino/a* is preferable,
in my view, to *Hispanic*, representing as it does popular usage, while *Hispanic*
retains associations from its birth in the corridors of the federal bureaucracy
and among political elites. I refer to other nonwhite people in the same context – for example, to people of African descent as African Americans and use
other terms of identity applied to them, for example, Negro, Black and Afro-
American, in political context. I refer to nonwhite people collectively as 'people
of color'.

In chapter 2, I analyze the political development of student activists during
the early 1960s and their ideological development away from the outlook of
the Mexican-American Generation. The focus is on the events, conferences,
and ideas leading up to the 1968 high school student strike in Los Angeles.
Chapter 3 focuses on two key conferences that resulted in the shaping of the
Chicano ideology and the formation of El Movimiento Estudiantil Chicano
de Aztlán. It concludes with an analysis of the factors contributing to the de-

cline of the Chicano student movement.

The remaining chapters contain a critical analysis of two of the most significant contributions made by the Chicano student movement in which I was a
direct participant. The first was the creation of La Raza Unida Party, the first
Mexican American political party in the history of the United States. Chapter
4 is an account of the rise and fall of that party. Chapter 5 offers a critical analysis of the most lasting contribution of the movement, the emergence of the
Chicano intellectual generation in the context of the development of Chicano
Studies programs in institutions of higher education and the development of
the National Association for Chicano Studies. Chapter 6 describes the difficulties that faced the Chicano Movement in the wake of the Reaganite conservative revolution of the 1980s and the development of Hispanic identity as
a reflection of that conservative influence, while the Epilogue charts the rapid
growth – and growing diversity – of US Latino communities and argues that
Latinos must play a key role in building a new US movement for multiracial
democracy.

Notes

1 Clayborne Carson, *In Struggle: SNCC and the Black Awakening of the 1960s*, Cambridge,
   Mass. 1981.
2 Alfredo Lopez, *The Puerto Rican Papers: Notes on the Re-Emergence of a Nation*, New York
   1973.
3 Todd Gitlin, *The Sixties: Years of Hope, Days of Rage*, New York 1987; see also his *The
   Whole World Is Watching: Mass Media in the Making and Unmaking of the New Left*,
   Berkeley 1980.
4 Richard Flacks, *Youth and Social Change*, Chicago 1971, pp. 7–8.
5 Julian Foster, 'Student Protest: What Is Known, What Is Said', in Julian Foster, ed., *Protest!
   Activism in America*, New York 1970, p. 36.
6 Seymour Martin Lipset, 'Youth and Politics', in Robert K. Merton, ed., *Contemporary Social
   Problems*, 3d edn, New York 1971, p. 776. Also see Lipset's *Rebellion in the University*,
   Boston 1977.
7 David L. Westby, *The Clouded Vision: The Student Movement in the United States in the
   1960s*, Cransbury, N.J. 1976, p. 39.
8 Ibid.
9 Sohnya Sayres et al., eds, *The Sixties Without Apology*, Minneapolis 1984.
10 Gitlin, *The Sixties*, p. 4.
11 George Katsiaficas, *The Imagination of the New Left: A Global Analysis of 1968*, Boston
   1987.
12 David J. Garrow, *The FBI and Martin Luther King, Jr.: From 'Solo' to Memphis*, New York
   1981.

13 Juan Gómez-Quiñones, *Mexican Students Por La Raza: The Chicano Student Movement in Southern California 1967–1977*, Santa Barbara 1978.

14 Rodolfo Acuña, *Occupied America: A History of Chicanos*, 3d edn, New York 1988, p. 333.

15 Armando B. Rendon, *Chicano Manifesto: The History and Aspirations of the Second Largest Minority in America*, New York 1971.

16 Acuña, *Occupied America*, p. 324.

17 Ibid.

18 Ibid., p. 325.

19 Luis Valdez, interview, 11 August 1982.

20 Frances Leon Swadesh, *Los Primeros Pobladores: Hispanic Americans of the Ute Frontier*, Notre Dame 1974.

21 These terms have included *Americans of Mexican descent, Latin-Americans, Spanish-Americans, Texicans, Mexican-Americans, Mexicanos, Mexicans, Hispanos*, and *Californios*.

22 Leo Grebler, Joan W. Moore, and Ralph C. Guzman, *The Mexican American People: The Nation's Second Largest Minority*, New York 1970. Chapter 17 is 'Intermarriage as an Index of Assimilation', pp. 405–19.

23 Manuel H. Peña, *The Texas-Mexican Conjunto: History of a Working-Class Music*, Austin 1985.

24 Swadesh, *Primeros Pobladores*, p. 206.

25 The Census Bureau does not have a separate racial category for Mexican Americans. They and other 'Hispanics' are defined as Caucasians.

26 Lewis Feuer, *The Conflict of Generations: The Character and Significance of Student Movements*, New York 1969, pp. 529.

27 Richard Flacks, *Social Problems*, New York 1970, p. 354.

28 Richard Flacks, 'The Liberated Generation: An Exploration of the Roots of Student Protest', *Journal of Social Issues*, vol. 23, no. 3, 1967, p. 55.

29 Feuer, *Conflict*, p. 11.

30 Ibid., p. 14.

31 Katsiaficas, *Imagination of the New Left*, pp. 22–27.

32 Included in my definition of Mexican Americans are those born in Mexico who emigrated to the United States as children and who are therefore products of US schools and other US institutions.

1

From Segregation to Melting-Pot Democracy: The Mexican-American Generation

Mexican Americans became an oppressed minority group as a consequence of the expansion of the US Empire in the nineteenth century, and that fact has had a profound impact on their political and intellectual development. The subjugation of Mexican Americans, beginning with the Texas–Mexico War of 1836 and the US–Mexico War of 1846–48, has never been considered a moral or constitutional issue by US society or even by liberals. Like the Native American peoples, Mexican Americans were subjected to a process of colonization which, in addition to undermining their culture, relegated the majority of them to a permanent pool of cheap labor for US capital. As a 'conquered' and nonwhite people, they were never the beneficiaries of the fruits of capitalist development. Even the once privileged Mexican gentry who welcomed the white colonizers with open arms soon lost their social status and political power with the formation of a new class structure.[1]

Like African Americans, Mexican American working-class children able to attend school were placed in segregated schools. But in contrast, Mexican Americans never had access to even the sort of higher education provided by segregated institutions like the Negro colleges. Access to white colleges and universities was generally restricted to the small Mexican American middle class largely centered in San Antonio, Texas and to the children of the Hispano elite in New Mexico. The Treaty of Guadalupe Hidalgo, signed after the defeat of Mexico by the United States in 1848, granted Mexicans remaining in the new US territories certain rights pertaining to property, religion, culture, and education – rights that were never honored or enforced by the US government. The eventual result, particularly due to lack of educational opportunities, was a negligible Mexican American middle class and intellectual sector as racial, class, and gender oppression became the reality for the vast majority of Mexicans and Mexican Americans relegated to the ranks of cheap labor.

At the turn of the twentieth century, the Mexican American population began to increase dramatically. Data on Mexican immigration were not then accurately reported by the government, but reliable estimates by historians and social scientists have put the number of immigrants from Mexico at 24,000 between 1900 and 1909 and at more than 82,000 during the 1910–14 period of the Mexican Revolution.[2] The Revolution was not the only stimulus to emigration, however, since many more thousands left Mexico after the Revolution ended.

The crucial factor in Mexican emigration was in fact capital's demand for cheap labor in the Midwest and Southwest. World War I caused significant shortages of white labor, and Mexicans and Mexican Americans were needed in the expansion and development of the steel industry in Chicago and Pittsburgh, and in agriculture and in the southwestern economy in general. In addition to shortages of white labor, the passage of legislation excluding Asian immigration had eliminated Asian workers from the cheap labor pool. According to the US Census, the Mexican population had reached 1,225,207 by 1930.[3]

The children of Mexican immigrant workers attended segregated public schools along with their Mexican American cousins, and both groups underwent a profound process of 'Americanization' and indoctrination into the 'American way of life'. Despite segregation, they thus learned the values, beliefs, and ideas of the dominant culture at the same time that they suffered from anti-Mexican racism. But like the majority of youth in the United States, the contradictions between what they were taught in school about 'American Democracy' and the realities of their people's racial and class oppression were not apparent to most of them.

Historically, schools, including segregated schools, have been central institutions in perpetuating ideological hegemony in the United States. Mexican American working-class youth have therefore been subject to a socialization process that reinforces the dominant ideology and undermines competing ideologies. The architects of public and private school systems in the United States have defined the role of the schools as

> the deliberate indoctrination for American democracy of children and youth. … A proper business of education, both public and private, in this country is to imbue young Americans with intelligent devotion to their country's basic principles and ideas. Indoctrination for American democracy is [a] proper … and necessary, business of American education. It is a plain duty of schools and teachers to give vigorous support to the ideological pattern that sustains them.[4]

This has historically meant teaching the virtues of capitalism and the 'American way of life'. In teaching such virtues, the schools have also served as agents of cultural imperialism by contributing to the erosion of the indigenous cultures of the Southwest through the assimilation of Mexican immigrant and Mexican American youth. Schools have historically also kept Mexican Americans 'in their place' as cheap labor by pushing youth out of public schooling at an early age through the tracking system. This process has included placement of Mexican-American youth in classes for the mentally retarded or for slow learners and channeling them into manual training rather than academic courses. Stigmitized as dropouts, working-class youth have thus historically been assured of walking the same path as their parents in the ranks of the unemployed and underemployed proletariat.[5]

Of course, some working-class Mexican and Mexican American youth resisted this ideological Americanization. Emma Tenayuca, for example, as a young woman led a strike of Mexican pecan workers in Texas during the 1930s. She subsequently became a communist and later served as the cochair of the US Communist Party in Texas. Tenayuca and other youth who engaged in class struggle did so as workers and not as student activists, since they were generally no longer in school. Once out of school, they came in contact with communists and socialists in the workplace or in the community and became aware of radical ideologies.

The origins of student activism among youth of Mexican descent in the United States, however, can be traced to 1929 when Ernesto Galarza, then a 24-year-old first-year graduate student in history at Stanford University, spoke out in defense of Mexican immigrant workers. Galarza was not a member of any Mexican American student organization or group, for no such organizations then existed in American institutions of higher education. During his undergraduate years at Occidental College, which he entered in 1923, Galarza knew only five other Mexican or Mexican American students attending colleges and universities in Southern California. He was the first Mexican American to enter Stanford and during those years he continued to be the only Mexican American there.[6] He was therefore considered a 'novelty' and a 'curiosity', because white students 'didn't know what a Mexican looked like or what to expect of him.'[7]

As an eight-year-old, Galarza had fled to the United States because of the Mexican Revolution. With his mother and two uncles he worked in the fields of California's Sacramento Valley. Experiencing the exploitation of child labor then common in the United States, he became intimately aware of how Mexican immigrant workers were oppressed by those who owned the fields.

The racism that manifested itself around immigration spurred Galarza to fight attempts to restrict immigration from Mexico. Immigration had emerged as a political issue that pitted those ostensibly concerned with keeping America 'racially pure' (while protecting white American workers from foreign competition) against those who argued that cheap Mexican labor was essential to the expansion of capital in the Southwest. The former were in favor of restricting immigration from Mexico through extension of the same legislation that had excluded Asians prior to the 1920s. Like Asians, Mexicans were perceived as a 'peril' and a threat to the social and cultural fabric of American society.[8]

Galarza spoke out in a political atmosphere poisoned by fear that the US was being 'invaded' by hordes of non-white peons from the Western Hemisphere. Vulgar racist hostility against Mexicans was a staple of newspapers, magazines, and scholarly journals, especially between 1926 and 1930, when public hearings were conducted by House and Senate committees on Mexican immigration. Those in favor of restricting immigration represented various patriotic societies, eugenicist organizations, and a significant sector of organized labor. Patriots and eugenicists argued that 'Mexicans would create the most insidious and general mixture of white, Indian, and Negro blood strains ever produced in America ... ' and that most of them were

> hordes of hungry dogs, and filthy children with faces plastered with flies ... human filth ... [They are] promiscuous ... apathetic peons and lazy squaws [who] prowl by night ... stealing anything they can get their hands on.[9]

A professor of zoology at the University of California characterized Mexican immigrants as Indian peons 'without the trace of Caucasian blood … ' who were 'ignorant, tractable, moderately industrious, and content to endure wretched conditions of life which most white laborers would not tolerate.' His conclusions were that Mexicans were a 'menace to public health, … [a] serious burden upon our charities, … [of] low mentality', inherently criminal, and therefore a degenerate race that would afflict American society with 'an embarrassing race problem.'[10]

Others compared Mexicans to Blacks in the South – and in equally negative terms. One eugenicist, for example, argued that because Mexicans were 'eugenically as low-powered as the Negro … ' and were 'superstitious' savages who did not understand 'health rules', they suffered from widespread venereal disease and were therefore a health menace.[11] The politicians who supported the restriction of Mexican immigration also based their arguments on vicious racist stereotypes. Senators Hiram Johnson of California and Thomas Heflin of Alabama, for example, argued that Mexicans were a danger to American society because they were a 'mixed breed', 'low type', and 'docile' people.[12]

Rather than defend fellow workers, labor unions supported restriction of immigration because they believed that Mexicans took jobs away from white workers. Anticommunist politicians and organizations categorized Mexican immigrants as part of the 'Red menace'. The US Bureau of Immigration conducted intense deportation hunts for 'aliens' and 'subversives' who, it asserted, were holding jobs that should belong to Americans. Although ostensibly aimed at 'Reds', the main victims of this campaign were actually Mexicans since deportation efforts were focused on Southern California – the area with the densest Mexican population in the United States. Local political leaders like Los Angeles County Supervisor John P. Quinn advocated the large-scale deportation of Mexicans on the grounds that they were 'criminally undesirable' and part of the 'Red problem'.[13]

At a public meeting of the National Conference on Social Work, Galarza responded to these attacks with his own criticism of both the 'racial purists' and the 'economic expansionists', the former for mustering 'the familiar artillery of racial dilution and the color flood', and the latter for 'pressing the equally old argument that the very economic structure of the United States rests on the blood and sweat of the [Mexican] immigrant' without any sincere or serious concern for their welfare. He directly challenged the notions that the 'Mexican problem' stemmed from a backward and inferior Mexican culture and that Mexicans were taking jobs away from white workers. Mexicans, he pointed out, were 'not innately married to an animal standard of living ... ' but were compelled to live in bad conditions by severe unemployment:

> The Mexican is the first to suffer from depression in industrial and agricultural enterprises. ... [D]esperation grips many of them and the old familiar phrase, packed with a penetrating helplessness, goes the round: 'Va a estar duro el invierno' (It is going to be a hard winter). I flatly disagree with those who maintain that there is enough work for these people but that they refuse to work, preferring to live on charity. On the contrary ... there are more men than there are jobs. The women storm the canneries of the Sacramento Valley by the hundreds in search of the jobs that are counted by the dozens.[14]

Galarza then criticized the capitalists for their self-serving praise of Mexican workers as fundamentally important to the building of the western United States:

> It is amusing to read the praises of those opposed to the restriction of immigration. ... [I]t is said ... an empire has been created largely by the brawn of the humble Mexican, who laid the rails and topped the beets and poured the cubic miles of cement. But this acknowledgement is misleading – and tardy. For some obscure reason these builders of colossal fortunes have done their jobs and gone their ways still clothed in rags. ... If it is true that the Mexican has brought to you arms that have fastened a civilization on the Pacific slope, then give him his due. If you give him his earned wages and he proves improvident, teach him otherwise; if he is tuberculous, cure him; if he falls into indigence, raise him. He has built you an empire![15]

Galarza and the handful of other working-class students of Mexican descent – those few fortunate enough to attend college in those years – were indeed exceptional. Most Mexican American youth were not able to complete the elementary grades, and were thus in no position to seriously contemplate a higher education. The intense exploitation of Mexican and Mexican American workers contributed directly to the exclusion of youth from formal schooling after the third or fourth grades. Mexican and Mexican American children were forced to leave school in order to augment the family income. This was especially true in the more isolated rural areas.

With the exception of those few from the Hispano elite families of New Mexico and the small Mexican American middle class of San Antonio – the handful of working-class youth who gained access to institutions of higher education did so as a result of the active support of individual teachers, clergy, or social workers who were sympathetic and in a position to identify youth with exceptional intelligence. This had been the case with Ernesto Galarza. In his autobiography, Galarza expressed fond recollections of teachers who had contributed to his intellectual development and had introduced him to the white world outside the *barrio*.[16] Among them were his first school principal who 'warmed knowledge into us and roasted racial hatreds out of us', and the teachers who never 'scolded or punished' Mexicans for speaking Spanish. He also mentioned a white union official who 'affectionately' encouraged him to be a scholar and teachers who allowed him the flexibility necessary to continue working for the family while simultaneously attending school. He credits the YMCA, which opened to him the 'rest of the wide world around Sacramento'. And finally, there was his high school political science teacher, who talked him out of making his career in the canneries and into thinking seriously about a college education.

Galarza, unlike most of his generation, did not attend segregated schools, but recalled undergoing the same process of assimilation. He was never allowed to forget that he was in school to become a 'good American'. Interestingly, however, he never believed that Americanization was forced on him. On the contrary, he seems never to have had to confront vulgar racists or teachers concerned with 'scrubbing away what made him originally foreign'. By the time he entered college as an undergraduate, he felt there was something 'ahead of him' because he was being helped by friends and 'warm responsible people'. At Occidental College he vividly recalls his professor as being neither 'soft' nor antagonistic because of his Mexican-ness.

The process of assimilation experienced by Galarza in the mid-1920s did not undermine his Mexican identity. At Occidental College, as during his earlier schooling, he was able to maintain direct contact with his people. He did this by working in the canneries around Sacramento during the summer and in the fields near Los Angeles during the school year. However, he did observe that other youth of Mexican descent were undergoing a crisis of identity that manifested itself as a 'generation conflict', created by the contradiction of being both Mexican and American at the same time. These young people faced an 'either-or' choice. Their parents continued to exhibit a strong loyalty to Mexico, while the children tended to reject what they perceived as 'Mexican' and adopted what they thought to be 'American'. As Galarza put it,

> The children begin to feel contempt for field labor and disdain for the sweat and grime which permeate the life of their parents. Along with this goes a cooling of the loyalty to the home country. Pride of birth is forgotten and in its place creeps a desire to imitate their play-fellows in what appeals to them as distinctly American. What is worse, they forget the mother tongue. And while this is going on they fail to find a secure place in the social scheme of their adopted country. Color counts heavily against them. As Mexicans, they are denationalized and they find themselves in a difficult borderland through which it seems that all second generation immigrants must pass.[17]

As the issues surrounding the 'Mexican problem' became more pronounced in US politics, those entrusted with the Americanization of Mexican immigrants began to take their jobs more seriously, especially those who had the responsibility of educating the children in the segregated 'Mexican schools'. White administrators and teachers, unlike those isolated individuals Galarza had known during his own schooling, gave Mexican and Mexican American youth a much heavier dose of Americanism. In addition to teaching the virtues of American democracy, they also taught that Mexican culture was a major factor in the 'backwardness' of Mexican Americans. Both racists and antiracists adhered to the view that the problems of the Mexican and Mexican American child were rooted in the cultural traditions of a society that was semifeudal – if not altogether feudal – a society suffering from the absence of the 'progressive' values inherent in the US capitalist system. This type of socialization in the schools contributed greatly to the identity crisis among Mexican American youth.

The 'Mexican schools' were intended to give Mexican American youth the opportunity to adjust to the American way of life, and the teachers were the agents of this Americanization. They were expected to participate in Mexican American community activities much as anthropologists would study 'strange people, strange languages and strange customs'. Mexican American mothers and their children were perceived by even the more liberal teachers as culturally handicapped and intellectually inferior because of the 'primitive' conditions of the Mexican home:

The people in the Mexican schools … are far from representative of the higher classes of Mexico, or even of the middle classes, but rather of the lowliest type. They are primitive people close to nature and elemental in customs and home life.[18]

Some of the more advanced experts of the 'Mexican problem', the social scientists who published works about Mexicans, reflected a similar perspective. Sociologist Emory Bogardus, for example, one of the more sympathetic and liberal academics of the 1920s and 1930s, came to similar conclusions in his study of Mexican American youth. To him, the fundamental problem of 'second generation Mexicans', that is, those born in the United States, was their 'lack of environmental stimuli'. As a result, he described Mexican American youth as passive and concluded that they were not as aggressive as Japanese or Black youth. Mexican culture, he argued, did not produce the kind of leadership necessary to show young people the way: 'They have not had the skilled leadership in organization work, as the Japanese have had. Neither have they had popular speakers to challenge and arouse them, as the Negroes have had. The underlying community organization has been exceedingly simple.'[19]

Because Mexican American youth lacked the aggressiveness that was supposed to be characteristic of the American way of life, Bogardus reasoned that they naturally remained in the unskilled working class of their parents, a status that then compelled Mexicans to 'congregate in the less desirable and low sections of a city.' Segregation was therefore interpreted as the natural result of the Mexicans' self-imposed isolation from the mainstream of American society. Bogardus and others who, in their own way, were sympathetic to the plight of Mexican Americans, argued that segregated schools were good for Mexican American youth:

In the American or non-segregated schools, the Mexican children are often at a disadvantage. They arrive at school age with little or no knowledge of English, and hence do poorly until they learn English. They thus fall behind, and become discouraged before they have a chance to show what they can do. They do not show up well in classes beside American children who have better home conditions, and more parental help and stimulation. Sooner or later they cease to try, and drop out of the school. They are victims of conditions which normally lead to mental conflicts and inferiority complexes.[20]

The response by Mexican Americans was to challenge segregation in the courts. It was the first time in US history that any racial or ethnic group had taken a legal approach in struggles for educational equality. In Texas and California, Mexican Americans were involved in numerous desegregation court battles. The first case was *Jesús Salvatierra v. Independent School District* in Del Rio, Texas, in 1930. The town's school board was sued on the grounds that Mexican American students were being deprived of the resources given to white students. Attorneys with the League of United Latin American Citizen's (LULAC), a civil rights organization (founded in 1929), played a prominent role in the case. The district judge issued a ruling in favor of Salvatierra, but the state's higher courts later overturned his decision on appeal from white opposition.[21]

The next case took place in 1931, in San Diego, California. In *Roberto Alvarez v. the Board of Trustees of the Lemon Grove School District*, Mexican Americans sued the school district when the principal of the local elementary school prevented seventy-five Mexican American children from enrolling in an all-white school. The court ruled in favor of Roberto Alvarez. In contrast to the outcome of the Texas case, this decision was not challenged in the state's higher courts and the children were admitted to the white school. But the Lemon Grove case did not result in the termination of segregation elsewhere in California.

Other school boards throughout the state continued to implement existing segregation policies until the 1946 *Mendez v. Westminster* decision. Prior to this case, the city of Westminster in Orange County, California, had separate public schools, movie theaters, public pools, and restaurants for whites and Mexicans. The parents of eight-year-old Sylvia Mendez sued the school district when she and her brothers were denied enrollment at the 17th Street School in Westminster because of their dark skin and Spanish surname. They won their case. In contrast to the *Alvarez* decision, the *Mendez* case contributed directly to ending segregation throughout the state through the passage of legislation, signed by Governor Earl Warren, prohibiting segregation in California.

All of the segregation cases fought in the courts by Mexican Americans were based on national origins and language, not race. But *Mendez v. Westminster* set an important legal precedent for ending racial segregation throughout the United States eight years later. Thurgood Marshall, who had filed an amicus brief in *Mendez* on behalf of the National Association for the Advancement of Colored People (NACCP), used legal arguments from the *Mendez* case to win the historic *Brown v. Board of Education* desegregation case in the US Supreme Court in 1954.

The YMCA's Role in Americanization

The struggles against segregation did not result in the end the Americanization of Mexican American youth in the schools or outside the schools throughout the Southwest. By 1930 numerous conferences had been held and studies published about the conditions of poverty in Mexican American communities. This led to the eventual 'discovery' that poverty and segregation fostered special problems among the youth of Mexican descent because of their extreme isolation from the American mainstream. Both church and government social welfare agencies began to receive funds earmarked for work in the Mexican American community, and especially for the prevention of juvenile crime. One of the more significant church-related agencies was the YMCA, whose central branch in Los Angeles received a gift of $30,000 in 1934 for the specific purpose of creating boys' clubs in the predominantly Mexican communities of what came to be known as Watts.

The Young Men's Christian Association was founded in Britain in 1844 by two Protestant clerics as an evangelical Christian missionary movement to spread a 'Christian influence' and convert 'young men to Christ' through 'spiritual and mental improvement … by any means in accordance with the Scriptures.'[22] The founders perceived youth as the 'most dynamic class' since they represented both the positive and negative of any society and would eventually develop into either able-bodied leaders or criminal elements. By 'capturing' young men for Christ, the YMCA would save them from the evils of the industrial city, assure the 'spread of Christianity in its purest form', and thus 'save' the world.[23]

Although ostensibly interdenominational, the YMCA was predominantly Protestant in orientation. As a society of religious laymen committed to the Protestant ethic, the YMCA received generous support from a capitalist class anxious for an instrument of social and moral discipline after the founding of its US section in Boston in 1851. Theodore Roosevelt, J. P. Morgan, Cornelius Vanderbilt, Russell Sage, and John D. Rockefeller were but a few of the YMCA's benefactors during its formative years. Rockefeller in particular donated large sums of money to sustain the YMCA's foreign work in China, the Philippines, and Latin America.[24]

In the United States, the YMCA became directly involved in programs aimed at helping European immigrants adjust to US society. This was done through the creation of Americanization programs:

[T]he associations developed a large americanization program during [the] years of the greatest immigration in all American history. In their endeavors to help new Americans find themselves, associations in the larger cities adapted their programs to meet the needs of these young men strangers by providing employment services, instructions in the English language and in American institutions, and citizenship.[25]

Because of its successful work with Europeans, the YMCA eventually began to work with Mexican immigrants as virtually an extension of the Protestant churches. It became especially involved in areas near the Mexican border when the Mexican Revolution erupted in 1910, assisting the various Protestant churches that had initiated missionary programs to provide social, medical, and educational services to Mexicans who were escaping the Revolution. The YMCA's ultimate purpose, however, was to turn these refugees into good Americans and good Protestants. The president of the Presbyterian Synod reflected the prevailing attitude among Protestant leaders when he explained the importance of these services to Mexican immigrants:

The thousands of Mexican immigrants on our border are just now in a most receptive mood. Mentally, socially, religiously, they are in a state of transition, and the forces of evil are at work among them. The question which is to be decided within the next few years is whether they are to be won to anarchy or to Americanism; to Bolshevism or to Democracy; to Trotsky or to Christ.[26]

In its quest to save the Mexicans from the evils of 'un-American' ideologies, the YMCA spent $40,000 to distribute Spanish-language pamphlets espousing Christian values and warning against the evils of socialism.[27] Hand-in-hand with its antisocialist efforts, it adopted a policy of 'cultural amalgamation' that was consistent with the assimilationist 'melting pot' ideology of contemporary Americanization programs.[28]

The Mexican Youth Conference

The central branch of the YMCA in Los Angeles used its $30,000 grant in 1934 to hire a young Mexican American social worker named Tom García to organize summer conferences and boys' clubs in Mexican American communities. Described by his YMCA superiors as a 'clean-cut, intelligent and conscientious young man' who was physically attractive and 'successful in his personal relationships' but without 'conceptual skills', García recruited working-class youth who were students at local high schools and colleges and active in church-related youth organizations.[29] The young men recruited by García were those considered to be good students and athletes with leadership potential. Most of the young men were already familiar with the work of the YMCA through participation in sports programs like the Hi-Y Club, which often attracted the better athletes.[30]

The first Mexican Youth Conference was held soon after García was hired and was patterned after YMCA conferences which had previously been held for older boys. The conference was basically a summer weekend camp with an emphasis on recreation and sports. The purpose of the conference, nevertheless, was to develop 'character, good citizenship and desirable values among Mexican youth.' By 1934, the YMCA had ceased to be the 'right arm' of the Protestant churches and had no religious program per se, other than providing the atmosphere for 'interdenominational fellowship'. YMCA officials did not consider García's work to be a priority; it was merely a token effort to do some good for Mexican American 'boys'. One of García's superiors described his own attitude toward the project in these terms:

[I] felt some pride that the Y was demonstrating in token fashion a caring concern for minorities. ... I do not believe, however, that the Y had a policy relating to Mexican youth or saw itself as a 'defender' in any sense. ... [T]he García-Watts project ... was probably more opportunistic than consciously pursuing a chosen course or reflecting a stated policy.[31]

Nevertheless, the absence of a stated policy of political and religious indoctrination did not mean that these young men were not exposed to ideas and concepts that mirrored a particular philosophical, political, and sociological framework for the interpretation of both the 'Mexican problem' and the nature of American democracy and institutions. The YMCA officials who supported the García project in Watts were products of liberal capitalist ideology, and in addition to stressing the melting pot concept of assimilation, they promoted the belief that American institutions were egalitarian and democratic. As one official recalled, they made 'conscious attempts ... to apply the principles of liberal education and sociological concepts of the time. We could all identify with Dewey, Hartshorne, and May, the laws of learning and the elements of character development.'[32]

These concepts were of course not new to the youth who participated in the conferences and the various boys' clubs. Their YMCA activity simply reinforced what they had been taught in the schools and in the church. By the time they became involved in the Mexican Youth Conferences, their political consciousness had already been formed.

In addition, these young men were encouraged to take advantage of the educational opportunities afforded by 'American democracy' through participation in the annual Mexican Youth Conferences and in the boys' clubs organized by García. YMCA officials, because of their contacts in various institutions of higher education, were able to create these opportunities and make it possible for many, especially those who served as leaders, to be admitted to colleges and universities, and later to gain access to professional jobs that had not previously been accessible to Mexican Americans.

The Mexican Voice

Although the official purpose of the Mexican Youth Conferences was sports and recreation – and, of course, good citizenship – they provided the young men with the opportunity to engage in collective dialogue about the 'Mexican problem'. Four years after the first conference, several of them, headed by Félix Gutiérrez, a student at UCLA, decided to extend the scope of these discussions. Applying his skills as a journalist, which he had acquired while working part-time for the *Pasadena Chronicle*, Gutiérrez started putting out a mimeographed newsletter that he called *The Mexican Voice*.

Gutiérrez made it clear that the newsletter's purpose was to establish year-round communication among conference participants as a forum for their ideas and opinions on the issues facing Mexican youth and the Mexican population in general. In addition, the newsletter would report the activities of YMCA boys' clubs in the area and 'news of accomplishments by Mexicans' that would inspire 'unencouraged youngsters' to excel in school and motivate them toward constructive activities and away from gangs and juvenile delinquency. Gutiérrez affirmed that *The Mexican Voice* would promote good citizenship by advocating 'a more active participation in civic and cultural activities by those of our national descent.' The newsletter later evolved into a polished and professional-looking publication, which carried the subtitle 'Inspirational, Educational, Youth Magazine'. The consistent theme of the publication throughout its life was progress for Mexican American youth through the attainment of a higher education. A nineteen-year-old junior college student described this program:

> Education is the only tool which will raise our influence, command the respect of the rich class, and enable us to mingle in their social, political, and religious life. ... [A] college education is absolutely necessary for us to succeed in the professional world. ... [I]f our opinion is to be had, respected, our income raised, happiness increased, we must compete! *Education is our only weapon!* [33]

Gutiérrez wrote his editorials under the pen name Manuel De La Raza and entitled them 'Nosotros' to underscore his own commitment and that of the publication to a Mexican identity. He consistently criticized those of Mexican descent who attempted to pass as 'Spanish':

> Rather discouraging has been a trend ... among both our Americans of Mexican descent and others ... [of] calling any accomplished Mexican-American ... or well-to-do above average either in professional or trade circles ... 'Spanish' or 'Spanish-American'. ... The whole inference [is] ... THAT NOTHING GOOD COMES FROM THE MEXICAN GROUP. The inference ... is that only the talented, the law abiding, the part Mexican, the fair complexioned, the professionals and the tradesmen are 'Spanish'. The drunkards, the delinquents, the very dark, the manual laborers, the *pachucos*, the criminals and those in the lower socio-economic scale are the Mexicans. ... Newspapers carry this trend, prominent politicians ... [and] Anglo Americans in general are guilty of this, but worst of all, our own Mexican-Americans are making this distinction! Let's have more pride in our own group. We are all the same, whether we have been here ten generations or one. We have common goals. ... [L]et us be proud of our heritage. [34]

Gutiérrez perceived the building of 'pride in our race' as one of the most important goals of *The Mexican Voice* and therefore made sure that the academic and athletic accomplishments of Mexican youth were always acknowledged in it as proof that Mexicans were 'as good a race as any other.'

But although Gutiérrez advocated taking pride in Mexican identity, he simultaneously urged Mexican Americans to identify as Americans first and as Mexicans second. After meeting with the Mexican consul at a time when Mexicans were being repatriated to Mexico, he expressed criticism of a speech made by the consul because it stressed that all Mexicans owed their first loyalty to Mexico. In an editorial in *The Mexican Voice* written after that meeting Gutiérrez responded:

'A Mexican will always be a Mexican.' In China, Japan or in New York, sure. But after the second or third generation that's hard to believe; especially here in our country. Go to Los Angeles, San Francisco, Pasadena, Santa Barbara, and see the young students of our ... descent – gay, carefree, thinking of success, interested in American activities, playing American games, speaking and using American terms, having the same ideas and ideals, using American sportsmanship, enjoying American customs, loving American food. ... We wish our Consul could visit our modern 'Mejicano' and see him or her go around with American friends, taken for one, treated as one and feeling as one.[35]

In the same editorial Gutiérrez stressed that *The Mexican Voice* 'sticks for Americanism' and that the future of his young generation was in the United States and not in Mexico.[36]

Others echoed the themes Gutiérrez sounded in his editorials. In an article entitled 'Are We Proud of Being Mexicans?', Manuel Ceja, a star athlete at Compton Junior College, formulated the question of pride in this way:

Why are we so afraid to tell people that we are Mexicans? Are we ashamed of the color of our skin, the shape and build of our bodies, or the background from which we have descended? The Mexican youth in the United States is, indeed, a very fortunate person. ... Where else in one country do you have two cultures and civilizations of the highest type that come together to form one? With the ability to use the Spanish and English languages one has innumerable doors opened for ... [success]. Then why is it that we as Mexicans do not command respect? What can one individual do about this situation? He can uplift the Mexican name by constant work – hard work with others who have the same high ideals and aims but securing an education, not just high school but a college one, by being a clean-cut fellow, trustworthy and dependable with the highest moral aims. A Mexican boy can and must provide a favorable opinion wherever he goes. A Mexican must be a Mexican. His heritage of rich Aztec and Spanish blood has provided him with characteristics born of a high cultural civilization. When this rich background has been tempered with the fires of the Anglo-Saxon understanding and enlightenment, you will have something which will be the envy of all.[37]

As much as those who wrote in the pages of *The Mexican Voice* stressed pride in Mexican culture and identity, they nevertheless agreed with the conclusions of Bogardus and other experts on the 'Mexican problem', that the root of the problems facing Mexicans in American society was a backward Mexican culture. As Paul Coronel, the president of the 1940 YMCA Mexican Youth Conference, put it, 'We have concluded that our Mexican youth are not meeting the social and intellectual requirements of our highly progressive American civilization. ... We are blaming no one else but ourselves ... for our backward conditions.'[38]

Coronel did acknowledge that poverty was a fundamental problem in keeping Mexican American youth from attending school and that segregation was a source of their demoralization. He also implied that racism, although he did not use that term, contributed to their demoralization because they were aware that even Mexicans with 'good training' were unemployed. But, in the final analysis, the problem of lack of schooling was in his mind due to 'the lack of inspiration and encouragement in our homes.' The solution was to stimulate and inspire Mexican youth to the 'realization that they have a place in our American society ... no matter how favorable or unfavorable our living conditions may be.'[39]

The Mexican Voice also had an impact on YMCA youth active outside of California. Rebecca Muñoz, a student at Arizona State Teachers College, wrote that the publication was evidence that an 'intellectual awakening' was taking place among Mexican youth. According to her, their generation was 'becoming conscious of the fact that' they were part of 'a revolution of amalgamation' that was taking place in the US. In her view, and in that of others like her, the Mexican Youth Conferences were the start of a youth movement that would result in the betterment of the Mexican people in the United States.

This movement was contributing, she reasoned, to making Mexicans less 'race conscious' and making it possible for them to take their 'rightful places' in the society. She echoed the sentiments of Gutiérrez and others who were critical of an older generation that still maintained a loyalty to Mexico:

> I have always thought that the beauty of this great democracy lies in the freedom of thought and expression which grants these people the privilege of thinking as they wish, but oftentimes we see these people working a great harm for themselves by passing up great opportunities for their self-betterment because of a mistaken sense of loyalty to their cultural background.[40]

This Mexican American youth movement was defined by Paul Coronel in terms that were essentially moral rather than political or religious:

> Our youth movement is fundamentally non-sectarian and non-political. We are not interested in interfacing with any religious beliefs or political theories which characterize radical youth movements in our present day of political and economical [sic] struggle. Though we are extremely interested in the progress of our Mexican youth, we are not using measures which are offensive and radical. ... We are using calm, determination, sincerity, and a strong sense of responsibility to achieve our ends.[41]

Guadalberto Valadez, Coronel's successor as president of the Mexican Youth Conference, defined the goals of their movement in a ten-point platform published in *The Mexican Voice* in 1941.[42] This platform stressed the various themes that had been consistently underscored at the conferences and in previous issues of the publication, beginning with Gutiérrez's editorials. In particular, the goals were to 'better conditions among our Mexican race' through pride in Mexican identity, commitment to social work in Mexican communities, inspiration to a higher education, and improvement of race relations between 'Mexican-Americans' and 'other racial groups'. The platform was based on the 'impervious necessity of producing good American citizens of Mexican descent' so they could appreciate 'the great nation we are privileged to live in.'[43]

They would accomplish all this by developing themselves into leaders of their people and into professionals who could serve as positive role models for

Mexican youth. In the words of Félix Gutiérrez,

> Our job is uplifting our people, ejecting [sic] confidence into their veins, bolstering their depleted prides. And how can we do this? By becoming teachers, social workers, writers, lawyers, doctors, business men, trained workers, and working in every way possible for their benefit and betterment. Remember, we understand them because we are one of them and only we can bring out the best in them! We are they; they are us![44]

The Mexican-American Movement, Incorporated

Many of the original participants of the YMCA Mexican Youth Conferences had completed undergraduate college programs by 1941. Many of them had become social workers or teachers and attempted to implement the idealism and goals formulated while they were students. As professionals they became more aware of the issues facing their people. A handful of them, those who had remained in close touch since their participation in the conferences and who had worked closely with *The Mexican Voice*, concluded that in the final analysis the problems of Mexican American youth were only a part of the broader issues affecting their communities and the society at large. They decided that it was necessary to reach out to more people by creating an organization that was not limited to youth. Further, although many of the key leaders were Protestants, they were convinced that their relationship with the YMCA had been an impediment in reaching more youth from predominantly Catholic Mexican American communities. They were acutely aware of the strained relationship between the Catholic and Protestant churches at the time, and of the need to work closely with the Catholic Church if indeed they were to be successful in developing a broader base.

Divorcing themselves from the YMCA was a difficult decision for the group, since most of the individuals – if not all – had obtained their professional jobs through the direct assistance of the YMCA; some were even employed by the YMCA itself. Initially, YMCA officials – especially those who had nurtured the intellectual and political development of the individuals involved – reacted unfavorably to the formation of an independent organization. They warned of the dangers inherent in such a move and expressed concern that an independent organization of Mexican youth would be vulnerable to infiltration by leftist groups:

More than once in the past ten years it [the Mexican Youth Conference] has been threatened when un-American groups or movements have tried to develop an entering wedge. There was a time once before when there was a question as to whether the YMCA would continue to back the [Mexican] work, and a very un-American group anxiously waited our action and stood ready to put some real money into its development. ... I do not know of any other organization which would have guided the movement as it has, helping the movement to grow, yet letting it take its own course.[45]

The danger of infiltration was a direct reference to the efforts of the Communist Party youth organization, which allegedly had once tried to take over the leadership of the Mexican Youth Conference. Ultimately, the YMCA officials – although grudgingly – 'gave their blessing' to the creation of an independent organization. The formation of the Mexican-American Movement, Inc. (MAM) was subsequently announced by Paul Coronel in 1942.

We began as a conference, we went into a general movement and now we are in the process of organization. The hinge upon which our work moves is the very responsible local council. No longer will we rely entirely on regional conferences for the work in the various areas. The local councils are made up of Mexican-Americans and non-Mexican-Americans who are interested in the problems of the Mexican people residing in this country.[46]

The group was incorporated as a nonprofit organization and listed a total of forty-two members, most of them past participants in the Mexican Youth Conferences. Their advisory board was composed of prominent Mexican Americans and white professionals, ranging from progressives like Ernesto Galarza, by then a high official of the Pan American Union in Washington, D.C., to one official of the conservative Daughters of the American Revolution. Although it was to be an independent organization, the founders made clear that its objectives would be similar to those of the YMCA, the Boy Scouts of America, Catholic Social Services, and other agencies working for the 'betterment of Americans'. As evidenced by the makeup of the advisory board, the organization was to seek the involvement of both Mexicans and 'Anglo-Americans' who were committed to combating the 'backward conditions and attitudes' in Mexican communities and to improving race relations.

The major goals of the new organization, as listed in the official handbook, conformed to those of the Mexican Youth Conferences. Basically this meant that it would be 'politically non-partisan' and 'non-sectarian', that it would reflect a commitment to the solution of problems through education, and stand for the improvement of American society by 'raising the social level of the Mexican American people', all in the context, of course, of a belief in 'American institutions and in the democratic way of life.'[47]

In 1943, World War II was at its height and thousands of soldiers of Mexican descent were dying on the battlefields. Tragically, their younger brothers and sisters were being attacked on the streets of Los Angeles by white sailors and marines on leave. Those confrontations, which became known as the 'zoot-suit riots', were manifestations of a vulgar anti-Mexican racism promoted by the Hearst newspapers, which publicly condoned and supported these racial attacks.[48]

The sector of Mexican American youth most affected by the violence were the *pachucos* or street youth from the *barrio* gang subculture that had originally emerged in the Texas border town of El Paso and which, by the 1940s had spread throughout the Southwest and as far as Chicago. Many of the *pachucos* dressed in a style characterized by baggy slacks and long-tailed coats – 'zoot suits'. *Pachucos* were considered troublemakers by some MAM members, who perceived them as 'giving Mexicans a bad name'.

However, the zoot-suit riots compelled many members of the MAM organization to re-examine the problems of Mexican American youth more critically, and to place them in the context of 'prejudice, segregation, discrimination, and social inequality'. By the time of the riots, many of them were working in government agencies concerned with equal employment in war-related industries. There, they experienced firsthand what job discrimination against Mexican American workers was. Paul Coronel, MAM's first president, interpreted the cause of the riots in the following terms:

Much has been written on the 'Pachuco' problem. Delinquency and crime waves have always victimized racial groups but it seems minority groups are always the hardest hit. The youth riots have arisen from our Mexican-American communities and now our ... young are faced with second generation adjustments.... The neglect of these sociological problems can be traced back to the first days of Mexican immigration ... [and] ... the failure of our institutions to assimilate the Mexican citizens into the channels of American citizenship. Their purpose has been one of antagonism and hatred towards that very society which bred them. ... American people have not regarded the Mexican-American as an equal, racially or economically. Our American institutions, our schools, community, churches, etc. have regarded the Mexican as a problem and not as an asset to our American society. The American communities have followed a policy of segregating the Mexicans from the normal process of our American life.[49]

Coronel asserted, however, that Mexican Americans were also to be blamed for contributing to the conditions which created the conflict. Coronel criticized Mexican parents for not encouraging education, for failing to adopt United States citizenship, and for not leaving behind Mexican cultural traditions that made integration into the mainstream of American life difficult. *The Mexican Voice* editorial criticized *pachucos* who participated in the riots for giving Mexican Americans a bad name. He made it clear, however, that *pachucos* were products of the United States, not Mexico.[50]

MAM believed that the new leadership of Mexican American professionals would come from its own ranks, as well as from returning World War II veterans with the courage to boldly identify as Mexican Americans. This leadership would educate other 'hyphenated' Americans about the contributions Mexican Americans had made to society.

They perceived World War II as the single most significant event that would make possible the acceptance and integration of Mexican Americans into US society. Even though none of MAM's key leaders had served in the armed forces, approximately one-half of the membership had. The MAM leadership felt that the notable participation of Mexican Americans in the armed services was the best thing that had ever happened to Mexican American youth, because the war had given them the opportunity to associate with others of different racial and ethnic backgrounds:

The services have helped our Mexican-American. It has dressed all alike and given opportunities for advancement on merit and work. It has given many of our shy inferior feeling Americans of Mexican descent a chance to learn something, a chance to fit into the scheme of things, a chance to belong. This war ... is doing what we in our Mexican-American movement had planned to do in one generation. ... It has shown those 'across the track' that we all share the same problems. It has shown them what the Mexican Americans will do, what responsibility he will take and what leadership qualities he will demonstrate. After this struggle, the status of the Mexican Americans will be different.[51]

In 1944, MAM held its first convention in Los Angeles. Approximately one hundred people attended: representatives from the local power structure, educational institutions, and the federal government were present. The majority of the 'distinguished guests' were perceived by MAM as prospective supporters of the organization. The convention was to be the first step in developing the solid financial backing needed to build and expand the organization.

The convention also served as an opportunity for the leadership to further clarify the nature and goals of the organization. Because of its liberal and civil rights orientation, MAM had been criticized and attacked by right-wing groups and individuals as a 'communist' organization. MAM leaders were not aware of the fact that the FBI was investigating MAM as a possibly subversive organization.[52]

At the convention MAM confirmed its role as a social service organization. It was explained that the label 'Mexican American' was chosen over those like 'Latin American' and 'Spanish-American' because it reflected the fact that they were Americans of *Mexican* origin. This label therefore served to identify the purpose of the organization: to struggle on behalf of all Mexicans in the US (whether born in Mexico or the United States). Coronel attempted to allay any fears that MAM was either a 'race-baiter' or inflammatory organization attempting to cause disorder: 'We are not here to defend the Mexican race or put it down. ... The essence of our work is intelligence, understanding, sympathy, cooperation and a mutual understanding.'[53]

He made it clear that MAM had taken a stance against segregation in the schools and other public places, but that it would not pursue militant or aggressive methods in addressing the issue. MAM would protest discrimination against Mexican Americans, but would not pursue legal action because that would be beyond the purview of the organization. The fundamental objective of MAM was education:

[W]e are perfectly good examples of people who are in schools, in colleges, in universities, in the professions, who have gained their place because they have earned it. We can't gain our place by simply hollering at the weaknesses or talking about the discrimination against us. ... [W]e accept the shortcomings that we have and we work from scratch up.[54]

Richard Ibañez, an attorney and MAM supporter, emphasized to the delegates that the movement was founded upon the same democratic principles that underpinned the institutions of the United States. In a very real sense, he stated, MAM's objective was simply to work for the application of those principles to Mexican Americans:

> In short, the Mexican-American movement is based upon the philosophy of democracy because democracy is an attempt ... to give dignity and respect to the individual, but if an individual is deprived of economic standing, if an individual has no voice in the society in which he lives, if an individual cannot have the same opportunities that others have merely because he may have a different shade of color, then we can't practice democracy in reality can we? Therefore, the Mexican-American Movement has been established for the purpose of making it possible to have in fact democracy and that ... generally, is the purpose of the Mexican-American Movement. ... [A] great task lies ahead of this young virile organization. It is a noble work that deserves the support of every individual who truly believes in giving the dignity and respect to the individual.[55]

The MAM convention succeeded in making an impact. The *Los Angeles Times* and *La Opinión*, the Mexican newspaper in Los Angeles, provided extensive coverage of the convention and put MAM's work in a positive light. One representative of the local government praised MAM as 'Democracy in Action' and its work as 'founded on sound democratic bases'. Paul Coronel was jubilant about the results of MAM's first convention:

> What we did ... climaxes our 9 to 10 years of arduous labor. We have certainly gotten now the public's attention and we now command the respect of prominent Mexican and Anglo-American leaders. ... I won't be surprised if in the near future we shall face a financial boom. We have proven and tested our intentions and motives. The people will respond to the growing power that the M.A.M. is developing.[56]

In a letter to another MAM member, Coronel reported that MAM had also had an impact on educators:

The M.A.M. now holds deep respect by leading educators in this state and in Washington. Just recently, they called me from the San Bernardino County School office asking me to say something to a very dignified leader from the Federal Department of Education. This is the second time that we have been invited to such an important conference.[57]

The very success of the convention stimulated Coronel to come to grips with the political implications of MAM's work. He believed that the time had come to re-examine its 'non-political' stance, although not to change its commitment to remain 'non-sectarian'. He argued that the time had come for MAM to go beyond the discussion stage in political or quasi-political involvement. It was time to bring about a concrete delineation of MAM's objectives in social and political work. But it was first necessary to place any political stance in proper perspective:

As I now see the M.A.M. expanding, the term *non-political* should not mean that we do not pursue political party affiliations or existing administrations. … We have a wonderful opportunity to help push or even direct the establishment of United States Housing authorities in certain areas where Mexican families would be concretely benefited. Our endorsement of useful needed organizations like the FEPC [Fair Employment Practices Commission] does not brand us as ultra-liberals or otherwise. We must identify ourselves with social organizations which will really and factually improve the social standards of the Mexican people, otherwise the Mexicans themselves will not place much value on our work and ideals. We should continue to work with leading educators to help them understand the colossal errors found in the present policies of segregation. … To say we can't meddle in such business is to defeat the purpose for which we exist. … The non-sectarian statement should be carefully handled. … No matter how we look at it, most people are religious and we must never be branded as anti-Christian or as being indifferent to Christian ideals.[58]

Plans were also outlined for the expansion of MAM into Colorado, Arizona, Texas and New Mexico. MAM members also participated on the Coordinating Council of the Latin American Youth Congress, which was attempting to develop a political action group that would serve the political needs of Mexican Americans. MAM's newspaper, *The Mexican Voice*, was renamed *Forward*. The organization also began to call for the development of community councils that could become bases for political mobilization. Among other things, the councils would 'support bills and ... candidates who voice the will of the community. We can use our vote, not as a threat, to coerce, to fight, but to express our will.'[59]

Despite these plans, MAM never reached the zenith that its leadership anticipated. World War II proved to be a disruptive event, and, in a sense, it always overshadowed the movement. The end of the war did not produce the wave of veterans interested in social activism upon whom MAM had counted heavily. Very few of even those veterans who had been MAM members before being drafted returned to participate in the organization. Reunification with families and the pressures of resuming full-time careers or college studies made it hard for them to assume additional activity and responsibility. The fact that the organization had survived for the duration of the war was credited to the leadership of Paul Coronel and a handful of other members.

As MAM's membership and overall participation began to decline, attempts were made to rejuvenate it by creating a youth component. MAM created a Youth Council, which it hoped would carry on with the same spirit and enthusiasm that had exemplified the earlier YMCA Mexican Youth Conference. The MAM leadership had expectations that the Council would successfully recruit 'new blood'. The organization had lost its momentum, however, and, as Coronel explained, a reawakening would require new people:

> I am beginning to feel we cannot depend on the old blood in our movement. The only thing that will awaken the movement and the people in it to the responsibility we owe our people is new blood. It is wonderful to speak to people and tell them what we're trying to do and feel the enthusiasm those people radiate. We have lost so much of that feeling.[60]

The incorporation of MAM as a nonprofit organization never generated the kind of funding necessary for its growth and survival. The anticipated donations from influential Anglos on MAM's advisory board and others in the power structure who had supported MAM's development never materialized. Since the inception of the organization, Paul Coronel had personally absorbed many of the costs of MAM activities. In the end he decided that he could no longer do so, and in 1950 MAM ceased to exist. Tragically, Paul Coronel and Félix Gutiérrez suffered untimely deaths shortly thereafter.

Into the Fifties

MAM's failure to survive did not mean the end of efforts to pursue the goals of the organization. Former members of MAM became involved in the formation of other community and educational organizations in Mexican American communities. Those who became teachers, for example, founded the Association of Mexican American Educators (AMAE). Manuel Ceja and Manuel Banda were the most prominent among them.[61] Those who became social workers contributed to the founding of the Community Service Organization (CSO), an organization inspired by the teachings of a radical Jewish grass-roots organizer by the name of Saul Alinsky. Others became active in community and electoral politics.

It was in those new organizations that former members of MAM came together with returning World War II veterans who shared their ideas about a Mexican American identity and social and political equality for their people. AMAE, CSO, and the American G.I. Forum, another new organization created by and for Mexican American World War II veterans who had been denied veteran's benefits,[62] joined hands with the League of United Latin American Citizens to promote the interests of Mexican Americans in education, housing, and social services. Veterans also became directly involved in electoral politics throughout the South and Midwest and contributed to the formation of groups like the Mexican American Political Association (MAPA) in California and the Political Association of Spanish Speaking Peoples (PASSO) in Texas and Arizona.

Collectively, these groups came to represent the new professional sector of an emerging Mexican American middle class with a progressive politics in the liberal capitalist tradition. They also advocated an ethnic politics rooted in the dialogue about questions of Mexican and American identities that were first articulated in the pages of *The Mexican Voice*. As such they became part of what I call the Mexican-American Generation. They shared the ideas and goals of those who founded the League of United Latin American Citizens in Texas.[63]

The student activists who participated in the YMCA Mexican Youth Conference and later created MAM followed in the footsteps of Ernesto Galarza and simultaneously departed from his ideological trajectory. They were all youth from the Mexican or Mexican American working class, but although Galarza was concerned about the identity crisis facing Mexican American youth, he also participated in the politics of class struggle, becoming the first organizer in the US labor movement with a Ph.D. In contrast, the founders of MAM committed themselves to building a Mexican American professional sector and entering the ranks of the middle class.

This fact does not diminish the significance of the Mexican Youth Conferences and MAM. They made a historic contribution as the first organized effort of student activists to confront the issues facing their people in the United States. The YMCA exposed them to ideas, ideas that were in contradiction to the widespread racist attitudes towards Mexicans and Mexican Americans. They were also ideas, however, that promoted the myth of American democracy and implicitly, if not explicitly, the virtues of capitalism and the evils of socialism and communism. Finally, it must be borne in mind that the Mexican-American Generation was a product of the politics of the 1930s and 1940s. The Roosevelt presidency put America back to work and saved the working class from the despair of the Depression. WPA programs directly helped Mexican American workers. World War II opened new doors for them by providing veterans with the G.I. Bill – federal financial assistance to get higher education – and therefore upward social mobility. It appeared to that generation that Mexican Americans were finally about to profit from democracy and the 'American way of life'. Their hopes were deceived, however. By the 1950s, Mexicans in the US had lost much of the ground they had gained in employment during the war. Anti-Mexican sentiment, fueled by the racism and McCarthyism permeating the postwar period, prevented consolidation of their wartime gains.

Notes

1 Leonard Pitt, *The Decline of the Californios: A Social History of the Spanish-Speaking Californians, 1846–1890*, Berkeley 1970, describes the process in California. For New Mexico and Texas, see Roxanne Dunbar Ortiz, *Roots of Resistance: Land Tenure in New Mexico*, Los Angeles 1980, and David Mantejano, *Anglos and Mexicans in the Making of Texas, 1836–1986*, Austin 1987.

2 Mario Barrera, *Race and Class in the Southwest: A Theory of Racial Inequality*, Notre Dame 1979.

3 Ibid.

4 Benjamin Floyd Pittenger, *Indoctrination for American Democracy*, New York 1941, p. 1.

5 David Montejano, *Anglos and Mexicans in the Making of Texas, 1836–1986*, Austin 1987.

6 Carlos Muñoz Jr., 'Occidental's Barrio Boy', *Occidental College Quarterly*, Summer 1987.

7 Lecture by Ernesto Galarza, Chicano Studies Library, University of California, Berkeley, 1976.

8 S. J. Holmes, 'Perils of the Mexican Invasion', *North American Review*, pp. 615–23.

9 House Committee on Immigration and Naturalization, Western Hemisphere Immigration, 71st Cong., 2d sess., 1930, p. 75.

10 Holmes, 'Perils', pp. 617–20.

11 C. M. Goethe, 'The Influx of Mexican Amerinds', *Eugenics*, Jan. 1929, p. 6.

12 Committee on Immigration, Western Hemisphere Immigration, p. 436.

13 Abraham Hoffman, *Unwanted Mexican Americans in the Great Depression*, Tucson 1974, p. 47.

14 Ernesto Galarza, 'Life in the United States for Mexican People: Out of the Experience of a Mexican', in *Proceedings of the National Council of Social Work*, 1929.

15 Ibid.

16 Ernesto Galarza, *Barrio Boy: The Story of a Boy's Acculturation*, Notre Dame 1971.

17 Galarza, 'Life in the United States'.

18 Katherine K. Murray, 'Mexican Community Services', *Journal of Sociology and Social Research*, vol. 17, no. 6, July–Aug. 1933, p. 547.

19 Emory S. Bogardus, 'Second Generation Mexicans', *Journal of Sociology and Social Research*, vol. 13, no. 3, Jan.–Feb. 1929, p. 277.

20 Ibid., p. 281.

21 Carlos M. Alcala and Jorge C. Rangel, 'Project Report: De Jure Segregation of Chicanos in Texas Schools', *Harvard Civil Rights-Civil Liberties Law Review* 7, March 1972; Arnoldo De León, *They Called Them Greasers: Anglo Attitudes Toward Mexicans in Texas, 1821–1900* (Austin 1983); Guadalupe San Miguel, Jr., *'Let All of Them Take Heed': Mexican Americans and the Campaign for Educational Equality in Texas*, Austin 1987.

22 Sherwood Eddy, *A Century with Youth: A History of the YMCA from 1844 to 1944*, New York 1944, p. 5.

23 Ibid.

24 Eddy, *Century with Youth*, p. 8.

25 C. Howard Hopkins, *History of the Y.M.C.A. in North America*, New York 1951, p. 479.

26 R. Douglas Brackenridge and Francisco O. García-Treto, *Iglesia Presbiteriana: A History of Presbyterians and Mexican-Americans*, San Antonio 1974, p. 128. See also E. C. Orozco, *Republican Protestantism in Aztlán*, Santa Barbara 1980, for a critique of the role of the Protestant churches in Mexican American culture.

27 Alfred White, 'The Apperceptive Mass of Foreigners as Applied to Americanization: The Mexican Group', Thesis, University of California, Berkeley, 1923, p. 52.

28 Jesse Howell Atwood, *The Racial Factor in Y.M.C.A.'s: A Report on Negro-White Relationships in Twenty-Four Cities*, New York 1946, p. 16.

29 Taylor Reedy and Harold A. Wagner, former YMCA officials, letters to the author, 11 August 1982 and 15 January 1982.

30 Manuel Ruiz, Jr., for example, one of the first Mexican Americans to obtain a law degree in the United States, was a member of the YMCA Hi-Y Club during the time he was captain of the Manual Arts High School track team in 1923 in Los Angeles. Manual Ruiz, Jr., letter to the author, 23 July 1982.

31 Taylor Reedy, letter to the author.

32 Ibid.

33 José Rodriguez, 'The Value of Education', *The Mexican Voice*, July 1938.

34 Manuel De La Raza [Félix Gutiérrez], 'Nosotros', *The Mexican Voice*, 1943.

35 Manuel De La Raza [Félix Gutiérrez], 'Nosotros', *The Mexican Voice*, Oct.–Nov. 1938, pp. 16–17.

36 Ibid.

37 Manuel Ceja, 'Are We Proud of Being Mexicans?', *The Mexican Voice*, August 1938, p. 9.

38 Paul Coronel, 'Where Is the Mexican Youth Conference Aiming?', *The Mexican Voice*, February 1940, p. 1.

39 Ibid.

40 Rebecca Muñoz, 'Horizons', *The Mexican Voice*, July 1939.

41 Paul Coronel, 'Where Is the Mexican Youth Conference Aiming?' p. 1.

42 Guadalberto Valadez, 'The Principles of the Mexican Youth Conference', *The Mexican Voice*, Winter 1941.

43 Ibid.

44 Manuel De La Raza [Félix Gutiérrez], 'Nosotros', *The Mexican Voice*, Nov.–Dec. 1939.

45 J. V. Root to Félix Gutiérrez, letter, 20 April 1942.

46 Paul Coronel, 'As We Move', *The Mexican Voice*, Summer 1944.

47 *Handbook of the Mexican-American Movement, Inc.*, n.p., n.d.

48 Mauricio Mazón, *The Zoot Suit Riots: The Psychology of Symbolic Annihilation*, Austin 1984.

49 Paul Coronel, 'The Pachuco Problem', *The Mexican Voice*, 1943, p. 3.

50 Ibid., p. 4.

51 Manuel De La Raza [Félix Gutiérrez], 'Nosotros', *The Mexican Voice*, Spring 1942.

52 Guadalberto Valdez, 'The President Speaks', *Forward*, 12 May 1946 and interview, 29 August 1978.

53 Proceedings (unpublished), First Annual Convention, Mexican-American Movement, 8 October 1944, p. 63. Author's files.

54 Ibid., p. 67.

55 Ibid., pp. 122–23.

56 Paul Coronel to Stephen A. Reyes, letter, 11 November 1944.

57 Paul Coronel to Stephen A. Reyes, letter, 9 March 1945.

58 Paul Coronel to Stephen A. Reyes, letter, 12 April 1945.

59 Forward, 12 May 1946, p. 1.

60 Paul Coronel to Angelo Cano, letter, 10 August 1949.

61 Carl Allsup, *The American G.I. Forum: Origins and Evolution*, Austin 1982.

62 Association of Mexican American Educators, 'A Brief History of the A.M.A.E.', n.d., author's files.

63 Moises Sandoval, *Our Legacy: The First Fifty Years*, Washington, D.C. 1979.

2

The Militant Challenge:
The Chicano Generation

By 1950 the Mexican and Mexican American population in the United States had increased significantly – doubling in California, for example. World War II had resulted in an influx of Mexican and Mexican American labor from rural areas to the urban centers of the South and Midwest. The economic prosperity generated by the war had made possible some upward social mobility for a small sector of the Mexican American working class. But most Mexican Americans remained rooted in the semi-skilled and unskilled proletariat. Although many of the wartime employment gains they had made in industry had been lost by the end of the 1940s, Mexican American workers continued to make some progress through their participation in trade union activity, including militant strikes, throughout the Southwest.[1]

Mexican women played important roles in these labor struggles. The 1950 miners strike in Silver City, New Mexico provides a dramatic example. The strike lasted almost two years. When the miners were prohibited from picketing, their wives took over the picket lines and succeeded in keeping the strike alive, while the men reluctantly did the housework at home. The police attempted to break their picket lines by arresting those they identified as the leaders, and several of the women were beaten by police. Nevertheless, the women stood their ground. The classic movie *Salt of the Earth* captured the drama of the strike and also underscored the issues of gender roles in the family. It was made during the McCarthyist anti-communist hysteria, and the filmmakers were part of the Hollywood Ten group of directors and script-writers who were blacklisted as communists in the film industry.[2]

The urbanization of the majority of Mexican Americans during this period was a major contributor to their 'Americanization'. The children of the Mexican American working class in particular came into direct contact with mainstream American culture through the dominant political institutions in the cities. Urbanization resulted in the acceleration of the acculturation and assimilation process and consequently the legitimization of the liberal capitalist ideology that underpinned the politics of accommodation and integration pursued by middle-class Mexican American organizations such as the League of United Latin American Citizens. These organizations had challenged the segregation of Mexican American children in the public schools beginning in 1929 and won several victories in the courts in the 1940s over *de jure* school segregation, decisions that had been hailed by LULAC as major victories for 'Democratic assimilation'.[3]

Mendez v. Westminster was the most famous of those cases. An eight-year-old girl by the name of Sylvia Mendez and her younger brothers were not allowed to attend an all-white Westminster, California elementary school because they were dark-skinned Mexicans. Her parents and the parents of three other Mexican American children sued the school district in 1946. The Ninth US Circuit Court of Appeals ruled in favor of the Mendez family on the grounds that the 'separate but equal' doctrine violated the US Constitution. The court's ruling in this case ended legal segregation in the state of California. Several organizations joined the appellate case as *amici curiae*, including the NAACP, represented by a young Thurgood Marshall. He would later use this case as the precedent for the *Brown v. Board of Education* case of 1954 that ended racial segregation in the South. De facto segregated schooling nevertheless remained the reality for most Mexican American youth in California and throughout the Southwest.[4]

The Mexican-born and Mexican American rural proletariat continued to be the most oppressed sector within the ranks of labor. Under the leadership of Ernesto Galarza it struggled against the far greater power of Southwestern agribusiness. Galarza, who as a student activist in 1929 had spoken out in defense of Mexican workers, had gone on to become the first Mexican American to earn a PhD in history and political science at Columbia University.[5] However, during the postwar years he became a labor organizer instead of pursuing an academic career. His first experience as an organizer was with the

Southern Tenant Farm Union led by the socialist H. L. Mitchell. He organized African American and white workers in Louisiana was later assigned by
Mitchell to organize Mexican American farmworkers in California in 1949.
Together with Mitchell, Galarza struggled within the labor movement to obtain support for organizing farmworkers. In 1950, the AFL-CIO endorsed
their efforts and appointed Galarza the executive secretary of the newly created National Farm Labor Union. César Chávez's father became a member of
Galarza's union.[6]

The politics of class struggle in the fields and in the cities did not move
students of Mexican descent to participate in those struggles or to follow in
Galarza's footsteps. The politics of the 1950s were not conducive to radicalism
anywhere, especially to participation in social struggles that could be easily
characterized as 'communist inspired'. Like other young people of their generation, Mexican American student activists – the few in existence – were influenced by the politics of super-patriotism generated by the war against Hitler
and fascism and reinforced by the Cold War against new enemies, Stalin and
communism. The decade witnessed the rise of right-wing ideologues like
Senator Joseph McCarthy of Wisconsin, who spearheaded an anticommunist
crusade across the nation, and the passage of right-wing federal legislation like
the McCarran-Walter Act, which resulted in the deportation of Mexican labor activists considered subversive of US national interests.

The Mexican American student presence on college campuses increased
during the decade as a direct result of the G.I. Bill. Among the thousands of
returning Mexican American veterans who took advantage of this opportunity to pursue a higher education were Américo Paredes, Octavio Romano-V.,
and Ralph Guzmán. They were destined to become, along with Galarza, significant contributors to Mexican American intellectual life.

Few returning veterans who went to college became involved in organizing Mexican American students on campus. Those who did become political
activists limited their involvement to mostly local community struggles and
joined middle-class and professional organizations. They did not choose to
identify themselves as students but as veterans. The politics of the times notwithstanding, the anti-Mexican racism in the larger society, although not as
ugly as it had been during the 1920s and 1930s, compelled a few of the more
progressive of them to speak out in defense of their people in the context of
the liberal reformist political tradition typified by the LULAC organization
and further developed by the new middle-class and professional organiza-

tions of the post–World War II era. Veterans played central leadership roles in those organizations. Their political consciousness was shaped by patriotic Americanism and the anticommunism then permeating society. They did not reject their Mexican origins but, like the generation of the 1930s, emphasized the American part of their Mexican American identity. In their minds, political accommodation and assimilation were the only path toward equal status in a racist society. Integration in education and at all levels of society would result, they believed, in the acceptance of their people as first-class citizens.

They acknowledged that Mexican Americans were victims of racism, but they did not promote a nonwhite racial identity for their people. Instead, they promoted the image of Mexican Americans as a white ethnic group that had little in common with African Americans. Some ignored their nonwhite Native American racial background for fear of being put in the category of 'people of color' and thus suffering the same discrimination as African Americans. They believed that by minimizing the existence of racism toward their people, they could 'deflect' anti-Mexican sentiment in society. Others rejected their nonwhite origins altogether and promoted a 'Spanish' or 'Latin American' identity.[7] As products of a racist society, others simply held anti-Black attitudes. Mass protest, confrontation, radicalism, and coalition politics with other people of color were therefore rejected as alternatives in the pursuit of civil rights and equal opportunity in jobs and education.

They perceived US society as democratic: all Mexican Americans had to do was to vote and elect their own to political office. LULAC, MAPA, and CSO, for example, were indeed able to elect a few of their members to office, but on the whole, Mexican Americans remained underrepresented in the political process and largely powerless. This was especially true in California.

From the ranks of the more progressive members of the Mexican-American Generation emerged intellectuals who had a more critical attitude toward US democracy. Ralph Guzmán personified these intellectuals. Like many of them he was a World War II veteran who had attended college on the G.I. Bill and had participated in the development of new middle-class organizations. He was a prominent member of CSO and worked as a journalist for the *Eastside Sun* community newspaper, where he first spoke out against injustices suffered by Mexicans and Mexican Americans.[8] He also served as director of the civil rights department of the Alianza Hispano-Americana, and in that capacity he engaged in litigation against the segregation of Mexican American children in the schools. During the 1950s he was one of the few Mexican Americans who spoke out against McCarthyism. In recognition of his work for civil rights, he became the first Mexican American appointed to the Board of Directors of the American Civil Liberties Union (ACLU). Guzmán received much support from another World War II veteran, Edward Roybal, the first Mexican American to be elected to the Los Angeles City Council. Roybal jeopardized his re-election by courageously defending the rights of free speech and association during the McCarthy era and publicly criticizing the use of 'Red Scare' tactics against those who defended Mexican Americans against racist attacks. One of the most progressive members of the Mexican-American Generation, Roybal was a cofounder of CSO and MAPA and later became the first Mexican American congressman from California.

When John F. Kennedy declared his candidacy for president in 1960, he called Guzmán and other leaders of the Mexican American middle-class and professional organizations for help. The Kennedy campaign thus marked the entry of this leadership into national politics. They played an important role in the campaign through the Viva Kennedy Clubs they organized in the southwestern states. The Kennedy campaign also recruited Mexican American college student activists into the Viva Kennedy Clubs and they became visible as well in middle-class organizations. Most importantly, it marked the beginning of a new era in politics that was to eventually produce the Chicano Generation: Mexican American student activists who would embark upon a new quest for identity and power characterized by a militant and radical politics.

The politics of the early 1960s differed markedly from those of the 1950s. The Kennedy presidency followed by the Johnson administration marked the end of McCarthyism and the beginning of a liberal political era in national politics. Liberalism nurtured the aspirations for political change on the part of African Americans and created cracks in the system of racial oppression in the South. The dramatic emergence of the civil rights movement generated reform in education and politics. Although chiefly aimed at benefiting African Americans, the movement created a political atmosphere beneficial to Mexican American working-class youth, for it gave them more access to institutions of higher education. Their access to college was no longer limited to patronage by the YMCA and the Protestant and Catholic churches, as had been the case in the 1930s, nor was it limited to veterans with G.I. Bill benefits, as it had largely been in the 1940s. There were now hundreds of youth of Mexican descent attending college as a direct result of federal educational programs made possible by the civil rights movement and implemented especially during the Johnson administration.

The growing numbers of Mexican American students on college campuses did not come close to representing a significant proportion of the Mexican American population: Mexican American youth remained severely underrepresented. Neither did they produce a visible Mexican American student activism. But from those numbers came a few student activists who, between 1963 and 1967, were inspired by Dr. Martin Luther King Jr. and participated in some activities and organizations of the civil rights movement. Some of them became active indirectly or directly as members of the Student Nonviolent Coordinating Committee. For example, Maria Varela became a key SNCC organizer in Alabama, where she established an adult literacy project.[9] She was from New Mexico and before joining SNCC had been a cofounder of Students for a Democratic Society at the University of Michigan. Elizabeth ('Betita') Sutherland Martinez, a civil rights activist of Mexican descent, became the director of the New York City SNCC office in 1964 and also worked in Mississippi.[10] Others participated in the 1963 March on Washington organized by Dr. Martin Luther King Jr. and the Southern Christian Leadership Conference. At San Jose State College in Northern California, a few Mexican American students joined a campus protest when a Black student was denied admission.[11] In 1967, at my campus, California State University at Los Angeles, I established a solidarity relationship between the United Mexican American Students (UMAS) and the Black Student Union.

Unfortunately, many others who had participated in SNCC and other organizations or who had been influenced by the civil rights movement came to the realization that Mexican Americans were not a concern of the Black civil rights leadership and its allies. The War on Poverty programs created by the Johnson administration did not initially address poverty in the barrios of the South and Midwest. The first organized student effort in the nation to bring specific attention to the needs of Mexican Americans and youth in particular took place on the San Jose State College campus in 1964 when Armando Valdez organized the Student Initiative (SI). Valdez was a member of Students for a Democratic Society and a supporter of SNCC.[12] He recruited some students from the handful of Mexican Americans on campus at that time and others from the ranks of white liberal student activists. The objectives of Student Initiative focused on pressuring the campus administration to create programs to recruit Mexican American students and tutorial programs to help them survive once they entered college.

Mexican American student activists were also exposed to a more radical politics during the early 1960s as left political organizations resurfaced from the underground where they had been driven during the McCarthy era. Communist and socialist youth groups became visible on college campuses as did nonsocialist New Left groups like SDS. Campus protest against the Vietnam War was also becoming visible, as manifested in the 'teach-ins' organized by white liberal and leftist faculty and students.

In 1964 Luis Valdez and Roberto Rubalcava, student activists at San Jose State, became associated with the Progressive Labor Party (PL); as an undergraduate student Valdez had been active in the Viva Kennedy Clubs and in MAPA. Valdez and Rubalcava traveled to Cuba as part of a PL delegation,[13] and their first-hand observation of the Cuban revolution inspired them to produce the first radical manifesto written by Mexican American student activists. The manifesto read in part:

> The Mexican in the United States has been ... no less a victim of American imperialism than his impoverished brothers in Latin America. In the words of the Second Declaration of Havana, tell him of 'misery, feudal exploitation, illiteracy, starvation wages,' and he will tell you that you speak of Texas; tell him of 'unemployment, the policy of repression against the workers, discrimination ... oppression by the oligarchies', and he will tell you that you speak of California; tell him of US domination in Latin America, and he will tell you that he knows that Shark and what he devours, because he has lived in its very entrails. The history of the American Southwest provides a brutal panorama of nascent imperialism.[14]

The manifesto represented a radical departure from the political thought of the Mexican-American Generation and a harsh critique of its political leadership:

> Spanish-speaking leaders are not leaders at all; Americanized beyond recall, they neither understand or care about the basic Mexican-American population, which has an identity of its own. As sons of Mexican manual laborers in California, we have traveled to Revolutionary Cuba ... to emphasize the historical and cultural unanimity of all Latin American peoples, north and south of the border. Having no leaders of our own, we accept Fidel Castro.[15]

Valdez returned from Cuba and after graduating from college joined the radical San Francisco Mime Troupe, where he continued to refine his critique of the assimilationist and accommodationist perspective of the Mexican-American Generation and worked to develop a new cultural identity and politics for Mexican Americans. Some of that thinking came to fruition when he joined the farmworkers' struggle in Delano, California in 1965 and founded the Teatro Campesino. Many of the ideas behind the conceptualization of the Chicano identity and the development of the Chicano Generation of the late 1960s emanated from the ideas of Luis Valdez and the cultural work of his Teatro Campesino. Key members of the Teatro were student activists he recruited from college campuses in Northern California.[16] One of the most prominent was Ysidro Ramon Macias, an undergraduate activist at the University of California, Berkeley. Macias became one of the Teatro's original playwrights; his influential play *The Ultimate Pendejada* dramatized the rejection of the assimilationism of Mexican-American identity and the emergence of Chicano identity.

However, Valdez and Rubalcava were unusual in the early 1960s. Most Mexican American student activists remained very much in the mold of the Mexican-American Generation's political thought and identity. Middle-class and professional organizations reached Mexican American youth by directly recruiting them into their organizations or indirectly influencing their ideological direction through participation in community youth programs. LULAC, for example, had a youth group called the Junior LULAC for youth between the ages of fourteen and eighteen. Its purpose was defined as carrying 'forth the work of the LULAC at the teen-age level' and serving as a training ground for the future leadership of the organization via participation in its 'social, civic, sports, and parliamentary activities'.[17] The LULAC constitution made clear that its youth auxiliary could not act 'contrary to the direction of the LULAC Supreme Council or the better judgement of' its adult leadership.[18]

Members of AMAE and MAPA and other professional Mexican American political activists, mostly social workers and teachers, promoted participation in the Catholic Youth Organization (CYO), Protestant church programs, and city youth programs. As in the 1930s, Los Angeles again became the site of a conference of Mexican American youth to provide 'citizenship training'. This time around the conference was not sponsored by the YMCA, but was organized by the Los Angeles County Human Relations Commission under the leadership of Mexican American World War II and Korean War veterans who had become social workers and teachers.[19] These conferences were held in the summer at Camp Hess Kramer and were patterned somewhat after the YMCA Mexican Youth Conferences of the 1930s. The first conference was held in 1963.[20] In addition to promoting good citizenship, the conferences were forums for discussion of problems in the schools and communities of the participants. Speakers came from the leadership of middle-class and professional organizations, and they exposed the student participants to the politics of the times. However, unlike the YMCA conferences of the 1930s, the Camp Kramer conferences did not result in a publication similar to *The Mexican Voice*.

Most of the participants were bright, 'clean-cut' high school students selected for their leadership skills. After entering college some of them became participants in the formation of Mexican American student organizations on ˇcampuses in the Los Angeles area. These new organizations promoted Mexican American identity and the theme of 'progress through education' defined by the 1930s student activists.

Before these student organizations emerged, however, several other events occurred which, in addition to the Southern civil rights movement, also had great impact on Mexican American student activists in the early 1960s. These included the dramatic emergence of the farmworkers struggle in California led by César Chávez, the land grant struggle in New Mexico led by Reies López Tijerina, and increasing discontent on the part of the Mexican American middle-class leadership with the Democratic Party and other dominant political institutions.

On 16 September 1965, the anniversary of Mexican independence from Spain in 1810, the National Farm Workers Association (NFWA) met at a local Catholic church hall in Delano, California and voted to join the striking Filipino grape pickers in the area. Four days later, members of the NFWA led by César Chávez joined their Filipino brothers and sisters on the picket lines with shouts of 'Viva La Causa!'[21] ˇLuis Valdez wrote the 'Plan de Delano' which proclaimed 'the beginning of a social movement in fact and not pronouncements.'[22] The 'Plan de Delano' defined the farmworker struggle as a non-violent revolution 'for social justice' led by the 'sons of the Mexican Revolution' and called for the unity of all poor farmworkers across the nation:

> The strength of the poor is also in union. We know that the poverty of the Mexican or Filipino worker in California is the same as that of all

farm workers across the country, the Negroes and poor whites, the Puerto Ricans, Japanese, and Arabians; in short, all the races that comprise the oppressed minorities of the United States.... We want to be equal with all the working men in the nation ... to those who oppose us be they ranchers, police, politicians, or speculators, we say that we are going to continue fighting until we die, or we win. WE SHALL OVERCOME.[23]

Student activists, especially those on some of the larger college and university campuses in California, were moved by the upwelling of the farmworkers' struggle to begin support activities on behalf of the farmworker movement.

The increasing discontent of the leadership of LULAC, MAPA, and other middle-class organizations also had a significant impact on student activists associated with those organizations. The nature of this discontent was not ideological but was initially related to the lack of upward mobility within the Democratic Party and other institutions, lack of Democratic support for Mexican American candidates for elective office, and the party's habit of taking the Mexican American vote for granted. MAPA and PASSO were in fact created by the middle-class leadership as a direct result of those realities. MAPA in California was the direct result of the Democratic Party's refusal to support the candidacies of prominent political leaders Edward Roybal and Henry Lopez for statewide office.

The 'Viva Kennedy' campaign in 1960 had been a watershed in the development of middle-class political organizations, since it marked the entry of their leadership into the arena of national politics for the first time. With the exception of California, Viva Kennedy Clubs had successfully mobilized the Mexican American vote for Kennedy. After Kennedy's election to the presidency, these leaders expected that some of their own would receive high-level appointments in the Kennedy administration. These expectations were frustrated. The Mexican American organizations were ignored by Kennedy and Democratic Party leaders. The leadership of MAPA bitterly criticized the Kennedy administration at the organization's fourth annual convention in November 1963, just days before Kennedy's assassination in Dallas. Edward Roybal criticized Kennedy for not doing anything he had promised during the course of the 'Viva Kennedy' campaign of 1960: 'It has taken the Kennedy Administration three years to appoint a coordinator on Latin American affairs and it has done nothing for Mexican Americans in the Southwest who helped the President get elected.'[24]

It was not until the Johnson administration that some Mexican Americans were appointed to a specially created presidential committee named the Inter-Agency of Mexican American Affairs, but this committee had no power nor was it an integral part of the administration. To add insult to injury, Lyndon Johnson's War on Poverty did not have Mexican Americans on its list of priorities but instead had a limited focus on the African American poor.

In Crystal City, Texas in 1963 the leadership of PASSO united with the predominantly Mexican American Teamsters union in a local election campaign. The result was the defeat of all the white candidates and the victory of all the Mexican American candidates endorsed by the two organizations. The Crystal City election was of historic significance: for the first time Mexican Americans had taken complete control of a city government in the Southwest. Crystal City was thus widely viewed as a 'revolt' against white political domination. Although those who took power were far from being radicals, their election did have a profound impact on student activists in Texas.[25] The Mexican American takeover of Crystal City's City Council lasted only two years, but it was training ground for José Angel Gutiérrez, at the time a nineteen-year-old undergraduate, who was to cofound MAYO four years later at St. Mary's University in San Antonio. He later returned to Crystal City to help found La Raza Unida Party, the first Mexican American political party in US history, and to lead a second electoral revolt with more permanence than the first.[26]

By 1966 the Mexican American middle-class leadership was prepared to take more public measures to express their discontent with the Johnson administration. On 8 April, at a conference called by the federal Equal Employment Opportunity Commission in Albuquerque, New Mexico, the presidents of LULAC, PASSO, and other organizations attacked the commission for not having a Mexican American leader as a member and for having only one on its Washington, D.C. staff. They also expressed displeasure that the commission did not take any action against the eight hundred major corporations in the Southwest that did not employ any Mexican Americans. The leaders presented eight demands to the Johnson administration for affirmative action on behalf of Mexican Americans.[27] After an hour at the conference, all fifty Mexican American leaders, representing organizations in all the southwestern states, walked out in protest.

The walkout in Albuquerque marked the first time that the middle-class leadership had engaged in an act of collective protest against the government. This action, while mild in comparison to what happened later in the 1960s, nevertheless had some impact on those student activists who were products of the Mexican-American Generation. It revealed a more critical political consciousness that was emerging among those who had not previously protested the contradictions of US democracy and who in particular had never used a civil rights tactic of public protest on behalf of Mexican Americans. The walkout did not represent a change in ideology on the part of the middle-class leadership, but it did encourage a more critical posture toward dominant political institutions among the Mexican American youth associated with those organizations.

A few of the middle-class leaders did make a radical departure from the ideology of the Mexican-American Generation. The most important of them was Rodolfo 'Corky' Gonzáles of Denver, Colorado. After a successful prize-fighting career, he had become a successful small businessman as a bail bondsman and was a Democratic Party politician well on his way to elective office. He had served as a Democratic precinct captain and was appointed the Colorado Coordinator of the 'Viva Kennedy' campaign in 1960. He served as the director of the War on Poverty program in Denver during the Johnson administration. By 1965, however, he had grown increasingly disenchanted with the Democratic Party leadership and resigned his party membership and posts as well as his position in the War on Poverty program. He explained his decision in a letter to the county chairman of the Democratic Party:

> The individual who makes his way through the political muck of today's world, and more so the minority representatives, suffers from such immense loss of soul and dignity that the end results are as rewarding as a heart attack, castration, or cancer.... can only visualize your goal as complete emasculation of manhood, sterilization of human dignity, and that you not only consciously but purposely are creating a world of lackeys, political bootlickers and prostitutes.[28]

After his resignation from the Democratic Party he founded the Crusade for Justice in 1965, the first Mexican American civil rights organization in the nation. He and his organization were to become extremely significant in the emergence of the Chicano civil rights movement.

On 5 June 1967, another major event took place that had an important impact on Mexican American student activists. It occurred in Tierra Amarilla, New Mexico where Reies López Tijerina had been leading a struggle to recapture lands that had been stolen from the Hispano people (Spanish-Americans who were direct descendants of the original Spanish colonizers of New Mexico).[29] Tijerina had founded the Alianza Federal de Mercedes as the organizational vehicle of that struggle. On 5 June, a group of armed men from the Alianza took over the county courthouse, taking twenty hostages who they held for about an hour and then released. A jailer and a state police officer were wounded. Later Tijerina's men fled into the mountains. The National Guard was mobilized, and it carried out a massive manhunt, complete with tanks. Forty innocent Hispanos were arrested. This was the first militant armed action taken by Mexican Americans anywhere in the Southwest for over a hundred years, and it became a source of inspiration for some student activists, especially in New Mexico.

With all these events taking place between 1964 and 1967, Mexican American student activism was becoming more visible on the campus as well as in the community. Federally funded War on Poverty programs in the community became training grounds for many students, and they became participants in local community politics. Some of them were influenced by the grassroots community-organizing approach of Saul Alinsky.

By 1966, student activists, though still relatively few in number, were seriously discussing the formation of distinct Mexican American student organizations on their campuses throughout the Southwest. By the fall of 1967 organizations had emerged on several college campuses in Los Angeles and on two campuses in Texas. At St. Mary's College in San Antonio, Texas it was named the Mexican American Youth Organization (MAYO).[30] At the University of Texas at Austin it was called the Mexican American Student Organization (MASO), later changing its name to MAYO.[31] In the Los Angeles area, chapters of the United Mexican American Students (UMAS) were formed at UCLA; California State College, Los Angeles; Loyola University; University of Southern California; California State College, Long Beach; and San Fernando State College. At East Los Angeles Community College, another group organized as the Mexican American Student Association (MASA).[32]

At about the same time, the Student Initiative organization at San Jose State College in Northern California changed its name to the Mexican American Student Confederation (MASC).[33] Chapters followed at Fresno State, Hayward State, and Sacramento State colleges. The following year, 1968, students formed a chapter of UMAS at the University of Colorado at Boulder,[34] and a MASC chapter at the University of California, Berkeley. By

1969 UMAS chapters were emerging in other parts of the Southwest. The first UMAS chapter in the Midwest was organized at the University of Notre Dame by Gilbert Cárdenas, a first-year graduate student in sociology and former undergraduate member of UMAS in California.[35]

Ideologically, most of these new student organizations had objectives similar to those of the Mexican Youth Conferences of the 1930s and the Mexican-American Movement of the 1940s. They emphasized the theme of 'progress through education', and concentrated on activities related to recruitment of Mexican American students and helping them stay in college. The new student organizations worked with Mexican American professionals to raise scholarship funds for needy students, and sought their advice on matters relating to the education of Mexican Americans. Some of the student activists themselves attended college with help from scholarships made available by middle-class organizations like LULAC. With few exceptions, the new student groups mirrored the political consciousness of the Mexican-American Generation of the 1930s and were committed to the development of a new generation of professionals who could play a leading role in the betterment of the Mexican American community within the context of middle-class politics.

These student organizations did not yet represent a student movement in political terms. But as they came into direct contact with community politics and learned more about the Chávez and Tijerina movements they came to represent a student movement in the making. By the end of 1967, the anti-war and Black Power movements had become other sources of growing militancy among some of the student leaders. The politics of the times were now characterized by mass protest, and the fact that the main protagonists in the unfolding drama were white and Black radical youth did not go unnoticed by the leadership of the Mexican American student organizations. Some of them joined with SDS and the Black student unions in planning campus protests.

But for the most part, UMAS, MASC, and MAYO stuck to Mexican American issues. They began to sponsor campus programs and demonstrations to support Chávez and Tijerina. Student caravans were organized to take food to Delano, where the headquarters of the United Farm Workers Organizing Committee was located. Student organizations provided much of the manpower on the picket lines at the Safeway stores and other markets during the grape boycott, and they demanded that colleges and universities boycott grapes. They brought Chávez, Tijerina, and Corky Gonzáles to speak on campuses throughout the Southwest.

The initial student support for the Chávez and Tijerina movements, how-ever, was largely related to pride in the fact that two Mexican American lead-ers struggling for social justice had achieved national recognition and extensive mass media coverage. In 1967 Chávez was the first Mexican American leader to appear on the cover of *Time* magazine. He was promoted by the mass me-dia and his followers as the 'Mexican American Dr. Martin Luther King Jr.' since he was also a disciple of the Ghandian philosophy of nonviolence. Luis Valdez, who had proclaimed Fidel Castro as his leader upon his return from Cuba in 1964, became the most ardent promoter of Chávez as 'our first real Mexican American leader ... [the one] we had been waiting for.'[36]

Support for Chávez also stemmed from the reality that many Mexicans and Mexican Americans had been farmworkers at some time in their lives. But the stark reality had to be faced that the farmworker movement was far from being a broad civil rights effort; Chávez was a union organizer and lent his increasing prestige and astute leadership abilities only to farmworkers – or to efforts that he saw as in the immediate interests of farmworkers. He consistently shunned responsibility for leading a movement broader than a union for farm workers, and he told student leaders that the issue of educational change was not on his agenda.[37] Many of his followers, however, including Luis Valdez, continued to embrace Chávez as the leader of all Mexican Americans and eventually as one of the leaders of the Chicano Movement.

Despite the inspiration provided by César Chávez and the farmwork-ers movement, student activists found it difficult to organize students solely around the issues related to the struggle of the farmworkers. The attention giv-en to the farmworker movement by liberal politicians like the Kennedys and by the mass media contributed greatly to the movement's rise and the making of Chávez into a respected national leader. But it also reinforced the exist-ing stereotype of all Mexican Americans as farmworkers. Although strongly supportive of the Chávez and Tijerina movements, student leaders on urban campuses were well aware that the vast majority of their people lived in cities. They therefore felt the need to build an urban movement to address the is-sues faced by the majority of Mexican Americans. Neither César Chávez and the farmworkers nor Reies Tijerina and the farmers of northern New Mexico truly addressed the needs of urban youth

Rodolfo 'Corky' Gonzáles did. Gonzáles, founder and head of the Crusade for Justice, a civil rights organization in Denver, Colorado was in his early for-ties but younger than Chávez and Tijerina; in addition he was a product of an urban *barrio.* He had parted company with the Mexican American middle-class organizations he had worked closely with in the past and now spoke directly, and forcefully, to the issues facing the youth. His charisma captured the imagination of young activists, students and nonstudents alike.

In 1967 he wrote an epic poem entitled *I Am Joaquín,* which was distributed to the UMAS, MASC and MAYO student leadership throughout the Southwest by La Causa Publications in Oakland, California. This poem was published in book form in 1972. *I Am Joaquín* did not offer its readers a well-defined radical ideology, but it did provide a critical framework for the developing student movement through its portrayal of the quest for identity and its critique of racism. More than a poem, it was an ambitious essay that attempted to dramatize key events and personalities from important moments of Mexican and Mexican American history, beginning with the indigenous ancestors prior to the Spanish conquest. It ended with the adamant assertion that people of Mexican descent and their culture would continue to endure.

I Am Joaquín filled a vacuum, for most student activists had never read a book about Mexican American history – especially one that linked that history with Mexican history. The few books available on some aspect of the Mexican American experience were not yet part of the curriculum in colleges, much less elementary and secondary schools. The only book that presented the history of Mexican Americans had gone out of print long before the 1960s. That book was *North from Mexico* by Carey McWilliams, a white liberal who had supported the Mexican American civil rights struggles in California before becoming the editor of the *Nation* magazine.

The most significant aspect of *I Am Joaquín* was that it captured both the agony and the jubilation permeating the identity crisis faced by Mexican American youth in the process of assimilation. As Gonzáles explains in his introduction, 'writing *I Am Joaquín* was a journey back through history, a painful self-evaluation, a wandering search for my peoples and, most of all, for my own identity.'[38] This search for identity and the dilemmas it posed are the key to understanding the Chicano student movement of the 1960s. To a large degree, the movement was a quest for identity, an effort to recapture what had been lost through the socialization process imposed by US schools and other institutions. To create a new identity, an alternative to the one defined by the Mexican-American Generation, the more militant student leaders sensed the need to take on that socialization process. These portions of *I Am Joaquín* were especially meaningful to the militant student leaders of the 1960s:

I am Joaquin,
lost in a world of confusion,
caught up in the whirl of a
  gringo society,
confused by the rules,
scorned by attitudes,
suppressed by manipulation,
and destroyed by modern society ...
I have come a long way to nowhere,
unwillingly dragged by that
    monstrous, technical,
      industrial giant called
        Progress
and Anglo success ...
in a country that has wiped out
all my history,
  stifled all my pride,
in a country that has placed a
different weight of indignity upon
    my
      age-
        old
          burdened back.
    Inferiority
is the new load ...
  I look at myself
  and see part of me
who rejects my father and my mother
and dissolves into the melting pot
    to disappear in shame.
    I sometimes
      sell my brother out
and reclaim him
for my own when society gives me
    token leadership
      in society's own name.[39]

Gonzáles did not advocate a specific identity for Mexican Americans in his poem: at the time he wrote *I Am Joaquín* he believed it possible to organize a movement regardless of the question of a specific identity:

> La Raza!
> Méjicano!
> Español!
> Latino!
> Hispano!
> Chicano!
> or whatever I call myself,
> I look the same
> I feel the same
> I cry
> and
> sing the same.[40]

It was Luis Valdez who first gave concrete direction to the development of a distinct Chicano identity and its emphasis on the nonwhite legacy of the Mexican American people. Valdez argued that there was only one identity appropriate to the oppressed Mexican American, and that identity was rooted in the nonwhite indigenous past and in the working-class history of the people. He wrote that the Spanish conquest of Mexico 'was no conquest at all', that although it did shatter 'our ancient Indian universe ... more of it was left above ground than beans and tortillas'.[41] Valdez thus stressed the Native American roots of the Mexican American experience and rejected those of the Spanish, who were European and white:

> Most of us know we are not European simply by looking in a mirror ... the shape of the eyes, the curve of the nose, the color of skin, the texture of hair; these things belong to another time, another people. Together with a million little stubborn mannerisms, beliefs, myths, superstitions, words, thoughts ... they fill our Spanish life with Indian contradictions. It is not enough to say we suffer an identity crisis, because that crisis has been our way of life for the last five centuries.[42]

Valdez, like Gonzáles, acknowledged that La Raza included all Mexican Americans, but he emphasized the working-class realities of the majority. As he put it,

> Our campesinos, the farm-working *raza* find it difficult to participate in this alien North American country. The acculturated Mexican-Americans in the cities, ex-*raza*, find it easier. They have solved their Mexican contradictions with a pungent dose of Americanism, and are more concerned with status, money and bad breath than with their ultimate destiny ... they will melt into the American pot and be no more. But the farmworking *raza* will not disappear so easily. ... We are repelled by the human disintegration of peoples and cultures as they fall apart in this Great Gringo Melting Pot.[43]

During the same year that Corky Gonzáles's poem was first distributed, a handful of student activists in Northern California, under the guidance of Professor Octavio Romano-V., an anthropologist at the University of California, Berkeley, published the first issues of *El Grito: A Journal of Contemporary Mexican-American Thought*, the first Mexican American scholarly journal to appear in the United States. One of their purposes in launching *El Grito* was to challenge the racist stereotypes of Mexican Americans that had developed and persisted within the social science disciplines. The journal was to be a forum for 'Mexican American self definition', a direct effort to deal with the question of identity, although in less political and more academic terms than those normally used by activists.

Identity and the discovery of one's roots were thus becoming crucial issues for student organizations as they emerged on campus after campus. And as student activists confronted the issue of Mexican American identity, they increasingly exposed the historic role of the schools in the undermining of Mexican American culture.

The Rise of Student Militancy

On the morning of 3 March 1968, shouts of 'Blow Out!' rang through the halls of Abraham Lincoln High School, a predominantly Mexican American school in East Los Angeles. Over a thousand students walked out of their classes, teacher Sal Castro among them. Waiting for them outside the school grounds were members of UMAS and various community activists. They distributed picket signs listing some of the thirty-six demands that had been developed by a community and student strike committee. The signs protested racist school policies and teachers and called for freedom of speech, the hiring of Mexican American teachers and administrators, and classes on Mexican American history and culture. As might be expected, the signs that caught the attention of the mass media and the police were those reading 'Chicano Power!', 'Viva La Raza!', and 'Viva La Revolución!' By the afternoon of that day, several thousand more students had walked out of five other barrio high schools to join the strike. The strike brought the Los Angeles city school system, the largest in the nation, to a standstill and made news across the country; a *Los Angeles Times* reporter interpreted the strike as 'The Birth of Brown Power'.[44] Over ten thousand students had participated by the time the Los Angeles 'blowouts' ended a week and a half later.

But the strike accomplished something much more important than shaking up school administrators or calling public attention to the educational problems of Mexican American youth. Although not one of its original objectives, the strike was the first major mass protest explicitly against racism undertaken by Mexican Americans in the history of the United States. As such, it had a profound impact on the Mexican American community in Los Angeles and in other parts of the country, and it generated an increased political awareness along with visible efforts to mobilize the community. This was manifested in the revitalization of existing community political organizations and the emergence of new ones, with youth playing significant leadership roles.

Overnight, student activism reached levels of intensity never before witnessed. A few Mexican American student activists had participated in civil rights marches, anti–Vietnam War protests, and had walked the picket lines for the farmworker movement. But the high school strike of 1968 was the first time students of Mexican descent had marched en masse in their own demonstration against racism and for educational change. It was also the first time that they had played direct leadership roles in organizing a mass protest. The slogans of 'Chicano Power!', 'Viva La Raza!', and 'Viva La Revolución!' that rang throughout the strike reflected an increasing militancy and radicalism in the ranks of UMAS and other student organizations. The nature of these concerns and the momentum built up among Mexican American students – both in high school and on college campuses – broke the ideological bonds that characteristically keep student organizations, and students in general, from questioning authority and the status quo. Membership grew as those organizations and their leaders became protagonists in struggles for change in

Mexican American communities. The strike moved student activism beyond the politics of accommodation and integration which had been shaped by the Mexican-American Generation and the community's middle-class leadership.

However, it was not student activists who conceived of the strike; the idea originated with Sal Castro, the teacher at Lincoln High School who had walked out with his students. Like Corky Gonzáles, he had become disillusioned with the Democratic Party and with Mexican American middle-class leadership. Also like Gonzáles, he had played a prominent role in the 'Viva Kennedy' campaign in 1960, serving as the student coordinator of the Southern California campaign. He was a Korean War–era veteran attending college on the G.I. Bill at the time. Like other veterans, he played a role in MAPA and was a founder of the Association of Mexican American Educators. He had been a firm believer in the 'American Dream' and was on his way toward a successful political career. In addition to the Kennedy campaign, he had worked on other campaigns and had been elected to the Democratic Party Central Committee.[45]

But by 1964 Castro had come to the realization that the Democrats did not have the interests of Mexican Americans at heart and that corruption was inherent in the political system.[46] A product of the barrio schools in East Los Angeles, Castro returned to the neighborhood as a teacher only to find that racism toward Mexican American youth remained virulent. Through the AMAE organization he worked hard to make reforms within the school bureacracy but was not able to accomplish much. Like other middle-class leaders, he saw that the civil rights movement ignored Mexican Americans and that they were low on the agenda of the War on Poverty and in education reform plans. But unlike most other middle-class leaders, Castro came to the conclusion that his people needed their own civil rights movement and that the only alternative in the face of a racist educational system was nonviolent protest against the schools. He therefore prepared to sacrifice his teaching career, if necessary, in the interest of educational change for Mexican American children.[47] The strike made Castro one of the movement's leaders.

The strike of 1968 went beyond the objectives of Castro and others concerned only with improving education. It was the first loud cry for Chicano Power and self-determination, serving as the catalyst for the formation of the Chicano student movement as well as the larger Chicano Power Movement of which it became the most important sector. In response to the strike, one of Mexico's foremost intellectuals, Carlos Fuentes, wrote that

Mexican Americans ... are reminding us all of the very powerful roots of our personality, of the very wide extension of our cultural image and of the community action that is required if that identity is to become something more than a passing reference in celebrations.[48]

After the strike the UMAS leadership urged the members to assume a more political role in both the community and on campus and to think in terms of being part of a student movement. In the first Mexican American student organization newsletter to be published and distributed throughout the Southwest, the UMAS chapter at California State College, Los Angeles, described its role:

UMAS is cognizant of the social, economic, and political ills of our Mexican people. The desire of UMAS is to play a vital role in the liberation of the Mexican American people from second class citizenship. To do this we see our role to stand united in the effort to affect social change for the better-ment of our people. We believe the ills that beset our people are not prod-ucts of our culture, but that said ills have been inflicted by the institutions which today comprise the establishment in the American society.[49]

This first newsletter urged students to participate in the Poor People's March on Washington scheduled for later in the spring of 1968 and to join the Mexican American delegation to it being led by Reies López Tijerina. It also called on students to support Sal Castro, who had been suspended by the Los Angeles Board of Education for his role in the strike and for his contin-ued support for change in the schools. Finally, UMAS advocated an 'internal and external' plan of action for the student movement:

[Recognizing] that the system cannot be changed overnight, we feel it is necessary that we work within the existing framework to the degree that it not impede our effectiveness. It is historically evident that working within the existing framework is not sufficient; therefore, our external approach will consist of exerting outside pressure on those institutions that directly affect the Mexican American community.[50]

The term *Chicano* appeared often – mostly interchangeably with *Mexican American* – but UMAS advanced no particular ideology for the student movement at this point. The newsletter made clear that UMAS was 'open to all students who want to contribute to the betterment of the Mexican American' and that it had 'no political labels'.[51] UMAS continued to stress educational issues, involvement in the community to assist high school students and defend them from harassment by racist teachers, the need to establish tutorial programs, and efforts to increase enrollments of Mexican American college students. These goals illustrate UMAS's emphasis on reaching out to and being part of the Mexican American community.

In the weeks following the strike, the leadership of each UMAS chapter in the Los Angeles area formed a coordinating body called UMAS Central. The first newsletter of this group called on Chicanos to take pride in their Mexican identity and on students to see themselves as a political vanguard.

> We have begun to recognize our role as an organizational agent through which Chicano students are able to recognize themselves as Mexicans and to take pride in it. We are the avant-garde of the young Mexican American liberation movement. We formulate a philosophy for our people and we provide the hope for the future of Mexicans of all generations. We recognize ourselves as a generation of doers as well as thinkers. ... We are resolved to perpetuate an atmosphere of respect and dignity for our people.... We are the agents of progress and unity. We demand social justice for a people too long oppressed.[52]

Militancy in the ranks of the developing student movement accelerated as a consequence of the response to the strike on the part of the power structure of the city of Los Angeles and the implementation of directives from the Federal Bureau of Investigation. On 4 March 1968, FBI Director J. Edgar Hoover issued a memo to local law enforcement officials across the country urging them to place top priority on political intelligence work to prevent the development of nationalist movements in minority communities.[53] Hoover's chief goal was to undermine the Black Power Movement, but his directive was considered applicable to other similar movements by the Los Angeles District Attorney, Evelle Younger, a former high official in the FBI and a Republican Party candidate for state attorney general at the time of the strike. The political intelligence units of the Los Angeles City Police and the Los Angeles County Sheriff's office were ordered to investigate the 'Brown Power' strike.

On 2 June 1968, three months after the strike and two days before

California's primary elections, thirteen young Mexican American political activists who had been identified as leaders of the emerging 'Brown Power' movement were indicted by the Los Angeles County Grand Jury on conspiracy charges for their roles in organizing the strike. The indictments charged that the thirteen activists had conspired to 'wilfully disturb the peace and quiet' of the city of Los Angeles and disrupt the educational process in its schools.[54] They were characterized as members of communist 'subversive organizations' or outside agitators intent on radicalizing Mexican American students. Each of the thirteen activists faced a total of sixty-six years in prison if found guilty.

None of the 'LA Thirteen' were in fact communists or members of 'subversive organizations'. They included Sal Castro, a teacher at Lincoln High School; Eliezer Risco, editor of a community newspaper called *La Raza*; and Patricio Sanchez, a member of the Mexican American Political Association (MAPA). Two were student activists, Moctezuma Esparza from UCLA UMAS and I, from California State University LA UMAS. Four were members of the Brown Berets: David Sánchez, Carlos Montes, Ralph Ramirez, and Fred Lopez. The others were activists working with community War on Poverty programs: Richard Vigil, Gilberto C. Olmeda, Joe Razo, and Henry Gomez. Instead of preventing the rise of another 'nationalist movement', the indictments of the LA Thirteen simply fueled the fire of an emerging radicalism among Mexican American students.

Although all of the indicted thirteen were men, as were the majority of the organizers, women played key roles as organizers in the walkouts. They organized important community and campus meetings essential to the planning of the walkouts and did much essential behind-the-scenes work in educating members of their community – and their own families – about the issues related to the walkouts and developed networks of organizations in support of the walkouts. Some of the key organizers among high school students were Paula Crisostomo, Mita Cuaron, Tanya Luna Mount, and Rosalinda Gonzalez; Vickie Castro was one of the college students.[55]

Several weeks after the walkouts, Mexican American graduating seniors at San Jose State College and members of the audience walked out during commencement exercises. Approximately two hundred people were involved in the demonstration. They denounced the college for its lack of commitment to the surrounding Mexican American community, as shown by the low enrollment of Mexican American students on campus. The walkout was also a protest against the inadequate training of professionals such as teachers, social workers, and policemen, who, after graduating, would work in the Mexican American community with no understanding of the culture and needs of that community, or – most important – of how their own racism affected their dealings with Mexican Americans.

Prior to the commencement, the student leadership had demanded that all graduating seniors be required to participate in intensive two-week sensitivity workshops so that they could learn something about Mexican American culture. The proposed workshops were to be taught by students from San Jose's Mexican American community who knew the problems awaiting anyone performing a job that required working with Mexican Americans. The student leaders called their protest the 'commencement' of a militant student movement that would struggle to change institutions of higher education responsible for perpetuating racism against their people. That walkout was the first protest activity undertaken by Mexican American students on a college campus.

Five months later, in November 1968, Mexican American students became part of a student strike at San Francisco State College, organized by the Third World Liberation Front (TWLF). It was marked by violent confrontations between students and the police, and many students were injured. The strike began over issues initially raised by Black students and lasted until March 1969. Although the students' demands mostly focused on the needs of Black students, one demand called for the creation of a Department of Raza Studies under the umbrella of a proposed School of Ethnic Studies. The TWLF also demanded open admission for all students of color. The San Francisco State strike was significant because it marked the first time that Mexican American and other third world student activists united to create a politically explosive 'rainbow' coalition.[56]

In October 1968, the Mexican American Student Confederation took over the office of Charles Hitch, president of the University of California system, to protest his refusal to discontinue the purchase of grapes while Chávez's farmworkers were on strike – part of a national campaign to boycott grapes in support of the UFW. The takeover of Hitch's office resulted in the arrest of eleven MASC members for trespassing and unlawful assembly. This was the first in a series of third world student confrontations with university authorities on the Berkeley campus, which eventually culminated in the formation of another Third World Liberation Front and student strike.

Patterning itself after the Third World Liberation Front at San Francisco

State across the Bay, the TWLF at Berkeley organized its own student strike, which lasted from January through April 1969. It was the first major third world student confrontation within the University of California system, and one of the most violent to occur at any of the university's campuses: many students were arrested or became victims of police violence.

In contrast to the strike at San Francisco State, Mexican American students played a leading role in the organization of the Third World Liberation Front and the strike on the UC Berkeley campus. The strike was aimed at exposing the university's lack of commitment to meeting the educational needs of third world people. Although there were many differences within the TWLF, the strike demands incorporated previous issues raised by both African American and Mexican American student activists. The TWLF demanded the creation of a Third World College with departments of Mexican American, Black and Asian-American studies. It also demanded sufficient resources for the proposed college to involve itself in minority communities and contribute effectively to their development. TWLF demanded that the new college be under the full control of its students, faculty, and representatives of the community; 'self-determination' was to be its principle of governance. Other demands called for open admission for all third world people and poor working-class whites and the recruitment of third world faculty and staff.

There were other high school student strikes throughout the Southwest during 1969, patterned after the 1968 strike in Los Angeles. In Denver, Colorado and Crystal City, Texas, high school strikes also resulted in significant political developments beyond the immediate issues of educational change. In Denver, the strike contributed to the further development of the Crusade for Justice and made Corky Gonzáles a national leader of the emerging Chicano movement. In contrast to the relatively violence-free student strike in Los Angeles, the Denver demonstrations resulted in violent confrontations between police, students, and members of the Crusade for Justice, and Corky Gonzáles was himself arrested. After his release he praised the striking students for risking 'revolutionary' actions to make history: 'You kids don't realize you have made history. We just talk about revolution. But you act it by facing the shotguns, billies, gas, and mace. You are the real revolutionaries.'[57]

In Crystal City, a high school strike contributed directly to the founding of La Raza Unida Party, a second electoral revolt in that city that resulted in the party's takeover of city government and the school system, and the making of José Angel Gutiérrez into another national leader of the Chicano Movement.

The movement was given further impetus by other events that took place in 1968, the year that was the turning point of the decade. The antiwar move-meent became a potent political force in national politics as mass protest against the war in Vietnam dramatically increased. Simultaneously, on the battlefields of Vietnam, US troops were being overrun in the Tet offensive, the largest Vietnamese attack of the war. As a result the Johnson adminis-tration was forced to agree to peace talks held in Paris later that year. It was also the year that Dr. Martin Luther King Jr. led the Poor People's March on Washington, which included a contingent of Mexican Americans. Later in the year Dr. King and Senator Robert F. Kennedy were assassinated.

Even more important, 1968 was also the year of international student up-risings from Paris and Berlin to Tokyo to Mexico City. In Mexico City, the site of the Olympics that year, over four hundred students were massacred by the Mexican army. In Paris, students battled police and brought the entire city to a standstill, touching off a month-long nationwide general strike of ten mil-lion workers. Between 1968 and 1969, Mexican American student militancy intensified as more and more of them became convinced that they were part of an international revolution in the making.

From the ranks of these militant students came artists, poets and actors who collectively generated a cultural renaissance and whose work played a key role in creating the ideology of the Chicano Movement.[58] In Oakland, California the first group of radical artists organized themselves as the Mexican American Liberation Art Front (MALAF). Elsewhere in the Bay Area, José and Malaquias Montoya, Esteban Villa, Renee Yanez, Ralph Maradiaga and Rupert García produced posters whose striking art reflected the movement's quest for identity and power. Yolanda Lopez and Graciela Carrillo organized the Mujeres Muralistas, or the Mural Art Women in the tradition of the Mexican revolutionary artists David Alfaro Sequieros, José Clemente Orozco, and Diego Rivera. By 1970 a distinct Chicano art movement was in full bloom throughout the Southwest.[59]

Poets and writers produced campus and community underground news-papers, which replaced student organizational newsletters as the main form of movement communication. These newspapers led to the formation of an independent Chicano Press Association.[60] In addition to Berkeley's *El Grito*, radical poets and writers created other magazines such as *Con Safos* in Los Angeles and *El Pocho Che* in San Francisco.[61]

Student activists also created numerous campus and community-based 'guerilla' theater groups patterned after the Teatro Campesino. By 1970 these groups had become part of a national Chicano theater movement called Teatros Nacionales de Aztlán.[62]

The student strikes in the community and on the college campus, in conjunction with the political upheavals of the late sixties, thus generated the framework for the eventual transformation of student activist organizations into a full-blown student movement and a larger civil rights movement with clear social and political goals and an ethnic nationalist ideology that came to be known as cultural nationalism.

Notes

1 See Zaragosa Vargas, *Labor Rights Are Civil Rights: Mexican American Workers in Twentieth-Century America*, Princeton, N.J. 2005.

2 See Vickie L. Ruiz, *From Out of the Shadows: Mexican Women in 20th-Century America*, New York 1998.

3 Edward Garza, 'LULAC: League of United Latin American Citizens,' Master's thesis, Southwest Texas State Teachers College 1951, p. 32.

4 Guadalupe San Miguel, Jr., *Let All of Them Take Heed*, Austin 1987.

5 Muñoz, 'Galarza,' p. 15.

6 Conversation with Delores Huerta.

7 Mario García, 'Americans All: The Mexican-American Generation and the Politics of Wartime Los Angeles, 1941–45,' in Rodolfo de La Garza et al., eds, The Mexican American Experience: An Interdisciplinary Approach, Austin 1985.

8 Rodolfo Acuña, *A Community Under Siege: A Chronicle of Chicanos East of the Los Angeles River, 1945–1975*, Los Angeles 1984, p. 121.

9 Clayborne Carson, *In Struggle: SNCC and the Black Awakening of the 1960s*, Cambridge, Mass. 1981, p. 119.

10 Betita Martinez, interview, January 1989.

11 Luis Valdez, interview, 11 August 1982.

12 Armando Valdez, interview, 6 January 1983.

13 Luis Valdez, interview.

14 Luis Valdez and Roberto Rubalcava, 'Venceremos!: Mexican-American Statement on Travel to Cuba,' in Luis Valdez and Stan Steiner, eds, *Aztlan: An Anthology of Mexican American Literature*, New York 1972, pp. 215–16.

15 Ibid.

16 Luis Valdez, interview.

17 League of United Latin American Citizens, Constitution, By-Laws, and Protocal, n.p. 1977, p. 24.

18 Ibid., p. 26.

19 Juan Gómez-Quiñones, *Mexican Students Por La Raza: The Chicano Student Movement in Southern California, 1966–67*, Santa Barbara 1978, pp. 16-17

20 Acuña, *Community under Siege*, p. 119.
21 Ronald B. Taylor, *Chávez and the Farm Workers*, Boston 1975.
22 Valdez, 'Plan of Delano', in Valdez and Steiner, eds, *Aztlán*, pp. 197–201.
23 Ibid.
24 Kenneth C. Burt, 'The History of the Mexican-American Political Association and Chicano Politics in California', unpublished MS, p. 62.
25 John Staples Shockley, *Chicano Revolt in a Texas Town*, Notre Dame 1974.
26 Armando Navarro, 'El Partido de La Raza Unida in Crystal City: A Peaceful Revolution', Ph.D. diss., University of California, Riverside 1974.
27 'Walkout in Albuquerque', *Carta Editorial*, vol. 3, no. 12, 8 April 1966, in Valdez and Steiner, *Aztlán*, pp. 211–14.
28 Stan Steiner, *La Raza: The Mexican Americans*, New York 1973, pp. 383–84.
29 Peter Nabokov, *Tijerina and the Courthouse Raid*, Berkeley 1970.
30 Navarro, 'La Raza Unida in Crystal City'; Navarro, *Mexican American Youth Organization: Avant-Garde of the Chicano Movement in Texas*, Austin 1995.
31 César Caballero, 'A Historical Review and Analysis of U.T. MAYO's Social Change Activities', unpublished paper, 1974.
32 Gómez-Quiñones, *Mexican Students Por La Raza*, p. 19.
33 Armando Valdez, interview.
34 United Mexican American Students, 'La Historia de UMAS', Boulder, Colo. 1970.
35 Gilbert Cárdenas Papers, author's files.
36 Luis Valdez, 'The Tale of La Raza', *Bronze*, vol. 1, no. 1, 25 November 1968.
37 In 1968 Chávez conveyed this message to a delegation of UMAS members who had gone to Delano in support of the United Farm Workers. The meeting was reported to the author in his capacity as president of UMAS.
38 Rodolfo Gonzáles, *I Am Joaquín: An Epic Poem*, New York 1972, p. 1.
39 Ibid., pp. 6, 10, and 51–52.
40 Ibid., p. 98.
41 Valdez, 'The Tale of La Raza'.
42 Ibid.
43 Ibid.
44 Dial Torgerson, '"Brown Power" Unity Seen Behind School Disorders: Start of a Revolution?', *Los Angeles Times*, 17 March 1968.
45 Salvador Castro, interview, 17 March 1982.
46 Ibid.
47 Ibid.
48 Letter from Carlos Fuentes to Prof. Donald W. Bray in response to his invitation to speak at a UMAS event at California State College, Los Angeles, after the strike. Bray had written to Fuentes on my behalf when I was president of UMAS.
49 Carlos Muñoz, Jr., *UMAS Newsletter*, California State University, Los Angeles, 17 April 1968, p. 1.
50 Ibid., p. 2.
51 Ibid., p. 1.

52 *UMAS Central Newsletter*, no. 1, 5 May 1968.

53 Baxter Smith, 'FBI Member Reveals Repression Schemes', *The Black Scholar*, vol. 5, no. 7, April 1974, p. 44.

54 Two years later, in June 1970, a California state appelate court dropped the charges against the thirteen activists. See *Salvador B. Castro et al., Petitioners, v. The Superior Court of Los Angeles County, Respondent; The People, Real Party in Interest*. 9 C.A. 3d 675; 88 Cal. Rptr. 500, 1970, pp. 675–720.

55 See Dolores Delgado Bernal, 'Grassroots Leadership Reconceptualized: Chicana Oral Histories and the 1968 East Los Angeles School Blowouts', *Frontiers*, vol. 19, no. 2, 1998, pp. 113–42.

56 See Jason Michael Ferreira, 'All Power to the People: A Comparative History of Third World Radicalism in San Francisco, 1968–1974', Ph.D. Dissertation, UC Berkeley, 2003.

57 Steiner, *La Raza*.

58 Tomás Ybarra-Frausto, 'The Chicano Movement and the Emergence of a Chicano Poetic Consciousness', in Ricardo Romo and Raymund Paredes, eds, *New Directions in Chicano Scholarship*, Santa Barbara 1977.

59 Rupert García, 'La Raza Murals of California, 1963 to 1970: A Period of Social Change and Protest', Master's thesis, University of California 1981. See also Shifra M. Goldman and Tomás Ybarra-Frausto, *Arte Chicano: A Comprehensive Annotated Bibliography of Chicano Art, 1965–1981*, Berkeley 1985.

60 Francisco J. Lewis, *The Uses of the Media by the Chicano Movement: A Study in Minority Access*, New York 1974.

61 Bruce Novoa, *Chicano Poetry: A Response to Chaos*, Austin 1982.

62 Jorge Huerta, *Chicano Theatre: Themes and Forms*, Ypsilanti, Mich. 1981

3

The Rise of the Chicano Student
Movement and Chicano Nationalism

The Crusade for Justice hosted a National Chicano Youth Liberation Conference in March 1969. It was held at the Crusade headquarters in Denver, Colorado. It brought together for the first time activists from all over the country who were involved in both campus and community politics. The conference was also significant because it brought together young people of all types – students, nonstudents, militant youth from the street gangs (*vatos locos*), and ex-convicts (*pintos*) – to discuss community issues and politics. The majority of those in attendance, however, were student activists, and most of them were from California. The conference emphasized themes related to the quest for identity, as popularized by Gonzáles and Valdez, which were eagerly received by students searching for an ideology for the emerging student movement.

Corky Gonzáles and his followers in Denver had developed the image of the Crusade for Justice as 'the vanguard' of the rapidly growing Chicano Civil Rights Movement. The Crusade, originally a multi-issue, broad-based civil rights organization oriented toward nonviolence, came to symbolize Chicano/a self-determination and espoused a strong nationalist ideology that militant youth found extremely attractive. Gonzáles articulated this nationalism in a clear and appealing manner:

> Nationalism exists ... but until now, it hasn't been formed into an image people can see. Until now it has been a dream. It has been my job to create a

reality out of the dream, to create an ideology out of the longing. Everybody in the *barrios* is a nationalist. … [I]t doesn't matter if he's middle-class, a *vendido*, a sellout, or what his politics may be. He'll come back home, to La Raza, to his heart, if we will build centers of nationalism for him. … [N]ationalism is the key to our people liberating themselves. … I am a revolutionary … because creating life amid death is a revolutionary act. Just as building nationalism in an era of imperialism is a life-giving act. … We are an awakening people, an emerging nation, a new breed.[1]

During the week-long conference, Gonzáles and his followers stressed the need for students and youth to play a revolutionary role in the movement. Conference participants were told that previous generations of students, after completing academic programs and becoming professionals, had abdicated their responsibility to their people, to their familia de La Raza. This abdication of responsibility was attributed to the fact that Mexican American students had been Americanized by the schools, that they had been conditioned to accept the dominant values of American society, particularly individualism, at the expense of their Mexican identity. The result had been the psychological 'colonization' of Mexican American youth.

To liberate themselves from this 'colonization', students needed 'revolutionary' role models. Street youth and ex-convicts would become the models. Conference speakers proposed that henceforth most crimes committed by Mexican Americans were to be interpreted as 'revolutionary acts'. The language and dress of the street youth, the *vatos locos*, would be emulated. *Carnalismo* (the brotherhood code of Mexican American youth gangs) would mold the lives of students and become a central concept in the proposed nationalist ideology. From the ranks of this new breed of youth would come the poets, the writers and the artists necessary for the forging of the new Chicano identity. This new identity would base itself on symbols of traditional Mexican culture and would reflect a total rejection of *gabacho* culture – the culture of the white Anglo-Saxon Protestant.

The conference participants developed a series of resolutions outlining the goals of Chicano liberation within the context of the nationalist ideology that Gonzáles put forward. The resolutions exhorted students to take up a struggle to unite all Mexican Americans regardless of social class. The basis for unity would be their pride in Mexican ethnicity and culture. It was reasoned that all Mexican Americans, regardless of how indoctrinated they were with the dominant values of US society, ultimately nurtured such a pride. Nationalism, therefore, was to be the common denominator for uniting all Mexican Americans and making possible effective political mobilization.

The resolutions also called for a struggle to win political and economic control of Mexican American communities. Economic practices based on capitalist goals and values were to be rejected in favor of humanistic values thought to be at the core of Mexican and Mexican American culture. Capitalist economic institutions were to be replaced by people's cooperatives. Independent Mexican American political groups were necessary to take the place of the Democratic and Republican party machines, since 'the two-party system is the same animal with two heads that feed from the same trough.'[2] The importance of the struggle for community control of the schools received special emphasis. Chicano studies programs were needed to teach Mexican Americans their history and culture. The resolutions advocated bilingual education to assure the continuity of the Spanish language and Mexican American culture. Mexican cultural values were to be the most 'powerful weapon to defeat the gringo dollar value system and encourage the process of love and brotherhood.' The resolutions also advocated self-defense and militant protest.

No resolution was proposed to deal with the issue of gender inequality. A handful of Chicana feminists organized a Chicana workshop for the purpose of drafting a resolution on the subject. But the majority of the women participants refused to approve such a resolution out of concern that it would become a divisive issue. The men at the conference reflected the male attitudes that permeated the movement at the time. They perceived feminism as a white women's issue and believed strongly that Chicanas should follow the Chicano leadership of the movement. The majority of Chicanas agreed. When the conference delegates reconvened to vote on all the resolutions that emerged out of the workshops, the representative of the Chicana Caucus reported that 'it was the consensus of the group that the Chicana does not want to be liberated.'[3]

Enriqueta Vasquez, a participant at the conference, expressed her disappointment at the consensus of the Chicana Caucus: 'As a woman who has been faced with living as a member of the Mexican-American minority group, as a breadwinner and a mother raising children, living in housing projects and having much concern for other humans plus much community involvement, I felt this as quite a blow. I could have cried ... then I understood why the statement had been made and I realized that going along with the feelings of the men at the convention was perhaps the best thing to do at the time.'[4]

The resolutions as adopted by the conference were put together in a document entitled *El Plan Espiritual de Aztlán* or *The Spiritual Plan of Aztlán.** The document was drafted by a committee that included Alurista, one of the better known radical poets from the ranks of the student activists. His poetry, like the work of Luis Valdez, emphasized the Native American aspects of the Mexican American experience.[5] The conference agreed that the conference participants would base all their political work on the premises and program outlined in *El Plan Espiritual.* The participants resolved to disseminate the document at all Mexican American functions on campuses and in Mexican American communities. The following manifesto prefaced the plan:

In the spirit of a new people that is conscious not only of its proud historical heritage, but also of the brutal 'Gringo' invasion of our territories, we, the Chicano inhabitants and civilizers of the northern land of Aztlán, from whence came our forefathers, reclaiming the land of their birth and consecrating the determination of our people of the sun, declare that the call of our blood is our power, our responsibility and our inevitable destiny. ... Brotherhood unites us, and love for our brothers makes us a people whose time has come and who struggle against the foreigner 'Gabacho' who exploits our riches and destroys our culture. ... We are Bronze People with a Bronze Culture. ... We are Aztlán.[6]

More than a thousand people had attended the Chicano Youth Conference. It was a week of serious deliberation – and singing and dancing as well. Maria Varela, one of the participants, described it:

'Conference' is a poor word to describe those five days. ... It was in reality a fiesta: days of celebrating what sings in the blood of a people who, taught to believe they are ugly, discover the true beauty in their souls during the years of occupation and intimidation. ... Coca Cola, Doris Day, Breck Shampoo, the Playboy Bunny, the Arrow Shirt man, the Marlboro heroes, are lies. 'We are beautiful. ...' [T]his affirmation grew into a *grito*, a roar, among the people gathered in the auditorium of the Crusade's Center.[7]

---

* *Aztlán* was the name used by the Aztecs to refer to their place of origin. Since the Aztecs had migrated to central Mexico from 'somewhere in the north', Chicano activists claimed that Aztlán was all the southwestern United States taken from Mexico in the 1846–48 US–Mexican War. This included California, Texas, New Mexico, most of Arizona, large parts of Colorado, Nevada, and Utah, and a piece of Wyoming.

The conference was a phenomenal success, going far beyond the expectations of Gonzáles and the conference organizers. For one thing, it made Gonzáles one of the leaders of the Chicano Movement. Moreover, the conference promoted solidarity among youth of different social backgrounds and from different parts of the US. Puerto Rican youth from Chicago and New York had also attended. Before the conference, very little communication had existed between Mexican American youth in different states, or even between regions of the same state. But it was no surprise that the majority of the participants came from California, because that was where the rapidly developing Chicano student movement first came to maturity.

The Santa Barbara Conference

Approximately a month after the Denver youth conference, the Chicano Coordinating Council on Higher Education (CCHE) held a conference at the University of California, Santa Barbara. CCHE had been organized as a state network of students, faculty and staff who were interested in creating programs to help Mexican American students attending California's colleges and universities. The goal of the conference was to develop a master plan for the creation of curriculum and the related auxiliary services and structures essential to facilitate Mexican American access to those institutions. The Santa Barbara conference was successful in developing such a plan (discussed further in chapter 5). The conference had an added significance, however, in that it was the first opportunity for young Chicano/as who attended the Denver conference to implement the ideas of *El Plan Espiritual de Aztlán*. Although not one of its original goals, the Santa Barbara conference also became the 'founding convention' of the Chicano student movement, which quickly spread across campuses throughout the United States.

At the Santa Barbara conference the student leaders moved to adopt a new name for existing student organizations, a name that would transcend localism and regionalism and align the student movement with the goals of *El Plan Espiritual de Aztlán*. The students envisioned the development of a Mexican American student movement that would play an important role in national as well as community politics. They therefore placed the issue of the name change in a context that would transcend California:

Since the movement is definitely of national significance and scope, all student organizations should adopt one identical name throughout the state and eventually the nation to characterize the common struggle of *La Raza de Aztlán*. The net gain is a step toward greater national unity which enhances the power in mobilizing local campus organizations.[8]

After intense deliberation on the implications and political significance of a new name, the students voted to drop their current organizational names throughout the state. Thus, the United Mexican American Students, the Mexican American Student Confederation, the Mexican American Youth Association, and the Mexican American Student Association eventually dropped names associated with a particular campus or region and became El Movimiento Estudiantil Chicano de Aztlán (The Chicano Student Movement of Aztlán), based on wide agreement that the new name should reflect the terms *Chicano* and *Aztlán*:

> *Chicano*, in the past a pejorative and class-bound adjective, has now become the root idea of a new culture identity for our people. It also reveals a growing solidarity and the development of pride and confidence.[9]

The adoption of the new name and its acronym, MEChA, signaled a new level of political consciousness among student activists. It was the final stage in the transformation of what had been loosely organized, local student groups into a single structured and unified student movement. A literal translation of the acronym MEChA was 'match' or 'matchstick'. Thus, in the minds of Mexican American student activists the obvious symbol was 'fire', with all its connotations of militancy.

In terms of identity and ideology, MEChA symbolized the emergence of a new generation of youth, La Raza Nueva or the 'new people' or 'reborn youth'. The adoption of this new name thus encouraged students to see themselves as an part of the new Chicano/a generation that was committed to militant struggle against US institutions that had historically been responsible for the oppression of Mexican Americans. Adamant rejection of the label 'Mexican-American' meant rejection of the assimilationist and accommodationist melting pot ideology that had guided earlier generations of activists:

> *Chicanismo* involves a crucial distinction in political consciousness between a Mexican American and a Chicano mentality. The Mexican American is a person who lacks respect for his cultural and ethnic heritage. Unsure of

himself, he seeks assimilation as a way out of his 'degraded' social status. Consequently, he remains politically ineffective. In contrast, *Chicanismo* reflects self-respect and pride in one's ethnic and cultural background. ... [T]he Chicano acts with confidence and with a range of alternatives in the political world.[10]

The new student movement wanted to build around the term Chicano the unequivocal rejection of middle-class striving for assimilation:

Chicanismo simply embodies an ancient truth: that man is never closer to his true self as when he is close to his community. ... Chicanismo draws its faith and strength from two main sources: from the just struggle of our people and from an objective analysis of our community's strategic needs.[11]

Chicanismo was seen as an extension of the concept of La Raza Cósmica by some Chicano miitants. The term had been coined by the Mexican philosopher José Vasconcellos in his book of the same title. This notion posited that the peoples of mixed indigenous and European bloods throughout the Americas would one day develop into a 'superior race'. This concept reinforced the idea that Chicanos were *La Raza Nueva*. In practice, however, it was not used in that context. Rather, it was used as Mexican Americans had used the term historically. *La Raza* simply referred to the 'people' and reflected a pride in being Mexican.

The Santa Barbara conference proposed two basic goals for the student movement. In the community, MEChA was to become organically tied to the everyday social and political life of the Mexican American communities, with the aim of developing those communities. On campus, MEChA was to become a permanent, well-organized power bloc for the purpose of redirecting university attention and resources to the needs of Mexican American students and Mexican American communities. In the community, close working relationships with community organizations were to be established, regardless of differences in ideology or orientation. Given the apolitical – and at times negative or conservative – attitudes towards politics within the Mexican American community, MEChA would treat politics in ways that would bring about an understanding of the necessity for political work:

The student movement is to a large degree a political movement and as such must not elicit from our people the negative responses that we have experienced so often in the past in relation to politics, and often with good reason. ... We must re-define politics for our people to be a means of liberation. The political sophistication of our Raza must be raised so that they do not fall prey to apologists and vendidos whose whole interest is their personal career or fortune.[12]

A critical element of this political education was the way in which the community viewed the colleges and universities. Chicano/as had to understand that these institutions were strategic agencies in any process of community development, and thus it was important to view them as *their* institutions:

What is needed at this time, more than anything else, is to firm up the rapidly growing identification of the university as a critical agency in the transformation of the Chicano community. Our people must understand not only the strategic importance of the university ... they must above all perceive the university as being our university.[13]

This position reflected MEChA's understanding that part of its own power on campus would have to derive from community support. If political and educational change were to be won on campus, the community outside the campus would have to be mobilized. The MEChA strategy was to establish itself as both a legitimate community organization and a student group. Legitimacy in the community would in turn depend on a successful effort to form alliances with professionals, workers, and street youth in the surrounding Mexican American communities of each local campus.

MEChA's second broad goal, that of establishing itself as a power base on campus, meant that it would have to undertake an ambitious effort to increase the recruitment of Mexican American students and to teach them the ideology of *Chicanismo*, politicizing them so that they would participate in protest activities on behalf of their people.

MEChA is a first step to tying the student ... throughout the Southwest into a vibrant and responsive network of activists that will respond as a unit to oppression and racism and that will work in harmony when initiating and carrying out campaigns of liberation for our people.[14]

The strategy called for students to be organized around social and cultural events that were designed to expose university indoctrination and propaganda based on the Protestant 'ethic of profit and competition, of greed and intolerance'.[15] MEChA would advocate replacing that ethic with the values associated with the 'ancestral communalism' of the ancient Mexican peoples. MEChA would appeal to the sense of obligation to family and community on the part of every student:

> MEChA must bring to the mind of every young Chicano that the liberation of his people from prejudice and oppression is in his hand and this responsibility is greater than personal achievement and more meaningful than degrees, especially if they are earned at the expense of this identity and cultural integrity.[16]

Finally, the MEChA strategy called for the organization to play a substantive role in the creation and implementation of Chicano Studies and support services programs on campus. Chicano Studies programs would be a relevant alternative to established curricula. Most important, the Chicano Studies programs would be the foundation of MEChA's political power base:

> The institutionalization of Chicano programs is the realization of Chicano power on campus. The key to this power is found in the application of the principles of self-determination and self-liberation. These principles are defined and practiced in the areas of control, autonomy, flexibility, and participation. Often imaginary or symbolic authority is confused with the real. Many times token efforts in program institutionalization are substituted for enduring constructive programming. It is the responsibility of Chicanos on campus to insure dominant influence of these programs. The point is not to have a college with a program, but rather a Chicano program at the college.[17]

Allies among sympathetic faculty and administrators were to be cultivated as links to the academic power structure. But an independent and autonomous MEChA would preclude any co-optation. Students would also be the ones to assure that Mexican American faculty and administrators would retain their allegiance to the movement:

Therefore students must constantly remind the Chicano faculty and administrators where their loyalty and allegiance lies. It is very easy for administrators to begin looking for promotions just as it is very natural for faculty members to seek positions of academic prominence. ... [I]t is the students who must keep after Chicano and non-Chicano administrators and faculty to see that they do not compromise the position of the student and the community.[18]

MEChA would mobilize community support on behalf those faculty and staff members who, because of their demonstrated commitment to student interests, might jeopardize their own jobs.

Since Chicano Studies programs were at the heart of MEChA's concerns, special measures were advocated – and special concerns were noted. The politics of expediency characteristic of college administrators constituted a particular threat. It was important that Chicano Studies programs not be put in the straightjacket of the usual, academic guidelines. Community input was deemed essential to preclude the complete control of programs by academicians – many of whom accepted a rigid academy–community dichotomy and who therefore would tend toward 'business as usual'. Adequate Chicano control of the programs could be assured only if people from the community, students and Chicano faculty were all directly involved in the decision-making process of the programs. Disolving the academy–community dichotomy would thus make possible Chicano programs that would become models of 'self-determination' and 'self-liberation'. 'Academy' and especially 'community' had to be conceptualized in new ways:

[T]he concept of 'community' is all-inclusive. The Chicanos on campus are an organic, integral part of the Chicano community. Among Chicanos on campus there can be no distinctions or separations because of personal occupational differentiations. ... [T]he Chicano community on campus is an extension of the larger community. The base of the Chicanos on campus is the Chicano community. ... The primary goals of the various programs must be to serve the interests of the Chicano people.[19]

As had been the case with the Denver conference, gender inequality was not included on the agenda of the Santa Barbara conference. In contrast to the Denver conference, however, Chicanas did not attempt to put it on the agenda and did not organize a Chicana workshop. This did not mean, however, that Chicana participants did not take notice of the way Chicanos ran the conference. Christina Vega, one of the two Chicanas representatives who served as MEChA chairs, made the following observation: 'Men were in large part in control of the conference.... it was usually a man who was up there talking. I started to get offended at one point by what I realized was a macho or male-chauvinist perception of women's role ... when I interacted with male participants, they saw me not as a chairperson of MEChA, but as a female. That was bothersome to me.'[20]

The Santa Barbara conference lasted three days and involved over a hundred activists. Most were undergraduates and leaders of campus organizations. But some were graduate students, and several were faculty members or administrators. The proceedings of the conference were subsequently published as *El Plan de Santa Barbara* (see the appendix). The plan was much more detailed and sophisticated than *El Plan Espiritual de Aztlán*. Yet the Santa Barbara document built on the ideological and philosophical foundations laid out in the Denver document. In one important respect, however, it went beyond the Denver document: it specifically focused on the role of the Chicano/a intellectual and identified the institutions of higher education as strategic targets for political change. The manifesto that prefaced *El Plan de Santa Barbara* was a militant challenge to the university; it announced that the Chicano student movement had officially arrived and intended to play a leading role in the Chicano Power Movement in California and in the United States:

> For all people, as with individuals, the time comes when they must reckon with their history. For the Chicano, the present is a time of renaissance, of *renacimiento*. Our people and our community, *el barrio* and *la colonia*, are expressing a new consciousness and a new resolve. ... [W]e pledge our will to move against those forces which have denied us freedom of expression and human dignity.[21]

The Decline of the Student Movement

The Santa Barbara conference ended on a high note of solidarity. MEChA did, in fact, play a prominent role in the new politics of protest and confrontation, both on the campus and in the community. The political consciousness of the students rose through the intensification of MEChA's political activity, and much was accomplished. Chicano Studies programs were established at California community colleges located in areas with a substantial Mexican American community, at all the state colleges, and at virtually all of the campuses of the University of California. In some schools they were instituted as regular departments, in others as research centers, and in still other schools as programs on specialized curricula within existing academic units.

Increased Mexican American access to the colleges and universities also became a reality as the student movement pressed for expansion of support services programs. The special focus given to recruitment of Mexican American students was successful as MEChA directly confronted the issue of who should control educational opportunity programs (EOPs). MEChA engaged in power struggles with white liberal and Black administrators, whose overriding emphasis on the recruitment of Black students was perceived as slighting Mexican Americans. In a few cases these programs were placed in the hands of Mexican American administrators, some of whom were former student activists. But on most campuses the EOPs were divided into two components, one with a Chicano administrator and one with a Black administrator. The results were mixed. On the one hand, Chicano control (or partial control) of the EOPs enabled MEChA to increase the Mexican American student presence on campus. On the other, Chicano influence contributed to bitter and intense conflicts between Mexican Americans and Blacks on several campuses, making viable coalition politics difficult, if not altogether impossible.

Institution-sponsored community programs were another tangible result of the student movement. In some cases, the institutions provided the funds for MEChA to establish community centers that served as a link between students and their communities. Through these centers students provided counseling and tutorial services for youth and adults. Some centers provided a meeting place for community organizations. A few centers also offered bilingual education classes to teach English and academic courses on the same credit basis as college and university extension programs. Many MEChA activists became involved in electoral politics and in community organizations struggling to make changes in the local schools. Alliances were made with other organizations – for example, with the Brown Berets, who were involved in combating police brutality and drugs in the Mexican American community.

The Brown Berets became the largest nonstudent radical youth organization in the Mexican American community. During their formative period soon after the Los Angeles high school strike of 1968, A few UMAS and later MEChA activists were important members of the organization during the formative period. David Sanchez, the founder and prime minister of the Brown Berets, Fred Lopez, Carlos Montes, and Ralph Ramirez were among the thirteen activists indicted for conspiracy after the student strike. They were students at East Los Angeles City College and California State College, Los Angeles. (Sanchez had been a model high school student leader who had been recruited by the conservative mayor of Los Angeles, Sam Yorty, into his city youth council.) Although the majority of the Berets were men, women played key leadership roles as well. Gloria Arellanes and Vickie Castro were two examples.[22] By 1970, its leadership and rank and file had become predominantly street youth. Sanchez and others who had been student activists dropped out of college to become full-time community activists, and they recruited members who were or had been members of gangs. Many recruits came from the ranks of *pintos* (ex-convicts), those who had served time in juvenile hall or prison. The Berets thus played a significant role in bringing street youth into the Chicano Movement.

The Brown Berets became a paramilitary organization and, because of it, developed an image as the Chicano counterparts of the Black Panther Party. As cultural nationalists, however, they had more in common with United Slaves (US), the militant Black nationalist organization headed by Ron Karenga. They did not share the Marxist/Maoist ideology of the Black Panthers, nor their internationalist framework. The Berets adopted, as their prime responsibility, the defense of the Mexican American community against police harassment and brutality. They were therefore heavily infiltrated by police intelligence agencies and COINTELPRO.

After the Santa Barbara conference, MEChA activists and Brown Berets participated in a community struggle against the Catholic Church that was led by Católicos por La Raza (CPLR). The organization had been founded by Ricardo Cruz, a law student who had been inspired by the 1968 student walkouts to become an activist in the Chicano Movement. Cruz criticized Cardinal McIntyre and archdiocese of the city of Los Angeles for its insensitivity to the human needs of the Mexican American community and its failure to support the grape boycott led by the United Farm Workers. CPLR publicly assailed the archdiocese for the building of a $4 million new ultramodern church, St. Basil's, in a wealthy part of the city, while simultaneously closing a predominantly Mexican American Catholic school in East Los Angeles. On Christmas Eve 1969, the CPLR lead a protest of several hundred people at St.

Basil's Church and attempted to disrupt the mass being given by Archbishop James Cardinal McIntyre. The police beat up and arrested twenty-one CPLR activists on three types of misdemeanor charges: inciting a riot, disturbing a religious service, and assault on a police officer. Among those arrested were Ricardo Cruz; Alicia Escalante, leader of the East Los Angeles Welfare Rights Organization; Tony Salazar, president of MEChA at UCLA; Armando Vasquez-Ramos, president of MEChA at Long Beach State College; Richard Martinez, chair of MEChA's LA region; and Brown Beret Fred Lopez.[23]

The Berets and MEChA became a significant part of the first major Mexican American demonstration against the war in Vietnam.[24] It took place in Los Angeles on 29 August 1970 the demonstration came to be known as the Chicano Moratorium.[25] It was cochaired by Brown Beret Prime Minister David Sanchez and Rosalio Muñoz, former student body president at UCLA and one of the first Mexican Americans to resist the draft. Other draft resisters were Manuel Gómez, a Brown Beret and student activist at Hayward State College and one of the most eloquent young poets of the Chicano Movement; Ernesto Vigil, one of the young leaders of the Crusade for Justice; and Lorenzo Campbell, a student activist at the University of California, Riverside.

The Chicano Moratorium drew over 20,000 people to Laguna Park in East Los Angeles. The rally started in a festive mood, but ended in terror when Los Angeles police and Los Angeles County sheriff's deputies attacked the crowd without provocation. Hundreds were injured and over two hundred were arrested. Those arrested included Corky Gonzáles and his contingent from the Crusade for Justice. Tragically, three Mexican Americans were killed. This police riot provoked the first violent Mexican American outburst in a major US city as thousands of protestors took out revenge by burning businesses and automobiles on Whittier Boulevard, one of the main thoroughfares in East Los Angeles.[26] In response to the police attack, Rosalio Muñoz issued a statement protesting the police violence and making it clear that the Chicano Moratorium committee would continue to protest the war and would not be intimidated by 'police totalitarian aggression'.[27]

Despite its achievements – or perhaps partly because of them – student activism had declined dramatically by 1971. New student organizations emerged that were more career-oriented, emphasizing individual advancement. They were also extremely apolitical. Students in engineering and architecture programs formed their own organizations, as did those majoring in health, pre-law, education, and other areas. MEChA had to compete with these new organizations for influence among Chicano/a students. However, most incoming students lacked the experience of being activists in protest actions or participating in political struggles that would have brought them closer to MEChA's ideological perspective. With protest and confrontation throughout the US on the downswing, mass demonstrations on behalf of Mexican American causes also declined. Most Chicano/a students no longer perceived MEChA as a viable organization for meeting their academic and social needs.

Meanwhile, the founders of MEChA had graduated. Some had entered graduate or professional schools where they became involved in student organizations independent of MEChA – organizations more attuned to professional career goals. A good example was La Raza Law Students Association, organized by Mexican American student activists in the law schools. Many of those who were graduate students when MEChA was founded and during the height of MEChA's activity had become part-time faculty – mostly in Chicano Studies or similar programs (since few Mexican Americans with doctorates were not available for these positions). But priorities shifted as these activists moved from involvement in the politics of confrontation to implementation of programs, and their emphasis often shifted to institutional politics.

Other former student activists became EOP recruiters, counselors, or administrators (often through EOP work-study programs). Consequently they also became part of the university bureaucracy and embroiled in institutional politics. Others had left the campuses and become politically active in community organizations. Still another factor in MEChA's decline was the fact that many of the activists had neglected their studies because of their political involvement. Many of these students were placed on academic probation and were thus forced to shift their personal priorities from MEChA to academic survival. Attendance at MEChA meetings suffered a noticeable decline.

Within the MEChA groups, students differed on priorities. Some argued that MEChA's priority was campus struggle concerning the issues directly affecting students. Others took the position that MEChA should concentrate its time and energy on community struggles and use its institutional base to generate resources needed in those struggles. These differences eventually widened, becoming more antagonistic, and this debate over strategy only added to the further decline of the student movement.

Other differences were due to personality conflicts among the leadership and also differences related to gender issues. Chicana students held a regional conference at the California State College at Los Angeles on 8 May 1971 to deal with gender issues. The conference consisted of two workshops. One was on the 'Political Philosophy' and the other was one 'Political Education'. The workshops dealt included the following topics: the 'struggle between men and women', the 'separation of *la familia y el movimiento*', 'new family concepts', and 'Church and family' and the 'historic role of women in all movement'.[28]

Efforts were made to revitalize MEChA at a statewide conference held at California State University, Northridge in December 1972. The conference held workshops on the future direction and goals of MEChA, on the concepts of *La Raza* and *Chicanismo*, and on the role of women in the student movement. Several major resolutions were passed. One required MEChA to support La Raza Unida Party. Another stipulated that women would have equal representation in the leadership of MEChA. Others called for MEChA to play a major role in the decision-making process of Chicano Studies and related Chicano programs; to boycott Coors beer in support of striking Mexican American workers; and to continue to support the struggle of the United Farm Workers Union.

The resolution of support for La Raza Unida Party reflected a concern to continue the ideology of *Chicanismo*. But it did generate some controversy because in a very important respect it conflicted with support for the farmworkers' struggle. Chávez and the UFW had consistently worked within the Democratic Party – indeed, the UFW's very existence depended on its ties to the Democratic Party. In return for support of pro-farmworker legislation and other reforms, the UFW endorsed and campaigned for Democratic candidates at the local, state, and national levels.

Ultimately, the conference's farmworker resolution was passed only because of the importance of the union to Mexican American farmworkers. However, the passage of both resolutions reflected contradictions within MEChA and further aggravated divisions within the organization, since some members opted to work actively in support of La Raza Unida while others continued to work actively in support of the farmworkers union (and indirectly for the Democratic Party).

The resolution on the role of women in the leadership of MEChA reflected a rapid acceleration of concern about the issue of sexism. Although women had always played an active role in the student movement, only two of them played a leadership role as MEChA chairs in California. The majority were consistently relegated to secondary roles. As had been the case at the Denver conference, Chicanas who identified themselves as feminists were harshly criticized for promoting what Chicanos perceived as white feminist ideas and issues. This was another key factor for divisions within MEChA.

Ana Nieto-Gómez was one of the most vocal and articulate feminists to emerge from the ranks of MEChA, and one of the two Chicanas who served as chairs of a MEChA chapter in California. She chaired the Long Beach State College chapter; the other was Christina Vega at UC Irvine. In response to the Chicano perception that feminism was a white women's issue, Nieto-Gómez defined Chicana feminism in this way:

When you say you are a feminist you mean you're a woman who opposes the oppression of not only the group in general, but of women in particular. … The feminist movement is a unified front made up both men and women – a feminist can be a man as well as a woman – it is a group of people that advocates the end of women's oppression.[29]

She placed the blame on the movement's Chicano Nationalist ideology for the failure of Chicanos to accept her definition of feminism: 'Cultural nationalism is against women … and men who aren't chauvinistic … it also separates us from other oppressed peoples.'[30]

Unfortunately most Chicanos in the student movement as a whole did not get the message, and as a result many Chicanas decided to spend their energies and time organizing their own conferences and developing their own feminist organizations on campus and in the community.

Chicana student activists were inspired by older Chicana feminists who had been long-time activists in Mexican American struggles prior to the emergence of the Chicano Movement. Francisca Flores (1913–1996) was a good example. In the 1950s, she was the editor of *Carta Editorial*, in which she expressed radical views during the McCarthy anti-communist hysteria. As a result, she was subject to numerous red-baiting attacks. In 1959 she became a co-founder of the Mexican American Political Association (MAPA). During the 1960s, she was inspired by Dr. Martin Luther King Jr., telling her nephew, Bill Flores, that "this is a man who will change America and we must march with him"[31] She then became the editor and publisher of *Regeneración*, a magazine she used to highlight the struggles of Mexican American women. She also co-founded the Comision Feminil Mexicana, one of the first feminist organizations of that decade. It was an organization that provided a 'platform for women to use for thinking out their problems, to deal with issues not customarily taken up in regular organizations … where women can discuss abortions without having to first discuss the emotional questions of moral issue.'[32] She also founded the Chicana Social Service Center in Los Angeles and served as its first executive director.

Alicia Escalante was another long-time activist in Los Angeles who became a role model for Chicana student activists. She founded the East Los Angeles Welfare Rights Organization, which was later renamed the Chicana Welfare Rights Organization. She focused on the issues that poor Mexican American women faced in California and throughout the nation. In 1969, she was one of thirteen angry welfare recipients who appeared as witnesses before an investigating subcommittee of the US Senate Committee on Nutrition and Human Needs. She was a single mother of five children. She bluntly told the senators that 'we are forced to feed our families rice, beans and other starches. Hidden hunger and periodic starvation appear in at least half the families of our community'[33]

In New Mexico, Elizabeth 'Betita' Martinez and Enriqueta Vasquez were two other activists who became role models for Chicana activists. Martinez was a veteran of the southern Civil Rights Movement and former member of the Student Nonviolent Coordinating Committee (SNCC). Vasquez was a veteran of local community struggles in Colorado and New Mexico. They were co-founders of *El Grito del Norte* newspaper in 1968. The initial focus of the newspaper was on the land grants struggle in northern New Mexico, but it soon expanded its coverage to Chicano/a struggles throughout the Southwest to become one of the best-known Chicano Movement community newspapers in the area. Martinez was the editor and Vasquez wrote a regular column devoted to the issues facing Mexican American women. She also produced six essays that are considered seminal contributions on the 'woman question' debate engaged by Chicana feminists.[34]

Dolores Huerta was the most famous of all the older women activists. She was the first Mexican American woman to get national recognition because she was a co-founder with César Chávez of the farmworker movement in California. She was also one of the vice presidents of the United Farm Workers Union (UFW). Huerta made clear the fact that women were a central force in the union. As she put it, 'We couldn't have a union without the women.… their sacrifices have been unbelievable. And the participation of women has helped keep the movement nonviolent.'[35]

Chicana student activists inspired by the older generation of Mexican

American women activists, like those mentioned above, created organizations to promote dialogue on the gender issues they confronted in everyday life. For example, Dorinda Moreno and other Chicana student activists at San Francisco State College founded the Concilio Mujeres in 1970 in the Mission district community of San Francisco. Its purpose was to 'provide psychological support for women and to develop educational, communicational, and politically oriented projects.'[36] On campus, the Concilio created a 'La Raza Women's' seminar for the Ethnic Studies curriculum. In the community it opened an office from which Concilio activists launched projects that included a library and research center on women's issues. Many of the materials from the center became part of the first Chicana bibliography published by the Chicano Studies Library at UC Berkeley, compiled by three Chicana student activists at Berkeley.[37] The Concilio also founded a women's *teatro* group called Las Cucarachas; Chicana *teatro* groups were also organized on college campuses. At San Diego State University, for example, Felicitas Nuñez and other Chicanas founded Teatro de Las Chicanas. Other Chicana *teatro* groups emerged throughout the Southwest aiming to dramatize the Mexican American woman's experience. Others organized 'Adelita' chapters named for the women who fought in the 1910 Mexican Revolution alongside their men.

The first national Chicana conference took place in Houston, Texas, in 1971. The majority who attended were Chicana student movement activists. According to Marta Cotera, one of the conference organizers, 'Approximately 80% of the women were in the 18–23 age bracket from various universities across the United States.'[38] It was the first time that Chicanas were able to focus and dialogue with each other on gender issues of common concern to women. The role of Chicanas in the Chicano Movement and in the family was the main theme of the conference. Workshop topics ranged from 'marriage Chicana style' to 'militancy or conservatism – which way forward?' to the Chicana perspective on the exploitation of women.[39] This conference contributed to making Chicanas more aware of the feminist discourse taking place throughout the nation and specifically by Chicano Movement feminists. Feminist discourse generated a dilemma for Chicanas. As Maria Baeza, a participant at the conference, put it, 'For some it created a conflict: should they advance the Chicano Movement agenda solely or should they try to create a space for themselves within the movement. Most Chicanos felt that feminism was a white women's struggle and that Chicanas should just focus on the movement and they should continue to be the *soldaderas* of the *revolucion* following the men's leadership.'[40] Marta Cotera, the organizer of the conference, went on to publish the first two books on Chicana history.[41]

Many of those activists who participated in that conference returned to their campuses, where they continued the dialogue on gender issues and feminism. By 1975 Chicana veterans of the Chicano Movement had made an impact on the younger generation of Chicana activists that emerged after the movement had declined. At the University of California, Berkeley, for example, Chicana activists became aware of the Houston conference and others that took place afterward. They read the early writings by Chicana veterans of the Chicano Movement, and, propelled by their own dissatisfaction with the sexist attitudes of Chicanos in MEChA, they formed their own organization. They called themselves Las Mujeres del Movimiento (Women of the Movement). Their first project became an educational symposium they called 'Educacion en Luz' (Spotlight on Education). They invited male and female scholars and community activists to speak on the status of research on the Mexican American experience. The keynote speaker for the symposium was Dorinda Moreno of the Concilio Mujeres, and Ana Nieto-Gómez, by then an assistant professor of Chicano studies at California State University at Northridge, was one of the other invited speakers. Graciela Rios, one of the Mujeres del Movimiento recalled how deeply touched and inspired she was by Nieto-Gómez: 'She spoke to the issues I was confronting at that time as a young Chicana in a way I was able to critically understand them.'[42]

After the conference, Chicana students joined MEChA in demanding to be included in the decision-making process of Chicano programs on campus reflected the ever increasing conflict between students and Mexican American faculty and administrators. Students had played a key role in the early phases of developing and implementing proposals for Chicano Studies programs on campus. (This was true even before the historic Santa Barbara conference, where the role of students was first 'officially' spelled out.) However, once Chicano Studies programs were approved and funded and staff and faculty had secured positions, the role of students in them became more and more peripheral.

In essence, students had supported the efforts to make the programs an integral part of the institution. However, once programs became part of the institution they came under the general rules and regulations governing all academic programs. In the case of Chicano Studies, this meant that exclusive control of curricula by the faculty was expected to ensure conformance with university policies. Students thus could no longer expect to play an influential role in the further development of Chicano Studies programs unless 'understandings' were reached with the program faculty.

Although some programs did make efforts to allow students a direct role in decision making, the usual outcome of institutionalization was the gradual decline of student participation in the governance of the programs. Distrust between faculty, administrators, and students evolved, creating a climate of divisiveness. Students often responded by criticizing the faculty for careerism and opportunism, while faculty members criticized students for not understanding the need to conform to institutional policy to ensure the survival of Chicano Studies programs.

Several other local, regional and statewide meetings and conferences marked efforts to revitalize MEChA and redefine its goals and objectives to be more in tune with the new issues and the changed situation. The general goals of the 1960s had been achieved. Chicano Studies programs had become a reality, and the EOPs and other support services programs had opened the doors to institutions of higher education for thousands of Mexican American youth from low-income families. Although many of these programs were relatively insecure, most new students saw them as part of the status quo and related to them as if they had always been there.

Thus, the issues and objectives outlined in *El Plan de Santa Barbara* could no longer have any meaningful impact on the new wave of students: The plan was not a program for the 1970s and beyond. The easily understood goals of MEChA's founders were not clear to the new MEChA activists, and confusion over goals and ideology began to develop. In response to this uncertainty, the new leaders began to ponder the future direction of the student movement. They attributed the decline of MEChA to the following reasons:

> The lack of vision and adaptability to a new situation made the organization stagnant and nonproductive. This was basically due to the fact that our goals ... were vague and undefined and that we were trying to build up an organization on false assumptions such as: (1) because we are all Chicanos we would be drawn together and automatically define our goals and directions: (2) that by simply directing our efforts and energies to the issues facing the Chicano, political consciousness would evolve. These assumptions have been detrimental to the Chicano's advancement for self-determination.[43]

Chicanismo, as defined in *El Plan de Santa Barbara*, had kept the movement generally united during its formative period. But this cultural nationalist ideology, as it was generally understood in 1969, proved unable to accommodate the different levels of political consciousness that characterized the student movement. The ideology of *Chicanismo* had settled the internal confusion over identity. But in spite of this tremendous accomplishment *Chicanismo* could not even begin to answer the substantive questions concerning the ultimate shape of a political ideology and strategy that could take into account the diversity of political orientations within the Mexican American community. There is no question that *Chicanismo* propelled the movement's politics against racism. But, as conceptualized in 1969, it did not offer a framework for the concrete analysis of the dominant political and economic institutions of US society and how they affected the different strata of Mexican Americans.

In addition, *Chicanismo* never offered the student movement adequate insight into the nature of the institutions of higher education and their role in society. Breaking some of the barriers to educational opportunity for Mexican Americans, by itself a formidable accomplishment, ultimately proved to be a very limited political goal. Interestingly, some student activists had recognized these limitations soon after the Santa Barbara conference. Those who had become influenced by other left political organizations criticized *Chicanismo* as a reactionary ideology. At a conference that took place at Merritt College in Oakland in July 1969, some of these students put it this way: 'What nationalism as an ideology does is deny class society and a class consciousness.'[44]

Others, especially those involved in liberal Democratic politics, sought a path toward the acceptance of a liberal capitalism that called for the integration of Chicanos into the existing political economy of society. They argued that Chicano political power was impossible without the development of Chicano capitalist institutions:

> [W]e fail to realize that we ... lack the power that makes and breaks politicians and turns proposals into laws. We lack monetary power ... which enables the Anglo-Saxon to buy votes and politicians. ... We must be able to manipulate politicians through campaign contributions. ... [W]e shouldn't hesitate to sell our vote to the highest bidder. ... The solution ... is for us to become just as capitalistic as the white man. Let's go build Chicano corporations and industrial empires; let's go into business and finance, not being afraid to use the methods that have put the 'man' where he is.[45]

These advocates of Chicano capitalism believed that Mexican American students should major in the natural sciences, business and finance, and engineering. The response to 'Chicano capitalism' was a call for a revolutionary Marxism that could provide a critical understanding of how capitalism ultimately functions to the detriment of all working people:

> [W]hite workers are exploited in the factory for their labor in the same manner that Chicanos, blacks, and other minorities are exploited. They suffer from racial discrimination ... but as a class of people. The ones who benefit from this system are a small percentage of the population ... who control the means of production. To have ... Chicanos become big industrialists wouldn't help the Chicano masses any more than the white worker is helped by the white industrialists. What has to be understood is that Capitalism thrives on the exploitation of man by man, and the only way that the oppression of the people will be eradicated is by the destruction of this system and not by its toleration.[46]

The conflict over political ideology intensified, coming to crisis at a statewide MEChA conference held at the University of California, Riverside campus in 1973. Students who urged that MEChA adopt a Marxist ideology criticized cultural nationalism on the following basis:

> Cultural nationalism ... points to a form of struggle that does not take into account the inter-connectedness of the world and proclaims as a solution the separatism that the capitalist has developed and perpetuated in order to exploit working people further. ... It promotes the concept of a nation without a material basis and solely on a spiritual basis and tends to identify the enemy on a racial basis, ignoring the origin of racism and that it is simply an oppressive tool of capitalism.[47]

In a heated exchange, the Marxist faction argued that MEChA had ceased to be an effective organization because it had evolved into a bureaucratic and reactionary group. It had lost its will to struggle, as evidenced by the desire of the majority attending the conference to avoid discussions of political ideology. On the second day of the conference the Marxists walked out, along with many of the new, apolitical students who had had an interest in becoming MEChistas. These new students lacked the experience to understand the political debate. The student movement never recovered from the effects of this split. After the conference, statewide MEChA communication and coordination came to a virtual halt, and MEChA chapters returned to an emphasis on local campus politics.

Most of the students who had adopted a Marxist position at the conference dropped completely out of MEChA. Some formed countergroups, while others became involved with community-based Marxist organizations. One group of Marxists in Los Angeles and Orange counties formed El Comité Estudiantil del Pueblo:

> We have come together ... parting from the conclusion that MEChA has reached its objective limits as an organizational form to wage struggle on the student level. This conclusion was reached through the reflection of our own practice in the Chicano Student Movement.[48]

El Comité was a collective that included Mexican and Puerto Rican students who had links to revolutionary student movements in Mexico and to the Puerto Rican Socialist Party, respectively. The collective operated under the direction of the National Committee to Free Los Tres and CASA (Centro de Acción Social Autónoma). The National Committee to Free Los Tres was formed after the arrest of three activists associated with La Casa del Carnalismo, a community organization whose primary emphasis was to drive dope pushers out of the community. The three activists and the National Committee to Free Los Tres accused the authorities of planting drugs in order to make the bust, with the purpose of subverting the organizing efforts of La Casa del Carnalismo. CASA, the other organization working with El Comité Estudiantil del Pueblo, had been founded by Bert Corona, a labor organizer, former president of MAPA, and long-time political activist, but it had been taken over by the leadership of the radical Los Tres organization:

> We clearly align ourselves with the organizations that put forth the correct political line in theory and foremost in practice, concerning the struggle for self-determination of our people. Both CASA ... and the National Committee to Free Los Tres have shown in practice, their vigilance over the democratic rights of our people through their daily work and open political defiance and resistance to repression in the form of mass demonstrations and mobilizations. ... [B]oth organizations are responsible for taking our

struggle to a national level. Also, in developing an independent political line that corresponds to the particular concrete conditions of our people.[49]

Based on its work within these community organizations, El Comité Estudiantil developed a set of political principles that clearly established its Marxist orientation:

(1) Struggle for Self-determination as a people against the imperialist system which denies us that right.
(2) University reform.
(3) Creation of Student-Worker Unity.
(4) Anti-imperialist solidarity with student struggles within the United States and throughout the world, particularly with Latin America.[50]

In contrast to MEChA's ideology of cultural nationalism, the ideology of revolutionary nationalism was an attractive alternative to some of the more radical students on campus. The National Committee to Free Los Tres explained the difference between the two outlooks in this way:

[S]ome Chicano Movement activists obsessively continue to hold on to the view that we must struggle against exploitation, racism, repression and for self determination, guided by the spiritual, cultural and moral values of our Indian ancestors. ... [They] also hold the view that since the white European Invader is our oppressor, we must reject any ideas ... that come from white people. ... But the problems our people face today ... require concrete solutions. ... Cultural practices, spiritual beliefs, love ... Chicanismo ... do not teach us how to organize a workers strike, how to organize and struggle against police brutality, how to stop the dragnet raids and mass deportations of our people, how to organize a student movement. ... It does not teach us how to create a society free of exploitation, how as part of the working class we can take power. ... Our children should not feel proud that they are Mexicanos only because of their color. The strongest national consciousness comes from a knowledge that the masses of our people have made great contributions to the progress and development of organized society, industry and agriculture [and] led ... great struggles to organize workers against exploitation. ... Teaching history in this manner ... creates strong pride in our heritage. But it also recognizes and respects the role of other nationalities as workers and ... teaches our people true internationalism. It exposes the class nature of US society [and] ... imperialism as the bloodiest, most brutal exploiter ... responsible for the underdevelopment of the Third World. ... [W]e also learn the true nature of racism as having an economic base. ... [R]evolutionary nationalism entails working class solidarity which knows no borders. A concept especially important to us who exist divided from our people by the border established by the imperialist US powers. True revolutionary nationalism can only be developed in this context. *Un pueblo sin fronteras* [a people without borders].[51]

The revolutionary nationalism defined by the National Committee required the rejection of the Chicano identity defined at the Santa Barbara conference. The concept *sin fronteras,* which for Bert Corona had meant that all workers had to be organized regardless of which side of the border their home was on, now became the basis for a struggle against the politics of Chicano identity. CASA members attempted to persuade other students that Chicano culture did not exist. They argued that the perpetuation of the Chicano identity was harmful because it divided Mexican students in the United States from student movements in Mexico. The National Committee eventually merged with CASA. The Comité Estudiantil del Pueblo ceased to exist as student activists became the dominant constituency and former student activists the leadership of CASA.

Meanwhile, another predominantly Chicano Marxist community organization, the August 29th Movement, had emerged, though its political orientation was very different from CASA's. Comprising mostly former and current Chicano student and youth activists, it had adopted a Marxist-Leninism that emphasized the teachings of Stalin and Mao. ATM attracted left-leaning students who disagreed with CASA's rejection of Chicano identity. Instead, ATM took the position that *Chicanismo* was very much a reality:

> We ... oppose those forces who say that 'there is no Chicano people'. ... These forces ... claim that Chicanos in the southwest are actually Mexicanos, a part of the country of México. They desire ... not the right to political independence, but re-annexation to México. To these forces, it must seem that the Chicano people have not yet 'earned' their right to be called a people.[52]

ATM credited the student movement of the 1960s with having played the most significant role in the development of the Chicano Movement. It acknowledged the decline of MEChA but saw a need to give it direction and to broaden its scope by emphasizing support for worker and *campesino* struggles. Using Stalin's definition of a nation from *Marxism and the National Question*, ATM developed a plan for the establishment of a Chicano nation within those territories of the southwestern United States that had a majority, or a sufficiently large, Chicano population. ATM called on Chicano student activists to join in the struggle to establish a multinational communist party in the US:

> In every revolutionary movement students have played an important role. We must realize that only one class, the working class, is capable of carrying the revolution to success. But students who believe in the objective of socialism can consciously work for that objective. ... [S]tudents must take up the disciplined study of the science of the working class, Marxism-Leninism. They must involve themselves with struggles on campus and take leadership roles in those struggles, to educate others as to the fact that our problems derive from the system of imperialism and can only end with the destruction of imperialism. ... [W]e must remember ... we were not always students nor will we always be students. There is a class struggle raging and there are only two choices before us, either the side of the imperialists ... or the side of the proletariat. Let us build a multinational communist party.[53]

CASA and ATM competed with each other in efforts to recruit student activists from MEChA and other organizations. At a few campuses a bitter struggle took place over the control of MEChA or of the Chicano Studies program. But for the most part these organizations failed to have much impact on the majority of Mexican American students. Their intense debates were usually couched in polemical language and alienated the average student, who had no familiarity with Marxist terminology. The result was the reinforcement of anti-Marxist attitudes among most students.

On a statewide basis the dominant forces within MEChA were cultural nationalism and liberal interest-group politics. MEChA continued to decline; few students attended meetings and on some campuses MEChA ceased to function altogether. Nine years after the Santa Barbara conference, MEChA held a statewide constitutional conference at Stanford University to revitalize the student movement and redefine its goals. In a letter to all MEChA leaders in California the conference organizers addressed the significance of the conference in the following terms:

> It is very important that all MEChAs in the state participate in the development of a new constitution. This conference will mark an important stage in the history of the Chicano student movement as it will be the first time since *El Plan de Santa Barbara* ... that Chicano students will come together to re-define the goals, objectives, and philosophy of *el movimiento estudiantil Chicano.*[54]

By these standards, the Stanford conference was a failure. It did not produce the new document that was to replace *El Plan de Santa Barbara*, nor did it redefine the MEChA's objectives and ideology. MEChA continued to exist on many campuses during the 1970s and was active in varying degrees. On some campuses it ceased to exist entirely, and efforts to revitalize it met with little success.

Outside California, the Chicano student movement developed somewhat differently in both organizational and ideological terms. Few student organizations in other states had changed their names to MEChA. In Texas the Mexican American Youth Organization retained its name and identity, and only one MEChA chapter emerged in that state (at the University of Texas at El Paso in the early 1970s). It was not until 1980 that another MEChA evolved in Texas with the founding of a chapter at the University of Texas at San Antonio. The first statewide MEChA conference in Texas took place in 1982. Eleven student organizations participated and agreed to become members of a statewide MEChA. MAYO, MASA, UMAS, Hispanic Student Alliance, AMAS and even a LULAC chapter, were listed in the MEChA 'Member Organizations' list of 1981–82.

In Colorado, only one MEChA chapter emerged and that was at the Metropolitan State campus. At the state's leading college, the University of Colorado at Boulder, UMAS never did change its name to MEChA despite strong support from Corky Gonzales and his Crusade for Justice throughout the state. The same pattern prevailed in Arizona and New Mexico. In the Midwest, UMAS did evolve into MEChA at the University of Notre Dame. But, although the Notre Dame MEChA chapter was active on campus and in the community, the name did not spread to other campuses in the Midwest.

The failure of the MEChA name to take hold outside California was the result of the uneven development of cultural, racial, and political consciousness among Mexican American youth throughout the Southwest and Midwest. For example, the proximity of Texas to the Mexican border has historically resulted in the survival of a distinct Mexican culture and folklore in that state. The identity crisis among youth in Texas has therefore never been as pronounced as in California. In the Midwest, Mexican identity has merged with that of other Latinos, mostly notably Puerto Ricans.

The lack of equal emphasis on the quest for identity outside California did not mean that the Chicano student movement was not significant elsewhere. In terms of the quest for power, the movement was important, especially in Texas, Colorado and New Mexico, where it contributed to the development of La Raza Unida Party and the political mobilization of the Mexican American people.

In spite of internal conflicts, the student movement made significant contributions. It played the principal role in the establishment of programs on campus which produced greater access for Mexican American youth to institutions of higher education – most notably, Chicano Studies and EOP programs. It developed the political consciousness of Mexican American youth. It was always at the center of the development of the broader Chicano Power Movement in California and elsewhere in the United States. From the ranks of the movement have come intellectuals and professionals who are beginning to play a role in leading US political and economic institutions. Some of these intellectuals have participated in organizational efforts to develop new perspectives that challenge the dominant ideology. (The most notable of them have explored and incorporated Marxist, neo-Marxist and feminist concepts into their analysis of the Mexican American experience.[55]) In the absence of a strong student movement, however, most of these intellectuals have assumed roles in institutions that reinforce the dominant values of capitalism. The critiques of 'ivory tower intellectualism' that characterized the militant period of the movement are not often heard today, and certainly do not carry the sting they once did.

As with so many other social movements, students were the catalyst in bringing about a polarization between those who were content with the status quo, or who argued for a 'gradualist' approach, and those who were committed to quickly bringing about substantive institutional change. The debate continues, because the contradictions still exist. But without a strong student movement, it is not always easy to distinguish between the professionalism and sophistication required to compel social change and the professionalism used to maintain the status quo.

Notes

1 Quoted in Stan Steiner, *La Raza: The Mexican Americans*, New York 1970, p. 385.
2 *El Plan Espiritual de Aztlán*.
3 Enriqueta Longeaux y Vasquez, 'The Mexican American Woman' in Robin Morgan, ed., *Sisterhood Is Powerful: An Anthology of Writings from the Women's Liberation Movement*, New York 1970.
4 Ibid, p. 379.
5 In addition to Alurista, other committee members were Jorge González, Luis Valdez, and Juan Gómez-Quiñones; all were from California. Jorge González, interview, 1979.
6 *El Plan Espiritual de Aztlán*.
7 Quoted in Steiner, *La Raza*, p. 389.
8 *El Plan de Santa Barbara: A Chicano Plan for Higher Education*, Oakland 1969, p. 51.
9 Ibid., p. 9. The name MEChA was proposed by Ysidro Ramon Macias.
10 Ibid., p. 50.
11 Ibid., p. 9.
12 Ibid., p. 54.
13 Ibid., p. 80.
14 Ibid., p. 54.
15 Ibid.
16 Ibid.
17 Ibid., p. 13.
18 Ibid., p. 59.
19 Ibid., p. 14.
20 Interview with Christina Vega, 24 January 1979.
21 Ibid., p. 9.
22 See Dionne Espinoza, 'Revolutionary Sisters', in *Aztlan*, vol. 26, no. 1, Spring 2001, pp. 17–58.
23 The other twenty-one activists arrested were Connie Nieto, Roberto Gandara, Luis Garza, Ramon Cruz, Larry Hahn, Pedro Arias, Douana Doherty, Joe Razo, Raul Ruiz, Lydia Lopez, José Camarena, Luis Pingarron, Gloria Chávez, and Victor Mendoza.
24 A smaller scale demonstration of several hundred people had taken place in 1969 in East Los Angeles.
25 See Lorena Oropeza, *¡Raza Sí! ¡Guerra No! Chicano Protest and Patriotism during the Vietnam War Era*, Berkeley 2005, pp. 145–82.
26 See Armando Morales, *Ando Sangrando: I Am Bleeding*, for an account of the riots, pp. 91–122.
27 Ibid., p. 118.
28 The proceedings of the conference were published in *Hijas de Cuautemoc*, no. 2, May 1971.
29 Interview, 1979.

30 Ibid.
31 Bill Flores, 'Elogio a Francisca Flores', *TQS: Contemporary Newsletter of Eclectic Chicano Thought*, vol 13, no. 3, May-June 1996.
32 Francisca Flores, 'Comision Femenil Mexicana', *Regeneración*, vol. 2, no. 1, 1971, pp. 6–7. Reprinted in Alma Garcia, ed., *Chicana Feminist Thought: The Basic Historical Writings*, New York 1997.
33 *Time*, May 16, 1969.
34 Lorena Oropeza and Dionne Espinosa, eds., *Enriqueta Vasquez and the Chicano Movement: Writings from El Grito del Norte*, Houston 2005, p. 207.
35 Jean Murphy, 'Unsung Heroine of La Causa', *Regeneración*, vol 1, no. 10, 1971, p. 20.
36 *Las Cucarachas Newsletter*, n.d., author's files.
37 Cristina Portillo, Graciela Rios, Martha Rodriguez, eds., *Bibliography of Writings on La Mujer*, Berkeley 1976.
38 Marta Cotera, 'La Conferencia de Mujeres Por La Raza: Houston, Texas, 1971', reprinted in Alma M. Garcia, ed., *Chicana Feminist Thought*.
39 Ibid., p. 156.
40 Interview with Maria Baeza.
41 Martha P. Cotera, *Diosa y Hembra: The History and Heritage of Chicanas in the U.S.*, Austin 1976; *The Chicana Feminist*, Austin 1977.
42 Interview with Graciela Rios.
43 MEChA, *Chicano Resource Journal*, Berkeley 1972, p. 10.
44 Juan López, *El Indígena*, vol. 1, August 1969, n.p.
45 Mario Vázquez, *El Nopal*, vol. 1, no. 5, 1969.
46 Nacho González, 'Power to the People', unpublished paper, n.d.
47 Unpublished position paper, author's files.
48 El Comité Estudiantil del Pueblo, 'Aprender es Luchar', pamphlet, n.p. 1974, p. 1.
49 Ibid., p. 5.
50 Ibid., pp. 4–5.
51 *Sin Cadenas*, vol. 2, no. 1, 1975, pp. 5–6. This publication was the propaganda organ of CASA, which eventually became the organization's newspaper, *Sin Fronteras*.
52 August 29th Movement, 'Fan the Flames', 1976, p. 10.
53 Speech by student activist, member of ATM, Hayward, California, mimeo, n.d., author's files.
54 Document in author's files.
55 For a discussion of this work, see Estevan T. Flores, 'The Mexican-Origin People in the United States and Marxist Thought in Chicano Studies', in Bertell Ollman and Edward Varnoff, eds, *Marxist Scholarship on American Campuses*, vol. 3 of *The Left Academy*, New York 1986, pp. 103–38.

4

The Rise and Fall of La Raza Unida Party

One of the major outcomes of the 1969 National Chicano Youth Liberation Conference in Denver, Colorado was the call for the 'creation of an independent local, regional and national political party'. The Democratic and Republican parties were denounced for not responding to the needs and aspirations of Mexican Americans. No name for the party was proposed, nor was it decided where the party would first be organized. The Mexican American Youth Organization in Texas was the first group to take the initiative. In May 1969, two months after the Denver conference, MAYO decided at a statewide meeting to focus its activities on the Winter Garden area of south Texas, a region of small agricultural communities with a large concentration of Mexican Americans. Before this project was approved, MAYO chapters had organized around a number of issues that concerned local Mexican Americans, but now the emphasis shifted to gaining control of community institutions. The first target was the school system of Crystal City, Texas as a step in the direction of building the independent Chicano political party called for by *El Plan Espiritual de Aztlán*.

The name of the new party was La Raza Unida.[1] This name was the choice of MAYO activists who had participated in the national convention of the Alianza de Pueblos Libres in Albuquerque, New Mexico in October 1967.[2] Reies López Tijerina had organized this conference in order to unite his organization with others representing the white New Left, the Black Power

Movement, and the Hopi Indian nation.³ But the conference was perhaps most significant for the discussion of La Raza Unida among the Mexican American activists in attendance.⁴

A week later, MAYO organized a La Raza Unida conference in El Paso, Texas to protest the exclusion of Mexican American community activists from President Johnson's Inter-Agency Committee hearings in that city. The success of the El Paso meeting convinced the MAYO leadership that La Raza Unida should be the name of their political party.

José Angel Gutiérrez was selected as the chief coordinator of the Winter Garden Project since he had grown up in Crystal City, a Winter Garden community of some 10,000 people, 80 percent of them Mexican, and the self-designated 'Spinach Capital of the World'. This was not the first time that Mexican Americans had struggled for political power in that city. In 1963 Mexican Americans, with the support of the local Teamster Union officials and PASSO, were able to win city council elections that, for the first time in the history of Texas, allowed Mexican Americans to exert political domination over the white minority population.⁵

Mexican American domination of the council was short-lived, however; they were ousted from office by the white power structure at the next elections two years later. Their election had not been the result of strong grassroots community organizing, and the lack of this support was an important factor in their defeat. White economic domination and racism, which had historically fostered a colonial relationship between oppressor and oppressed in south Texas, were formidable barriers to the successful governance of the city by Mexican Americans and could not be overcome without effective community organization.

Nevertheless, the temporary setback of the 'gringo' in Crystal City contributed greatly to the growth of political consciousness among Mexican Americans in Texas. Student activists led by José Angel Gutiérrez and Mario Compeán began to plan for the formation of a mass-based political party that could eventually become an alternative to the two major political parties in Texas. The takeover and community control of the school system in Crystal City was to be the initial step in the plan, to be followed by political control of city and county government throughout rural south Texas. Once political power was achieved, the next step would be the economic 'decolonization' of south Texas through termination of Mexican American dependency on white economic institutions and the development of 'Brown Capitalism'.

MAYO's strategy rested on organizing support for educational change as opposed to political change. Parents were to be the main source of this support and the family unit would to be the mass base of the party. A student protest against discrimination in the schools was to be the catalyst of this process.

In June 1969 Gutiérrez began preparing the groundwork for the project. Six months later, a successful student strike at the local high school provided the springboard for organizing. Gutiérrez, a gifted organizer, lost little time. His efforts, together with those of his wife Luz and several other key people, resulted in the creation of El Partido de la Raza Unida in January 1970. In subsequent elections, the party was able to elect its candidates to both the school board and the city council, soon gaining control of them. For the first time in Texas history, Mexican Americans controlled the schools in a heavily Mexican town.

These victories – interpreted as a 'Chicano takeover' of the town – stimulated interest in La Raza Unida Party in other areas. A MAYO national conference in Mission, Texas in December 1969 placed top priority on the development of the party. MAYO chapters were to dedicate themselves enthusiastically to the organization of party chapters throughout the state. By 1971, La Raza Unida Party had replaced MAYO as the leading organization in Texas grass-roots organizing. Chapters had also begun to emerge in Colorado, California, and other areas.

During the mobilization of Mexican Americans in Crystal City MAYO had developed a strong anti-white orientation. The student boycott had been a tactic within the strategy of direct confrontation with the white power structure. MAYO saw this as a way to maximize community support and dramatize the need for Mexican American separatism and for Mexican Americans to build their own political party. José Angel Gutiérrez described MAYO's goals this way: 'We sought to expose, confront, and eliminate the gringo. We felt it was necessary to polarize the community over issues into chicano versus gringos.'[6]

The 'gringo as enemy' would continue to be a key theme as efforts to build La Raza Unida Party intensified. But aside from promoting the 'gringo as enemy' concept, very little was done to develop the party's theory or ideology. The development of La Raza Unida in Texas was marked by a definite emphasis on the practical questions of strategy, tactics, and organization combined with a strong commitment to cultural nationalism, although the latter was not defined very clearly. This commitment appears in the party's main document

outlining its political program in Texas and in speeches and statements by
party leaders. According to Gutiérrez,

> I realize that books in themselves do not end oppression. In line with
> this realization I have omitted discussion of ideology and philosophy. My
> purpose is not to describe the philosophical underpinnings of the U. S. of
> A. This book is a limited manual on how to deal with the racist, imperialist,
> colonialized society of white people. Chicanos cannot live by theory alone;
> we must pick up the tools of our liberation. This book is a tool.[7]

According to the preamble to the Texas Raza Unida Party platform, the
party had four objectives. The first was 'to replace the existing system with a
humanistic alternative which shall maintain equal representation of all people.'
The second, was 'to create a government which serves the needs of individual
communities, yet is beneficial to the general populace.' Third was the creation
of 'a political movement dedicated to ending the causes of poverty, misery and
injustice so that future generations can live a life free from exploitation.' The
fourth was 'to abolish racist practices within the existing social, educational,
economic and political system so that physical and cultural genocidal practices
against minorities will be discontinued.' These basic objectives are to be accomplished through adherence to the concepts of carnalismo and la familia:

> [B]ecause we are the people who have been made aware of the needs of
> the many through our suffering, who have learned the significance of
> *carnalismo*, the strength of *la familia* and the importance of people working
> together; and recognizing the natural right of all peoples to preserve their
> self-identity and to formulate their own destiny.[8]

The document goes on to present the party's position on various issues.
The educational problems facing Mexican Americans in Texas were addressed in terms of the lack of quality education due to 'the unequal distribution of revenues', the school system's failure to recognize the need for
parental involvement and community control of the schools, and the absence of 'alternative and innovative methods to teach the culturally different
child'. The party argued that these educational problems would be resolved
if multilingual and multicultural programs were instituted at all levels of the
state's educational system, if the schools were integrated, and if affirmative

action policies were aimed at representation of Mexican American personnel throughout the system in their proportion to the state's population.

Other recommendations dealt with the centralization of educational funding by the Texas State Office of Education for more equitable distribution of revenues, and an emphasis on meeting the needs of poorer communities as opposed to the newer and better funded schools. Community control of the schools was to make possible the 'racial, ethnic and socio-economic composition of the community'. More specific reforms were advocated:

1. There should be free pre-school education and day care.
2. 'All sectors' of the community should be equitably represented in institutions of higher learning.
3. One-third of the Board of Regents of those institutions should be elected by their student peers with provisions for the 'proportionate representation of minority groups'.
4. School administrators should 'have a degree in education with a concentration in curriculum, guidance, or administration and where applicable with extension courses in ethnic studies.
5. Minority counselors should be hired.
6. Anglo personnel in schools with a majority Chicano student population should 'have a conversational knowledge of Spanish.'
7. The 'captive audience concept' of learning should be replaced by 'the concept of learning as a shared experience'.
8. 'Schools without walls' should be established.
9. Standardized tests biased toward Anglos should be eliminated.
10. The 'tracking and grading systems' should be replaced by 'guided individualized instruction'.
11. Textbooks written by 'minority committees serving as advisors to the Textbook Review Committee' should be adopted.
12. 'That history classes include a study of the oral traditions, songs, legends and folklore of the State'.
13. School districts with a five percent or more dropout rate should be reviewed by the State Educational Commission.
14. Financial support should be granted 'private Chicano and Black schools and colleges' on the same basis as to religious institutions.[9]

For the most part these reforms were not revolutionary – and to the more radical tendencies within the Chicano Movement they were simply bourgeois demands. The section of the platform dealing with the party's politics gives a better understanding of the dominant ideological tendency in the Chicano Movement in Texas. The platform offers a radical analysis of the political system, but in the final analysis it rests on the assumptions of liberal pluralism. The party argued that 'most of the problems facing the people are a direct result of' political powerlessness. Those problems would be solved by electing more Mexican Americans to office with the support of their own political party. For 'those who have power can make things happen and those who do not are helpless. If Mexican Americans are to change the status quo then they must have a clear understanding of the power relationships in this society.'

The basic power equation is simple: 'Those who have the most money are the most powerful and the ones who control the institutions' and can perpetuate their grip on power.[10] The problem that the Chicano and other movements faced is that those who want power can get it only 'by selling-out to the power wielders'.

It is this selling-out that has brought about most of what is wrong with the American system. Whoever gets into power by this route always belongs heart and soul to some rich man or corporation and will never be able to serve the best interests of the people. Because of this, individuals who aspire to positions of power and prestige become very opportunistic and self-serving.[11]

What must be done in light of the fact that political change cannot come from 'within the two party system'? A political party must be built that 'does not have the label of being corrupt', a party that is 'not controlled by private economic interests'. La Raza Unida advocated the following political reforms:

1. The implementation of voter education programs to maximize political participation among those who have been excluded from the electoral process.
2. Lowering of the voting age to eighteen and allowing eighteen-year-olds the opportunity to run for political office.
3. Allowing 'All ex-convicts who are free from parole and probation ... the right to vote'.

1. The abolition of all filing fees for political office.
2. Enactment of local laws requiring public officials to hold open meetings 'at a time and place which working people can attend'.[12]

These positions mark the extent of the analysis of politics developed in La Raza Unida's platform, which interestingly made no mention of separatism or cultural nationalism. And although the party offered an analysis of how political institutions are controlled by economic interests, it did not explain how this reality related to the nature of US society – for example, via the imperatives of capitalism.

The balance of La Raza Unida's platform touched on economic development, the system of justice in the United States, the role of women, immigration, the selective service system, international affairs, natural resources, transportation, health, welfare and housing, and the positions the party advocated remained very much within the context of working within the political/economic structure of capitalism. The Texas party acknowledged that 'economic development is at the heart of the social and human problems confronting minority peoples' but did not offer a critique of capitalism. Instead, reform measures were seen as necessary to eliminate economic problems:

1. The reduction of regressive taxation. [Although it did not say so explicitly, the platform implied that the rich should pay an equal share of taxes.]
2. Restoration of the 'element of competition to the economy'. This is defined as the break up of 'monopolies and trusts by vigorous anti-trust activity', the institution of competition between public and private corporations, and finally, the development of 'community cooperative ventures'.
3. The distribution of wealth on a more equitable basis.[13]

The party's analysis of the system of justice was based almost completely on a report by the United States Commission on Civil Rights that criticized the treatment of third world people in the US. Several reforms were advocated to eliminate abuses:

1. Abolition of the Texas Rangers and creation of civilian police review boards.

2. Participation on juries of those formerly excluded.
3. Allowing those who do not read or write English but are capable of speaking and understanding it to sit on juries.
4. Establishment of free legal services for those 'unable to afford attorney's fees'.
5. The recruitment of third world students to law schools.
6. The abolition of capital punishment and introduction of 'massive prison reform'.[14]

As had been the case with the Denver conference of 1969, the platform of La Raza Unida Party was male centered. It made clear the organization's view that Chicanas do 'not have the luxury of dealing exclusively with feminism and fighting male chauvinism'. Racism was considered more central to the struggle for Chicana equality than sexism:

> Raza Unida Party does not feel that a separate stand on the rights of women is necessary as it is explicit that women are included in the fight for equal rights. ... The strength of unity begins with the family. Only through full participation of all members of the family can a strong force be developed to deal with the problems which face La Raza. Women are actively participating at all levels of La Raza Unida Party. Fifteen per cent of the candidates running for State officer ... are women. Thirty-six per cent of those holding the position of County Chairmen are women. Twenty per cent of those holding the position of Precinct Chairmen are women.[15]

In contrast to the Denver conference, however, the party acknowledged that women as a whole constituted an oppressed group. The platform therefore expressed solidarity with the women's movement:

> The women, men and youth of La Raza Unida Party join their sisters in the women's movement in demanding equal rights for all peoples, but more importantly, in assuring that human rights are guaranteed to all citizens.[16]

On the issue of immigration, La Raza Unida recognized that 'illegal immigrants' were used to maximize capitalist profits and as 'scab labor to break up Chicano union organizing efforts'. The party called for implementation of a number of 'unifying alternatives' to solve these problems:

1. That those who have resided in the United States for at least five years and are eighteen and over be allowed to vote
2. That after five years' residence in the US all 'foreigners' be provided with social services
3. That legislation be passed to make a number of labor practices felonies:
    a. Employer threats to deport 'illegal aliens'
    b. Hiring of 'illegal aliens' at a wage lower than the prevailing wage
    c. Allowing 'illegal aliens' to work outside the constitution, by-laws, or contractual rules of the local trade union
    d. Using 'illegal aliens' as strikebreakers[17]

The Selective Service System was criticized for drafting minority youth to serve in the US Army. The party's position on military service evolved from the premise that 'the failure of the schools and the existence of poverty and racism have led a large number of minority youth to consider paid military service as the only method to achieve economic stability'. Instead of spilling their blood on foreign soil 'minority youth must be offered the opportunity to serve' in their own communities. In this way, the statement reads,

the truest meaning of the words 'to serve one's country' could be developed in the U.S. if the needs of the minority communities could become a priority, thus allowing the youth of the country to serve their brothers and sisters at home.[18]

La Raza Unida was next organized by Corky Gonzáles in Denver. The first Colorado meeting took place on 16 May 1970 at Southern Colorado State College, and Gonzáles was elected state chair. In June 1970 the Colorado party adopted a platform at its third nominating convention.

The Colorado platform consisted of brief resolutions that, although related to some of the points of El Plan Espiritual de Aztlán, were not couched in the context of the nationalist ideology of the Chicano Movement. 'Communal-style' housing was called for, which was to be in the interest of the people and not the corporations. The platform demanded 'free education' with Spanish as the first language and English as the second. It called for rewriting school texts to emphasize the contributions of 'the Mexican American or Indio-Hispano' and other 'minorities'. It requested 'seed money' to start cooperative stores under the ownership of the people, demanded the return land to the 'pueblos', and the suspension of all taxation.

The platform further called for job training programs to be controlled by the people, the elimination of 'racist placement tests', and the enforcement of nondiscriminatory practices in unions. It demanded the 'immediate investigation of the records of all prisoners' and the correction of any legal errors uncovered by the investigation. It called for the 'immediate suspension of officers suspected of police brutality' and the 'suspension of the city-wide juvenile court system' to be replaced by a 'neighborhood community control court'. The platform demanded rights for farmworkers and the re-evaluation of the Homestead Act. Finally, it called for the redistribution of wealth via 'economic reforms' and condemned the Vietnam War as a 'form of genocide' against Mexican American youth.[19]

The development of La Raza Unida Party in California took a different course. Although the Mexican American population was concentrated in the southern part of the state, the first chapter of La Raza Unida was formed in Northern California. The Oakland–Berkeley chapter had its first organizational meeting on 22 November 1970, a few days after general elections that had included a Mexican American running for governor on the Peace and Freedom Party ticket. The chapter made its attitude toward the Democrats and Republicans clear from the beginning, passing a motion that 'La Raza Unida Party will not support any candidate of the Democratic or Republican Party or any individual who supports these parties.'[20] The founding document of the chapter, published soon afterwards, went on to state:

> We, the people of La Raza, have decided to reject the existing political parties of our oppressors and take it upon ourselves to form LA RAZA UNIDA PARTY which will serve as a unifying force in our struggle for self-determination.
>
> We understand that our real liberation and freedom will only come about through independent political action on our part, independent political action of which electoral activity is but one aspect, means involving La Raza Unida Party at all levels of struggle, in action which will serve to involve and educate our people. We recognize that self-determination can only come about through the full and total participation of La Raza in the struggle.[21]

La Raza Unida's striking success in Crystal City and the previous call for an independent Chicano party at the Denver Youth Conference had inspired the formation of this first California chapter, and in fact one of the organizers of the Oakland–Berkeley chapter had served as chairman of the workshop on racism at the Denver Conference. By the end of 1971, chapters of La Raza Unida were scattered throughout the state – initiated by local activists, however, rather than as part of any coordinated statewide effort. The fact that the chapters in California developed spontaneously rather than systematically indicated a certain degree of fragmentation – a fragmentation that would characterize the party's brief but active existence in California.

The party's organizers in California devoted themselves to a variety of political work during 1971. Regional conferences were held in both Northern and Southern California to discuss platform and strategy and to stimulate the formation of additional chapters. A major effort was launched to achieve official ballot status. California law required a party seeking ballot status to register at least 1 percent of the state's total of registered voters under the party's name, or to file a petition signed by a number of voters equal to at least 10 percent of the vote cast for governor at the preceding election. For La Raza Unida, this meant a major campaign to register 66,334 voters.

La Raza Unida candidates ran in a number of local elections, although the party did not have ballot status. In 1971 a candidate for the Oakland Board of Education received 33 percent of the votes cast, and candidates ran in several other districts. The most highly publicized electoral campaigns in California took place in Los Angeles, where one of the party's cofounders, Raúl Ruiz, was the candidate. The first took place in 1971 in a race for State Assembly in the 48th District. The 48th District was heavily Democratic, and approximately 18 percent of its registered voters were Spanish-surnamed.

Ruiz, who at the time was publisher of *La Raza*, was a former student activist and one of the original organizers of the City Terrace chapter of La Raza Unida. He ran against the heavily favored Democratic candidate, Richard Alatorre, and a Republican, Bill Brophy. Ruiz's presence on the ballot forced a run-off between Alatorre and Brophy, which the latter won with 46 percent of the vote to Alatorre's 42 percent; Ruiz polled 7 percent and a Peace and Freedom candidate took 3 percent. Since Ruiz's votes would almost surely have been Democratic in a normal election, La Raza Unida received widespread publicity for having played a 'spoiler' role and demonstrating that the Democrats could no longer rely confidently on Mexican American voter support.

The second Ruiz campaign occurred in 1972 in the 40th State Assembly District in East Los Angeles. Ruiz ran against incumbent Democratic Assemblyman Alex García, while this time drawing 13 percent of the vote. Although Ruiz won a higher percentage of the vote than in his first campaign, the results were disappointing since the 40th District was more heavily Mexican American and thus expectations of victory had been much higher.

In the February 1973 issue of *La Raza* magazine, Raúl Ruiz analyzed the election and its results in a remarkably candid commentary that identified some of the unresolved problems facing the California Raza Unida Party:

> No matter how we rationalized, it was a disappointment not to receive more votes – especially from the Chicano community. There was not a single precinct that actually came close to giving us a majority. As a matter of fact, García established a pattern of overwhelming superiority throughout the district – this, also, unfortunately, and frankly quite surprisingly, was also true in the Chicano community.
>
> Garcia certainly was not a strong incumbent. As a matter of fact, he was probably the weakest. ... García had also established the worst record of attendance in the history of the State of California. ... Garcia does not speak good Spanish and he says little or nothing substantial in English. ... Then why did he win and why did he win so big, especially in the *barrios?* Another question we have to ask ourselves is 'If we did not win, did we actually succeed in politicizing and educating the community of their socio-political condition?'
>
> Now this does not mean that we are wrong in the establishment of a new political concept and structure. But it does mean that we have a difficult road ahead. We cannot expect to do away with a political party that has been using and confusing our people for many years, for over half a century, with a few months of campaign activity. I think it presumptuous, and as a matter of fact, insulting that we should consider our people's beliefs so lightly.
>
> The people might be wrong in their assessment of the Democratic Party but they nevertheless believe in it and support it with their votes. Our people have formed a traditional voting pattern as strong as their religious pattern. One could say that a Mexican is born a Catholic and a Democrat, neither of those institutions really serve him but he strongly defends and supports them.

It is true that winning the office for the sake of winning is not the all-consuming reason for our political existence because we believe that the political consciousness that the people receive from our contact with them is more important. This, though, cannot be employed so loosely as to imply that anything we do in our political activity in fact increases the awareness of the people politically. ... The fact of the matter is that we not only lost but we failed to politicize the people to any meaningful depth. ... We failed to recognize that new registrations, whether young or old do not necessarily create a dependable block of potential votes. ... Many will register because it's different, others because of emotionalism, others because you happen to ask them, and others because they were confused. A very small fraction registered into the party because of a definite political consciousness to create social change. Our partido is not as our name states but rather, it is a goal that all of us should strive to attain. La Raza Unida is still a dream.[22]

The themes sounded in this short article were to be heard over and over again in the increasingly acrimonious debate over the proper role of La Raza Unida.

The year 1972 was also important for La Raza Unida because of the state and national conferences that took place. The California meeting was held in San Jose in April 1972 and discussed a wide variety of issues, including creation of a unified statewide organization to eliminate regional antagonisms. The party had always operated as three separate regional networks: northern, central, and southern. Many of the participants were not prepared to give up their autonomy, however, so no proposal was adopted.

Three months later, some five hundred people gathered for a second statewide meeting in Los Angeles. The ideological tensions within the party were clearly manifested in debates on the proper emphasis to put on electoral activity and on whether the party should remain exclusively Mexican American or should aim at a broader Latino and third world constituency. The second issue was resolved in favor of a continued focus on the Mexican American community; but the proper role of electoral activity was an issue that would continue to plague the party.

In September, La Raza Unida held its first national convention in El Paso, Texas to create a national organization and determine the party's role in the presidential election. Many of the issues debated at the convention were overshadowed, however, by the struggle for national leadership between José

Angel Gutiérrez and Corky Gonzáles. The tension created by this struggle had surfaced prior to the convention in debates on electoral strategy. Members favoring ideological politics tended to support Gonzáles, while those who supported Gutiérrez did so largely because of his more pragmatic, 'non-ideological' approach (exemplified by the electoral orientation that had succeeded in south Texas). Division on this issue had resulted in the early departure of the regional delegation from Southern California at the California state conference in July. In response to the debate, the Southern California delegation distributed a position paper that I wrote to address the issue of the divisive Gonzáles–Gutiérrez struggle and suggest a way to keep the party united:

> [W]e in the Southern Region are aware of the differences that exist between el Partido in Denver and the party in Texas. It is our understanding that the 'Denver Perspective' is that we should not be concerned with winning elections. That we should strive only to develop a revolutionary vanguard party that aims to conduct 'political education campaigns'. The 'Texas Perspective' is being interpreted by some as one holding to the view that the Partido must strive to win elections and be willing to engaged in hard-nosed negotiations with non-Partido politicians for purposes of ripping off valuable resources needed to organize the Partido in some areas. … [I]n the final analysis the perspective of the vanguard party and that of the successful electoral party are not mutually exclusive. … [W]e believe that the local situation must dictate the … orientation of the Partido. … [W]here there are small Chicano populations and no real chance of winning elections, the vanguard perspective can perhaps be the best tool. … In those areas where there is a majority or near majority of Chicanos, then the effort must be made to win.[23]

On the surface, the national convention was a tremendous success, drawing hundreds of delegates from throughout the Southwest and Midwest. In spite of the stormy differences, many saw the convention as the completion of the necessary first step toward the creation of a viable national party. Beneath the activity and enthusiasm, however, others sensed that the differences were irreconcilable and would loom larger and larger as time went on. On one level, struggle for leadership between Gutiérrez and Gonzáles represented a struggle between two men. Both were charismatic leaders and had proven themselves to their own constituencies. Both had devoted followings and a strong feeling for power. And both were convinced that they had the correct approach to building the party. Underneath this seemingly personal struggle, however, were fundamental political issues.

The struggle was a regional one as well, with delegates from Texas and Colorado equally desirous to have the party's leadership vested in their home states. But even this struggle represented the choice between the same ideological issues represented by Gonzáles and Gutiérrez. Gonzáles, a dramatic figure with his all-black outfit and his ever-present bodyguards, had been moving away from the narrow cultural nationalism of the Denver Youth Conference (of which he had been the high priest). He now included themes of internationalism and class conflict – and paid at least lip service to the women's movement and the struggle against sexism. For Gonzáles, the struggle and therefore the role of the party, was ideological – the formation of consciousness.

José Angel Gutiérrez, on the other hand, remained steadfast in his 'pragmatic' orientation. He favored a focus on local issues and material, pragmatic solutions, arguing against diffusing the movement thrust by emphasizing international issues. His stance remained essentially non-ideological in the sense that he did not argue from a structured or broadly encompassing ideology. His appeals were still essentially nationalist, with little attention given to issues of class or gender oppression among Chicanos.

In the contest for national chairman of the party, Gutiérrez had the advantage that he had been the inventor of the model that others were attempting to copy. The Crystal City takeover proved that he could do what everyone else merely talked about: achieve independent Chicano political power. The convention delegates gave Gutiérrez the national chairmanship and made Gonzáles vice-chairman – an impossible working arrangement. The display of unity after the election proved to be strictly show. El Congreso de Aztlán, the national organizational structure established at the convention, failed to materialize. There was in fact no basis of unity on which to build a national organization.

The convention also vowed to pursue a completely independent path, refusing to endorse presidential or other candidates of the major parties. Gutiérrez had come to the convention prepared to espouse a strategy of supporting whichever presidential candidate offered Mexican Americans the better deal, placing La Raza Unida in a position to organize a 'swing' vote. The sentiment for steering an independent course was so overwhelming, however, that he never formally proposed the idea to the delegates.

The California delegation was divided in its loyalties. The ideological division, as reflected in the Gonzáles-Gutiérrez struggle, was present within the
delegation: the San Francisco Bay Area delegates and part of the Los Angeles
delegation supported Gonzáles, but most of those from Southern California
supported Gutiérrez.

The saga of La Raza Unida in California had largely played itself out by the
end of 1973. Frustration with the electoral strategy and persistent ideological divisions weakened many chapters. The California party's newly formed
Central Committee held its first meeting in October 1973, but by this time
the party had already declined substantially. The last significant effort made
by the party came in 1973, when it initiated an attempt to incorporate a predominantly Chicano unincorporated area of East Los Angeles. Raúl Ruiz and
a slate of La Raza Unida candidates were elected to the proposed city council but, since the incorporation initiative was defeated, their victory came to
nothing.

The Student Role in La Raza Unida

The Chicano student movement played a major role in the development of La
Raza Unida Party, with the party in Texas evolving directly from the Mexican
American Youth Oganization. The student movement also played a significant
role in the party's development in other parts of the South and Midwest.

The rank and file of La Raza Unida were mostly students or former student
activists of predominantly of working-class origin, and this was especially the
case in California. With the exception of Colorado, where the party was in essence the Crusade for Justice and its main leader was Corky Gonzáles, student
activists dominated the party leadership – in large part because they could
devote more time to party work than nonstudents. Most did not have family
responsibilities and were therefore the more consistent members on a day-to-
day basis. During periods of intense activity – for example, during a political
campaign – larger numbers of nonstudents, including people from the community, became involved. After the elections, however, nonstudent participation usually declined. (Campaigns, of course, also brought out more of the
usually less-involved students – students who participated only sporadically
in any kind of political activity.) Students, then, were located in organizational
positions that allowed them to play a leading role in La Raza Unida and to
decisively influence the party's ideological orientation, strategies, and tactics.

The students in La Raza Unida were often those who had had previous political experience or who were simultaneously involved in other types of organizations. A large proportion had worked in MEChA, MAYO, or other student organizations. Others came to the party from the ranks of the United Farm Workers Union, the Brown Berets, the Junior LULAC, Parent Involvement in Community Action, CASA, various antiwar organizations, Católicos por La Raza, *El Quinto Sol*, the Socialist Workers Party, the CSO, MAPA, the Community Alert Patrol, the Angela Davis Defense Committee, and the Communist Party. Students with previous political experience tended to be the more consistent and dedicated members of their party chapters. Because it drew members from such a variety of political backgrounds, La Raza Unida came to comprise various ideological tendencies ranging from cultural nationalism to revolutionary nationalism to liberal reformism.

Students typically joined the party as a consequence of the student movement's emphasis on community solidarity and involvement in community politics. But they often had other motives as well. Mexican American students could not help but be aware that they were a small and relatively privileged group, compared to most of their friends and acquaintances from the *barrio* and from high school. While still identifying strongly with the Mexican American communities from which they came, many developed feelings of guilt and isolation on campus, where they were always a small proportion of the student body and usually physically removed from the *barrio*. As a result, they often idealized the *barrio* and the organizers active there.

In California, for example, the idea that Mexican American students should concentrate on working in the community was perennially expressed at MEChA meetings and in Chicano Studies classes. La Raza Unida became one avenue for realizing these objectives, and its nationalist thrust provided a ready vehicle for the fulfillment of feelings of integration and solidarity with the community.

The student movement served as a network for sharing information about events and party activity. Thus, students were better able than nonstudents to learn about the development of La Raza in other areas. Attendance at frequent student conferences augmented this advantage. In addition, Gonzáles and Gutiérrez were frequent speakers on campuses as part of Chicano Cultural Week, Cinco de Mayo, and other student-sponsored events.

In California, the relationship between Chicano Studies programs and La Raza Unida Party was very direct. In both the City Terrace and East Los Angeles chapters, for example, some students received credit for fieldwork through participation in party activities. In Oakland, Chicano Studies programs at Laney and Merritt community colleges served as centers of La Raza Unida activity. At San Jose State University, the first wave of students to join La Raza Unida came from Chicano Studies classes. In Orange County, a number of students received credit for their work in organizing for La Raza Unida Party. Through Chicano Studies programs, then, students were at least partially able to synthesize their academic work with political involvement.

The large proportion of students in the party had important consequences. Certain characteristics of students were clear assets to the party, while others were liabilities. On the positive side, the party benefited from the energy that students were able to put into organizational work. Their schedules were generally more flexible than those of working people, and they were thus able to devote more of their time to party work. They were also relatively mobile, making it possible for them to attend out-of-town conferences and workshops. Students had a great deal of enthusiasm, at least in the early stages, and this was important in developing a new organization. Students also had specific skills to contribute. They had better writing skills than most people in the community and were thus better able to draft resolutions, work on publicity, and prepare announcements and newsletters. Many of them were articulate and could function as effective spokespersons for the party. They were often relatively knowledgeable about national and international issues and used this knowledge to teach other party members.

On the negative side, a number of disadvantages must be noted. While some students had been active in other political organizations, they often lacked knowledge of the local political system in which they tried to operate. They tended to be more theoretical and given to rhetoric in their statements; at times nonstudents felt that students were talking down to them. In some chapters, students were perceived as participating only to earn college credit. In reality, the more academically oriented students dropped out of the party early in order to maintain their grades. Others became overly involved at the expense of their schoolwork and were placed on academic probation; they had to learn to set priorities.

There was also a generation gap that made it difficult for the college-age students to communicate with older people in the community. In some chapters, many of the students were not from the surrounding communities, making it difficult for them to establish ties with local residents. Students in general were often perceived by community people as transients having no ties to the area and therefore unreliable. A former Raza Unida member who was also a student at the time recalled some of these problems:

> Students had no prior experience in a political party. They didn't know how one functioned or how to organize. They were very young and lacked maturity. We needed a mature leadership to do something with the energy. We spun our wheels a lot, didn't think through positions we made as to the consequences of what we said or did. ... Contradictions were never dealt with and we often took on more than we could handle. They were full of ideals without experience. ... We needed more working people to balance us and keep us from going off the deep end, which was a tendency we had. In the long run it hurt us because we got a lot of students, but as soon as they dropped out, there went the chapter. In an abstract sense students were committed to the community, but they were not personally committed. They would show up at meetings but didn't show up to do hard work. They never related face-to-face with the community like going door-to-door to convince people to register in the partido. They had an idealized conception of what the community was, but never met anyone that they imagined from the community. They refused to see that the community wanted what most American middle-class people have and want, such as material possessions, a car, a good education for their children, a vacation, enough food. They thought the community wanted something [else] such as a political philosophy. ... They very much idealized and romanticized the community, much like they do the *vato loco* today.[24]

Student participation in La Raza Unida thus posed a dilemma. Students were indispensable to the formation of the party, yet they also brought with them a host of characteristics, which, if not counterbalanced, generated weaknesses in the organization.

Another issue that posed a problem for the party – as for so many other movement organizations – was sexism. Women had always been an important component of most party chapters. In some cases, half or more of the members were women. Women were generally assigned to handle the more routine tasks within the organization, while men dominated decision-making and 'more important' work. Few efforts were made to encourage or allow women to assume leadership positions. Men tended to dominate the ideological discussions and the debates on substantive issues, a situation that many women found difficult to deal with.

Relatively late in the life of the party, women members began to organize themselves to deal with issues of special concern to women. But by that time the party had already begun to decline. In 1975 a women's group called La Federación de Mujeres del Partido Raza Unida was formed in Southern California to take up the concerns of women in the party. They expressed their principal concern in the following statement:

> La Federación de Mujeres del Partido Raza Unida does not view the men as the enemy but the system as being the oppressor. Our struggle is not a battle of the sexes but a common struggle for the true liberation alongside the men. The purpose of the Federación is to develop La Mujer into the leadership positions at A-1 levels of the Partido. … La Federación shall not be limited to only women but shall make every effort to involve men as well as educate them to the issues and needs of La Mujer. La Raza Unida Party is opposed to the domination of one sex by another and recognizes no distinction between men and women in the common leadership. Both women and men of La Raza must provide leadership.[25]

Ideology and Strategy

The political model that emerged in Texas can be described as a nationalist, independent third party, with no regard for class differentiation. The use of *La Raza*, as opposed to *Chicano*, in the party's name had the purpose of providing a broad designation that would be accepted by all people of Mexican origin in the US, and conceivably by other Latin American people who at some time in the future might come under the banner of the party. It was a commonly used term, a self-description rather than an imposition, and did not have the negative connotations among the Mexican American community associated with the term *Chicano*. The idea of a political party with the name La Raza Unida was thus one of a party based on the ideology of Chicano nationalism. Self-determination was the essential theme of the party, which to La Raza Unida meant taking control of existing institutions and creating new ones where required by Mexican American needs – far from the meaning of secession from the US as a Chicano nation that some have attached to the term.

In California the ideological currents flowing within the Chicano student movement blended well with this ideological thrust. The student movement was essentially a nationalist movement, and the idea of forming an alternative political party for Mexican Americans was very attractive. In terms of ethnic identification, most of the chapters of La Raza Unida in California unequivocally identified themselves as Chicano. The exception was the San Francisco Bay Area. There, chapters such as Oakland's had members who gravitated toward a 'Latino' identification because of the large number of Central Americans in the Bay Area.

When it came to translating the concept of an ethnically based party into a working reality, however, some fundamental problems had to be faced immediately. The Texas model had been effective in a region where Mexican Americans formed the overwhelming majority of the population, and where the takeover of local political power through voter mobilization was a real possibility. In California, however, there were few analogous situations, particularly in the dense urban areas where La Raza Unida was strongest. In spite of the different electoral situation, a considerable part of the energy of most chapters went into registering people to vote Raza Unida and into campaigning for local office. In spite of a few successes like the takeover of the Board of Education by La Raza candidates in the small city of Cucamonga, California, a strategy based on such an approach soon bogged down. The drive to place La Raza Unida on the state ballot never came close to being realized.

By January 1974, more than three years after the formation of the first California Raza Unida chapter in the Bay Area, barely 20,000 of the required 66,000 registrations needed for ballot status had been obtained. The campaigns for statewide office also achieved little, typified by the highly publicized races of Raúl Ruiz for State Assembly. The possibility remained that Raza Unida candidates could play a 'spoiler' role and shake up the Democratic Party, but this negative rather than positive goal could do little more than generate frustration and feelings of impotence in the long run. One could hardly expect to do any significant recruitment to a party whose role was to defeat liberal Democratic candidates and, in so doing, help elect conservative Republicans.

Given this situation, other strategies and ideological orientations emerged within the party, leading to open conflicts within the chapters and at regional conferences. The most salient strategy, advocated by the members who opposed the emphasis on registration and election campaigns, was to concentrate on increasing the level of information and awareness of political issues among Mexican Americans, or what was referred to as 'raising the level of political consciousness'. The Lincoln-Boyle Heights chapter and the Labor Committee

Chapter of La Raza Unida, both in the Los Angeles area, were among the most prominent to champion this approach. The advocates of this position felt that chapters should concentrate on specific community issues and carry out this work year-round. Campaigns, they contended, were too diffuse and led to peaks of activity followed by extended periods of inactivity. Tactically, proponents of this view also supported the increased use of militant and highly visible events such as marches, rallies, picket lines and similar demonstrations. Registration drives and election campaigns, including the campaign for incorporation of East Los Angeles, were labeled reformist. The true goal of La Raza Unida's political activity, they argued, should be educational: winning electoral campaigns was seen as a secondary goal.

This approach also presented some important problems, however. One had to do with the level of resources available to the party. Conducting political work around community issues during the entire year called for resources that were not available to the chapters. Such work could be carried out on a volunteer basis for a certain period of time, but it was difficult to sustain this type of activity over an extended period without a full-time staff. In addition, work of this nature could be carried out through already existing groups that were not organized as 'political' groups per se. The Labor Committee eventually pulled out of the party and became the base for the August 29th Movement, an organization with an explicitly Marxist-Leninist ideology: it eventually became part of the League for Revolutionary Struggle.

In addition to these differences over the party's strategy, there were even more fundamental conflicts over basic political ideology. Bits and pieces of various ideologies often found their way into the political debates and pronouncements of the Chicano student movement, and La Raza Unida shared this tendency. Among the political figures identified by ex-activists as having had some influence on their thinking and on the thinking of other party activists were Franz Fanon, Malcolm X, Saul Alinsky, César Chávez, Corky Gonzáles, Fidel Castro, Huey Newton, and Karl Marx and other classic Marxists (Mao, Trotsky, etc.). They were also clearly influenced by the Black Power elements of the Black liberation movement and by the antiwar movement, with feminism beginning to makes its impact as well.

For the most part, however, the influence of these thinkers and movements was fragmentary and unsystematic. At best, some of the more sophisticated activists made attempts to be eclectic, selecting what they felt to be most appropriate from numerous strains of political thought. In actuality, the only common ground among La Raza Unida activists was provided by (1) the perception of Mexican Americans as an oppressed people; and (2) the conviction that the Democratic and Republican parties did not respond to the needs of Mexican Americans.

Beyond these two broad themes, the most common ideological orientation by far was nationalism, with most La Raza Unida members placing heavy emphasis on cultural identification and cultural issues. Opposition to assimilationism and the desire to preserve a distinct cultural identity continued to lie at the heart of La Raza Unida's appeal. And it was in relation to this posture that the party members emphasized Chicano control of existing institutions and the creation of new ones. Excerpts from a position paper – presented at one of the conferences by Armando Navarro, then a graduate student and the principal organizer of the Riverside–San Bernardino–Upland chapter – illustrate the tone of many of the party's positions in California:

La Raza Unida marks the emergence of a new way of life for Chicanos throughout the United States. Its appearance signifies a major Chicano commitment to terminating the more than a century of oppression of Mexican people in the US, and a full Chicano realization that to end this oppression, Chicanos must seek new concepts, new strategies, and new organization. ...

To achieve this, La Raza Unida must become more than a political organization. It must symbolize the creation of a nation within a nation, a spiritual unification for effective action of all persons of Mexican descent in the United States. One principle dominates La Raza Unida thought – that the destiny of each Chicano is linked immutably to the destinies of every other Chicano. ...

Unity will only be achieved by the formation of an evolutionary doctrine which is compatible with the philosophy, culture, and life style of La Raza. This doctrine will seek to synthesize the diverse perspectives of La Raza so that ultimately one dominant perspective will prevail. ...

The evolutionary doctrine must be buttressed by nationalism. This nationalism will be predicated on the beauty and strength of the culture of La Raza. Cultural nationalism will act as a stimulus for the unification of La Raza. Cultural nationalism will be defined for the purpose of identifying the cultural values held in common by La Raza as a people. ... [C]ultural nationalism will provide the foundation, strength, and unity which is needed in engendering La Raza Unida's evolutionary doctrine. … La Raza Unida will use the culture as a common bond to bring about the unification of La Raza Cósmica.[26]

Side by side with this dominant nationalist trend was a more radical, Marxist tendency, unevenly represented in the different chapters. The Riverside–San Bernardino–Upland chapter reflected little or no Marxist influence, as was generally true of most of the chapters outside of Los Angeles and the Bay Area. The Oakland chapter had a strong left orientation, and included some independent socialists and several members of the Socialist Workers Party. The San Jose chapter included some Marxists, with the students more inclined towards a left ideological orientation than the nonstudents. The Labor Committee of the Los Angeles area, a chapter that was not confined to any particular geographic region but instead recruited from the entire Los Angeles region, was the only predominantly Marxist chapter in the state.

At the height of La Raza Unida's activity, the Marxist tendency was small and for the most part remained relatively quiet. As time went on, however, a trend toward a Marxist analysis began to develop in more and more chapters, although it was strongly resisted in many others. By 1975, for example, some members of the City Terrace chapter were joining Marxist groups such as the Communist Labor Party, the Socialist Workers Party, the October League, and the Communist Party USA. This move to the left by many of the party's members aggravated the ideological conflict within the party, usually resulting in the more radical members becoming frustrated and leaving the organization altogether.

Ideological debate between the Marxists and the nationalists tended to center on certain issues. Marxists were more often in favor of broadening the scope of the party's membership to include non-Chicanos. At the 1972 state conference in Los Angeles, for example, some of the members proposed that La Raza Unida be converted into a multiracial 'people's party', but this motion was rejected. Marxist members also argued for a greater focus on international issues, particularly anti-imperialist struggles in other countries like the Vietnam War. The original platform of the Oakland chapter, one of the most progressive in the state, called for immediate withdrawal of US forces from Southeast Asia, the granting of independence to Puerto Rico, and the release of political prisoners in Latin American countries. The nationalists, on the other hand, wanted to maintain the party's focus on local issues. However, those with an international orientation were able to exert a significant influence when they could demonstrate a relationship between an international issue and the Chicano community. The war in Vietnam, for example, became an important Mexican American issue and triggered a major Chicano demonstration in Los Angeles in 1970. The disproportionate number of Mexican Americans who were being recruited into the armed forces and dying overseas was an issue that easily generated broad concern and support. The march and rally became known as the Chicano Moratorium Against the War, reflecting the independence of the Chicano anti-war effort from the broader anti-war movement of the white New Left.

The Marxist and Marxist-leaning members of the party also tended to favor the 'consciousness-raising' approach to political work rather than a focus on electoral strategies. Harboring the feeling that political campaigns were 're-formist' and 'unrevolutionary', they were inclined to drag their feet on the registration drive for ballot status – a campaign that all La Raza Unida chapters were supposed to participate in.

The Marxist tendency added another important dimension to the party that the nationalist orientation lacked. It provided a fundamental critique of US capitalism, insisting that the problems of Mexican Americans – such as poverty, political powerlessness, racism, and cultural intolerance – were unlikely to be solved within the existing structure of society. In contrast, the nationalists never extended their analysis of Mexican American problems to the broad workings of US political economy, and thus never called for a fundamental restructuring of society. By attributing the problems of Mexican Americans to diffuse attitudes such as prejudice, the predominantly nationalist element within the party implied that solutions to racial problems could be found within the existing social framework. The party therefore failed to challenge the assumptions of liberal capitalist ideology and, in effect, left unchallenged the liberal tradition that dominates the political thought of Mexican Americans, as well as that of most other Americans.

The Decline of La Raza Unida

After 1973, La Raza Unida Party declined rapidly. By 1975 the few chapters that claimed to still exist had become paper organizations, with very little significant activity in evidence. The decline of the party can be traced to several powerful factors. Third parties in the United States have historically found it difficult to make any substantive impact on the two-party system – or even to survive. The 'winner-take-all' nature of US politics and the co-optative skills of the two major parties have combined to make most alternative party ventures short-lived or marginal affairs. Typically, third parties that develop a constituency find their more popular positions co-opted in some form by one of the major parties, depriving the new party of its best chance to grow. La Raza Unida Party had more fundamental, internal difficulties, however.

One reason for the party's decline was clearly its failure to secure official ballot status in California. The party had invested considerable resources in the registration drive to achieve ballot status, and failure to obtain the required number of signatures had a profoundly demoralizing effect. This demoralization was compounded by the emotional letdown after the poor voting results for Raza Unida candidates in the Raúl Ruiz campaigns in Los Angeles. In Texas, the campaign of Ramsey Muñiz for governor failed to legitimize the party in the minds of Mexican Americans. His arrest and imprisonment several years later on charges of drug smuggling from Mexico put the finishing touch on the party's demise in that state.

An even more fundamental factor in the decline of the party was the disunity manifested at the party's 1972 National Conference in El Paso. The power struggle between the backers of José Angel Gutiérrez and Corky Gonzáles had confirmed fundamental antagonisms within the party. This conflict prevented the formation of the national structure that had been the goal of the El Paso conference. The split of the California delegation between the two camps aggravated these tensions, with the Gutiérrez-Gonzáles conflict paralleling to a substantial degree the already existing division between the narrow nationalist and the broader, more radical ideological tendencies among California La Raza Unida members. Thus, the national conflict reflected and exacerbated the existing tensions within the state parties.

Perhaps the most difficult problem in trying to establish the party as a permanent institution, however, was its inability to achieve ideological unity. The original version of La Raza Unida Party had been developed in Texas, where local majorities made the goal of achieving community control through electoral politics a realistic strategy. The California organizers attempted to transpose the Texas model, but were unable to adapt it to California's very different circumstances, particularly those of the large urban areas. The resulting failure of the electoral effort left the party floundering in confusion, unable to adopt more viable alternative strategies. For example, the party never fully explored the possibility of a coalition-building strategy – which, in the context of California politics, might have been a more effective route to take. The fragmentation and localism of the California party, conditions that prevailed throughout its existence, made it impossible to even address strategic questions in any systematic manner.

At a more basic level, it is important to note that the party's ultimate goals remained vague. 'Self-determination' was the organization's overall goal, and while it served to bring people together, its ambiguity ultimately led to problems. The concrete meaning of the term was never spelled out. Did self-determination mean taking over existing economic and social institutions? Or did it mean the creation of new ones based on different principles? In the absence of an alternative vision of society, US political organizations inevitably fall back into some vision of liberal ideology, and La Raza Unida proved to be no exception. The failure to develop a true alternative is surely a testament to the strength of the prevailing ideology, and to the tenacious hold that its basic assumptions have on anyone who enters the political arena. However, the fragmentation and localism of the California party, traits that characterized it throughout its existence, made it impossible to deal with such strategic questions in any systematic manner.

Perhaps the most basic cause for the decline of La Raza Unida was that fundamentally it emerged as a product of the Chicano student movement and its fortunes remained closely tied to the movement on the campuses. The decline of the student movement inevitably meant a decline in its off-campus extension. While students brought many advantages to the party-building effort, these were offset by predispositions that one La Raza Unida organizer described as 'quixotic.'[27] As students turned their attention to matters other than movement activity, the party lost its most dynamic component and entered a precipitous decline.

The Experience of La Raza Unida

La Raza Unida student activists who remained in college generally went on to enter professional careers, often in the public sector. Among them one finds college faculty members, high school counselors, outreach specialists and organizers for community-oriented public agencies, teachers, lawyers, health-services professionals, and public administrators. Most of them seem to have entered careers in which they could pursue their goal of serving the community – convinced that they are making some social changes in at least a marginal way.

In terms of political affiliation, former La Raza Unida student activists went in several different directions. Some remained in the Marxist organizations with which they were already affiliated, or towards which they were moving while still in La Raza Unida, such as the Socialist Workers Party, CASA, ATM, the Communist Labor Party, the October League, and the Communist Party USA. Some of the more disillusioned members dropped out of any political activity altogether. The most common political paths, however, took ex-members either back into the Democratic Party or into a variety of more narrow, locally based issue-oriented organizations that carry on struggles around the criminal justice system, health, education, employment, immigration, and other matters of concern to Mexican American communities. They provide a reservoir of experienced activists who may at some future time be attracted to a broader, more programmatic and well-planned political organization, under the right set of political conditions and with a more coherent strategy than La Raza Unida was able to provide.

On balance, former activists tend to give a favorable assessment of their experience in La Raza Unida. Their participation in the party sharpened their awareness of social issues and gave them valuable political experience and skills that they have applied in other organizations. For some it led to a broader political consciousness and a sensitivity to international issues, as well as other issues that do not always affect the Mexican American community directly but that nevertheless have repercussions there. Friendships and personal networks were established through party work that have continued since then and which have facilitated other political work. The party experience made them realize that a more thorough analysis of racial problems and strategies for overcoming them are needed. Although it may not seem to have had a profound impact on US politics, the Partido de La Raza Unida did provide its members and others with a foundation of experiences and skills that may contribute to that end.

La Raza Unida Party should be seen as only one more experience in a tradition of Mexican American political activism and resistance that dates back to the mid-nineteenth century. This tradition has encompassed forms of political struggle ranging from electoral politics and union organizing to armed uprisings. Only documentation and critical analysis of such experiences in a historical context will contribute to the building of political movements that can transcend the limitations that constrain alternative political projects.

Notes

1 See the following studies, which were published after the first edition of *Youth, Identity, Power*: Armando Navarro, *La Raza Unida Party: A Chicano Challenge to the US Two-Party Dictatorship*, Philadelphia 2000; and Ignacio M. Garcia, *United We Win: The Rise and Fall of La Raza Unida Party*, Tucson 1990.

2 Armando Navarro, 'El Partido de la Raza Unida in Crystal City: A Peaceful Revolution', Ph.D. diss., University of California, Riverside, 1974, pp. 139–41.

3 The convention was held under surveillance by police intelligence agencies. See 'Extent of Subversion in the New Left: Testimony of Robert J. Thomas', *Hearings before the Subcommittee to Investigate the Administration of the Internal Security Act and Other Internal Security Laws of the Committee on the Judiciary*, United States Senate, 91st Cong., 2d sess., 20 Jan. 1970, pp. 45–53.

4 MAYO leaders José Angel Gutiérrez and Mario Compeán were present, as was Corky Gonzáles.

5 John Staples Shockley, *Chicano Revolt in a Texas Town*, Notre Dame 1974.

6 Quoted in Shockly, *Chicano Revolt*, p. 124.

7 José Angel Gutiérrez, *A Gringo Manual on How to Handle Mexicans*, Crystal City, Texas 1973, p. iv.

8 La Raza Unida Party of Texas, 'A Political Action Program for the '70s', n.p. 1972, p. 3.

9 Ibid., p. 12–14.

10 Ibid., p. 18.

11 Ibid.

12 Ibid., p. 23.

13 Ibid., p. 26.

14 Ibid., p. 30.

15 Ibid., p. 40.

16 Ibid., p. 39.

17 Ibid., p. 42.

18 Ibid., p. 46.

19 Richard Santillán, *Chicano Politics: La Raza Unida*, Los Angeles 1973, pp. 19–23.

20 *Rasca Tripas*, Oakland n.d., n.p.

21 Ibid.

22 Raúl Ruiz, 'La Raza Unida Party', *La Raza*, February 1978, pp. 4–5.

23 Carlos Muñoz Jr., 'On the Status of La Raza Unida Party in Califas, Aztlán: A Position Paper'.

24 Elena Minor, interview, 29 January 1979.

25 Richard Santillán, 'The Politics of Cultural Nationalism: El Partido de La Raza Unida in Southern California, 1969–1978', Ph.D. diss., Claremont Graduate Schools 1978, p. 189.

26 Armando Navarro, 'The Concept of La Raza Unida', paper presented at a La Raza Unida Party conference, Riverside, California, 1972.

27 Armando Navarro, interview, 12 December 1978.

5

The Quest for Paradigm:
The Struggle for Chicano/a Studies

Before the emergence of the Chicano student movement in the late 1960s, students and intellectuals of Mexican descent were rare in institutions of higher education, they were largely invisible. In contrast to the African American experience, Mexican Americans never had the benefit of institutions equivalent to the Negro colleges. Despite the limitations of the Negro colleges, they did contribute to the development of a visible African American bourgeoisie and, more to the point, an intelligentsia that was able to establish a Black intellectual tradition – long before any significant number of African American and Mexican American youth were able to gain access to white colleges and universities.

The few Mexican Americans who gained access to college were from the small Mexican American middle class, located mostly in Texas and in New Mexico. Most were men; there were very few women. The few from the working class who were fortunate enough to attend college did so with the direct assistance of members of the Catholic and Protestant clergy, although the Mormon Church played a significant role in some areas. This was the experience of the first generation of Mexican American student activists in the 1930s. Their connections with the YMCA and the Protestant churches opened doors to a college education for most of them. The Young Women's Christian Association (YWCA) did make attempts to encourage the few young Mexican American women who joined the organization to attend college in the 1930s It was the G.I. Bill that finally provided the opportunity for a higher education to a larger number of working-class Mexican American men who were veterans of World War II and the Korean War.

More Mexican American students reached college campuses during the 1960s due to the equal opportunity programs generated by the African American civil rights movement. Although the focus of those progrms was on African Americans, a small percentage of Mexican Americans, the majority of them men, were able to take advantage of them. In addition, the G.I. Bill made college accessible to Vietnam War–era veterans. Upon arrival on college campuses, however, they did not find there a Mexican American intellectual tradition or a focus on books on the Mexican American experience in the United States. That experience was ignored in the college curriculum. Mexican American history, for example, was not discussed in US history courses. One exception was at the University of Texas at Austin, where students were exposed to the work of several Mexican American scholars on the faculty. They were Carlos E. Castaneda, George I. Sánchez, and Américo Paredes. Castaneda and Sánchez were prominent intellectuals in LULAC, Sánchez having served as national president in 1942. Paredes was a product of the World War II generation of veterans who attended college on the G.I. Bill. Collectively, they were the founders of what I call the Mexican American intellectual tradition.

Typical of the Mexican-American Generation, Sánchez promoted the Americanization of people of Mexican descent in the United States, but he was the first Mexican American scholar to wage battle against the racism of white schooling. He spent much of his career from the 1930s on challenging the validity of IQ tests and exposing their bias against Spanish-speaking children.[1] In 1940 he published a book on the history of his people in New Mexico entitled *The Forgotten People*, in which he concluded that 'in the march of imperialism a people were forgotten, cast aside as the byproduct of territorial aggrandizement'.[2] This was the first book published by a Mexican American intellectual that was critical of US society, albeit not from a radical perspective but from the perspective of a liberal academic who strongly identified with his people:

> It has been found necessary and desirable throughout ... to point out faults and weaknesses in various sectors of the present situation. This is done in a spirit of constructive criticism.... [T]he deficiencies are revealed

and criticized with impersonal detachment and with all the scientific objectivity permitted to one who, at the same time, seeks emotional and mental identification with the mass of the people.... In this nation there is no excuse for human misery and ... good intentions cannot substitute for good deeds.[3]

As a scholar/activist Sánchez promoted social justice and equality for Mexican Americans long before the emergence of the Chicano student movement in the 1960s. But student activists outside Texas did not know about him or his work. Prior to his death, he lent his support for the creation in 1970 of the Mexican American Studies Center at the Austin campus of the University of Texas.

Following in the footsteps of Sánchez, Américo Paredes published a book entitled *With His Pistol in His Hand* in 1958; it documented a history of resistance and struggle on the part of Mexicans and Mexican Americans in Texas.[4] He and his work were also largely unknown outside Texas before the 1960s. Paredes was instrumental in the establishment of the Mexican American Studies Center at the University of Texas at Austin and served as its first director.

Outside Texas, Julián Samora, a sociologist at the University of Notre Dame, also focused on the Mexican American experience and contributed to the shaping of the Mexican American intellectual tradition. Samora was the first scholar of Mexican descent to focus his research on the problem of political leadership in the Mexican American community and on the co-optation of community leaders by white power structures.[5] He eventually established the Mexican American Studies Center at Notre Dame and in the early 1970s created a publication series at the University of Notre Dame Press with a special focus on the Mexican American experience, the first such series in the nation.

Outside the institutions of higher education there was Dr. Ernesto Galarza, a scholar activist who never pursued an academic career but who engaged in independent research and writing. His work evolved from his years of active participation as a union organizer in the labor movement, described in chapter 1. Galarza differed from other intellectuals of the Mexican-American Generation in his focus on a critique of capitalism and its exploitation of Mexican and Mexican American labor. Although he never identified as a Marxist, his writings on farm labor nevertheless had radical overtones. His first major book was *Merchants of Labor*, in which he exposed the Bracero Program:

> The bracero system might have been a higher stage in American civilization, as slavery was in the Roman. If so, the affluent society, imperial in its own fashion, could ponder its good luck. It had only to reach out across the border down Mexico way to tap a reservoir of millions of menials who longed to toil as managed migrants for a season.[6]

Sánchez, Paredes, Samora and Galarza inspired a few young scholars who were to emerge from the Chicano student movement of 1960s. Galarza's influence was limited to student activists involved in community struggles, since he never pursued an academic career. The few students who knew about these four were aware that their work had focused on some aspect of the Mexican American experience and therefore had some relevance to the development of Chicano Studies.

To most Mexican American student activists in California, however, the scholarship of these men fell short. The young militants were caught up in the process of radicalization and were unable to give their predecessors the recognition they deserved. The militant mass protest and confrontations of the 1960s, girded by an ideology of cultural nationalism, demanded the assertion of a strong Mexican identity and the rejection of anything resembling an assimilationist or integrationist strategy. They criticized Sánchez, Paredes and Samora as products of traditional academia. Their scholarship, some argued, was couched in the language of their academic mentors and did not challenge the dominant paradigms of their disciplines. For the most part, they all represented an integrationist-assimilationist perspective, which the Chicano student movement – MEChA, in particular – had vehemently rejected.

During the 1960s and even into the 1970s, young Chicano scholars made little attempt to understand the nature of the their predecessors' politics in the context of their times. There was a widely felt need to develop a different kind of scholar, one who could do research critical of US society and simultaneously contribute to the shaping of the Chicano consciousness called for by the student movement. The young radical intellectuals produced by the Chicano Movement were searching for a 'new' activist-oriented scholarship that would identify and initiate the kind of research demanded by the current phase of struggle for Chicano liberation.

The Origins of Chicano Studies

The 1968 high school walkouts coincided with ongoing United Mexican American Students (UMAS) efforts to establish Mexican American studies programs in local colleges and universities in the los angeles area. UMAS participation in the walkouts reinforced demands for those programs. The first Department of Mexican American Studies in the nation was created in the fall of 1968 at California State College, Los Angeles, as a result of demands by UMAS on that campus. These demands intensified as the Chicano student movement grew and became a central force in the emerging Chicano Movement. After the formation of MEChA at the 1969 Santa Barbara conference, the demand was for Chicano Studies instead of Mexican American Studies, reflecting the cultural nationalist ideology of the Chicano Movement. Even before the 1969 conference, student activists, working with sympathetic faculty and staff, developed proposals for the creation and institutionalization of Mexican American or Raza Studies programs at several California campuses during the 1968–69 academic year.

The proposals revealed a wide variety of perspectives on the purpose, scope, and structure of the proposed programs. They also differed in ideological perspective. On those campuses where militant student protest took place or where radical leadership was dominant, the proposals had a more political orientation. At San Francisco State College, for example, the site of the first violent student confrontations, students placed their proposed program within the following context:

> The purpose and goal of La Raza Studies is to provide education to Chicanos and Latinos ... excluded from the educational process.... The concept of education ... involves a new understanding of education [and] a powerful force in the renovation and reconstruction of the entire system of education ... to provide the community with the resources to deal with the problems it faces. The primary resources ... are individuals who are sensitive to the needs of their people, creative in their approach to problem solving, and equipped with the skills necessary to serve their community.[7]

At the University of San Diego, where radical student leader Angela Davis was studying with Marxist philosopher Herbert Marcuse, a joint African American and Mexican American proposal was made calling for an autonomous 'Third College' to be named after African revolutionary Patrice Lamumba and Mexican revolutionary Emiliano Zapata. The college was envisioned as a definite alternative to existing traditional academic units on that campus:

> We demand that [the] College be devoted to relevant education for minority youth and to the study of the contemporary social problems of all people. To do this authentically, this college must radically depart from the usual role as the ideological backbone of the social system, and must instead subject every part of the system to ruthless criticism. To reflect these aims … it will be called Lumumba-Zapata college. To enhance the beauty of the name, we demand that the architecture be Mexican and African style.[8]

At the University of California, Berkeley, MASC proposed the establishment of a Chicano Studies Department within the structure of a Third World College. The college had been one of the demands of the Third World Liberation Front (TWLF) during the student strike on that campus. Chicano Studies was envisioned in somewhat more academic terms but included a community involvement component:

> The present needs of the Chicano must be met in such a way as to provide relevant programs which will sustain self-confidence and provide a feeling of acceptance on the student's terms.… [B]i-lingual studies must constitute a part of the University's realistic recognition of community realities and innovative academic potential.… [A] part of the function of a department must be to prepare students for a more advanced participation in the University outside of the Chicano department, to develop student's abilities in a bilingual, bicultural manner … by focusing on an intellectual perspective of and about the Spanish-speaking communities, … to develop … abilities to serve their communities, [and] to develop a potential for self-fulfillment in at least two cultures.[9]

At California State College, Los Angeles, the proposal for a Mexican American Studies program had an emphasis on traditional academic and professional training. UMAS arranged with the campus administration for the appointment of Ralph Guzmán, at the time a professor in the Department of Political Science, to write the proposal. Guzmán placed the development of Mexican American Studies in the following context:

[T]he question is not whether ... such a program should be developed but whether the development of such a program would be systematic, orderly and in the highest tradition of scholarship or chaotic and make-shift.... [T]he latter alternative [must] be carefully avoided.... [T]he coordination of this program must rest upon individuals who possess not only high academic achievements but also demonstrated administrative skills.... This program ... is designed for students who elect to study this important minority group through the interdisciplinary approach or plan to engage in such professions as government service, education, social work, or others where knowledge of this subject would enhance professional opportunities.[10]

The Guzmán proposal did not receive the approval of UMAS student leaders. They rejected it because it departed from an explicit community and activist direction and instead emphasized the need for a program with a strictly academic and professional orientation. Guzmán called for a center similar to those that existed for Latin American Studies and other area studies. UMAS wanted an autonomous department with power equal to that of other departments. In what was perhaps the first of many unfortunate internal student-faculty struggles that came to characterize the development of Chicano Studies programs everywhere, the UMAS leadership prevailed and the students got their department.[11]

At the University of California, Los Angeles, the proposal also called for the establishment of a center, as opposed to a department, but with an emphasis on research. The center was to be called the Mexican American Cultural Center and was to develop along the following lines:

The principal objectives of the Center are the following ones: ... to encourage and support research into all areas of knowledge relevant to the Mexican American community.... To assist in the development of programs and research which will focus the unique resources of this University on the problems of the Mexican American community.... To assist in the development of new curriculum and bibliographical materials dealing with the culture, history and problems of the Mexican American.... To actively engage in furthering the involvement of the University with the Mexican American community.... In its roles as a coordinator between community and University and as a research and bibliographical resource the Center hopes to place this University in the forefront of institutions actively seeking solutions to the problems of the barrios of America.[12]

At the California State College at San Fernando (its name was later changed to California State University, Northridge) a proposal was submitted by Professor Rodolfo F. Acuña; it called for creation of a Department of Mexican American Studies with a traditional departmental status. The department's objectives were defined as follows:

To study the contributions of the Mexican-American to American culture and society ... promote better understanding among all Americans ... train those in professions such as civil service, police or social work, education, advertising, etc. to work more effectively with ... problems ... aggravated by the alienation of the Mexican-American ... encourage Mexican-Americans to seek higher education by creating a greater feeling of pride for their heritage and acquainting them with the culture that helped form their community ... enable all students, whatever their ethnic background, to specialize in the Mexican-American.[13]

The most ambitious of the proposals in terms of scope and structure was written by Professor Jesús Chavarría at the University of California, Santa Barbara. It called for a Chicano Studies Center to include a department, a research component, and a community-university component to develop cultural and 'urban-change' programs. The program had several objectives:

Through Chicano Studies, Chicano students intend to study and legitimize their cultural heritage, ... broaden and deepen the university's educational and cultural mission by enlarging its academic program, ... serve ... as a socializing process, ... affect the student's individual consciousness and contribute to the shaping of his sense of community, ... provide the student with the necessary technical and educational skills to interpret his social worlds ... especially that part of the world denominated 'the Third World'. The end result will be that students will be able to know themselves ... to change their community.[14]

These proposals reflected a consensus on the need of Mexican American students for the programs, as well as differences over the structure, objectives and ideology. Some advocates stressed the potential for such programs to help students resolve the cultural identity crisis fostered by the assimilation process. Others expected that the programs would develop into meaningful academic alternatives to established departments. Still others perceived such programs as a training ground for community organizers.

Ideologically, the spectrum ran from those like Acuña who defined Mexican American Studies as a curriculum that would emphasize the contributions of Americans of Mexican descent to US culture and society to those who defined it as a curriculum that would focus attention on racism and the structure of oppression, thereby promoting radicalism and class consciousness. None of the proposals touched on the need to integrate the experience of Mexican American women into the Chicano Studies curriculum. The proposals were all developed by men. One explanation is that whereas Chicanos with PhDs were practically invisible, Chicanas with PhDs were actually invisible. Unfortunately, none of the Chicano scholars involved in developing the proposals recognized the importance of gender at that time.

The Santa Barbara Conference

The civil rights movement had had a profound but one-sided impact on whites throughout the United States. Efforts to remedy discrimination or to establish equal opportunity programs tended to focus on African Americans and ignore other racial minority groups. Even in California, where Mexican Americans far outnumbered any other racially oppressed group, attention centered on African Americans. One result was the disproportionate placement of Blacks in administrative positions within Educational Opportunity Programs, which meant that – in qualitative as well as quantitative terms – the needs of Mexican Americans never received the attention they deserved. In 1968, soon after the end of the Los Angeles high school strike, a group called the Chicano Coordinating Committee on Higher Education was formed.

The founders included student activists, a handful of faculty, and administrators who were active in programs for equal opportunity in education, on committees developing proposals for Chicano Studies, or teaching the handful of Chicano Studies courses at a few scattered campuses in California. The majority were men. Only five of the twenty-three members of the CCHE Steering committee were women. CCHE's purpose was to develop a statewide network of community and campus activists who could put effective pressure on campus administrators to expand equal opportunity programs to give proper attention to the needs of Mexican American youth. CCHE also wanted the proposed Chicano Studies programs to develop directly under its control.

René Núñez, a community activist and director of a federally funded program called the Educational Clearing House in south central Los Angeles, came up with the idea of holding a statewide conference under the auspices of CCHE.[15] Núñez was one of the few Mexican Americans who shared the frustrations of CCHE members over the lack of focus on Mexican American youth by campus administrators running EOP programs. His program recruited 'high potential' minority high school students for the state college and university system. During his visits to high schools and college campuses throughout the state, Núñez became convinced that problems relating to student recruitment and retention and faculty hiring were similar throughout the system. He proposed a statewide meeting of student, faculty, and staff representatives from each campus where they could discuss those problems and come up with a plan of action to resolve them.

CCHE formed a steering committee to plan the statewide conference. In addition to Núñez, twenty-five representatives from the California community college, state college, and state university systems were selected to serve on the committee. The campus of the University of California at Santa Barbara was selected as the site of the conference because of its central location between Northern and Southern California. The conference was to be structured as a series of workshops that would produce a plan of action, or blueprint, for the struggle to secure equal access for Mexican American youth in higher education. In a letter to selected student leaders, faculty, and administrators, the CCHE leaders defined the purpose of the conference:

The purpose ... is to develop a 'Master Plan' for Chicanos in higher education which would at once serve as a guideline ... and would articulate the reality of the Chicano educational situation to the established system at large.... [It would] produce a document that can be used as a guide to recruit Chicano students, faculty, and administrators ... to deal with support programs, curriculum, etc. [and] ... present the needs of the Chicano community, as it relates to higher education, not as a series of demands, rather as an irrevocable law – an objective to be reached within a given time – a tangible reality.[16]

The development of a master plan for higher education was seen as vital to CCHE's efforts to provide direction and a philosophical framework for the emerging Chicano Studies and other programs. CCHE feared that without a plan of action built specifically around Mexican American interests the proposed programs would fall under the control of white liberals and Black administrators of EOP and ethnic studies programs. CCHE also wanted to avoid control by academic, career-oriented Mexican Americans who, in collaboration with administrators, might use the programs to obtain positions of power. CCHE believed that such co-optation could be avoided only if the programs were under the control of its members or those who shared its purposes and commitment to the rapidly developing Chicano student movement.

The conference was held in April 1969 at the campus of the University of California, Santa Barbara. The participants were carefully selected by the CCHE steering committee on the basis of demonstrated participation in campus struggles and expertise gained in formulating campus programs. The original intention was to limit the number of participants to one hundred. Twenty-nine campuses with active Mexican American student organizations were asked to send two student representatives each, which would have resulted in fifty-eight students attending. The remaining forty-two participants were to come from the ranks of faculty, administrators and community activists involved in programs aimed at encouraging Mexican American youth – whether in school or out – to pursue a higher education. In the end, however, more than one hundred delegates participated, with many more of them students than faculty or staff.

The Santa Barbara conference was organized around nine workshops, which fell into two main categories. One category was 'political operations'. These workshops concerned the questions of statewide communication and coordination, university-community relations, campus organization, and political action. Out of these workshops came the thrust for the formation of MEChA, the Movimiento Estudiantil Chicano de Aztlán. The other category was 'technical operations'. These workshops dealt with recruitment, support programs, funding, legislation, the Chicano Studies curriculum, and institutionalization. Out of this category of workshops came the proposal to refer to the programs as 'Chicano Studies' and not 'Mexican American Studies'. Existing Mexican American Studies programs were to become Chicano Studies programs, and those formed after the conference were to follow suit. A strategy for redirecting the focus of EOP programs to include appropriate attention to the needs of Mexican American students was also outlined. The creation of viable Chicano Studies programs, however, was perceived as the key to the successful implementation of all the goals of the conference:

> Chicano Studies represent[s], the total conceptualization of the Chicano community's aspirations that involve higher education. To meet these ends, the university and college systems of the state of California must act in the following basic areas: (1) admission and recruitment of Chicano students, faculty, administrators, and staff; (2) a curriculum program and an academic major relevant to the Chicano cultural and historical experience; (3) support and tutorial programs; (4) research programs; (5) publication programs; (6) community cultural and social action centers.[17]

The conference lasted three days and was an unequivocal success; the historic meeting produced results that went far beyond the expectations of the organizers. Not only did the conference meet the goals set for it, but other significant developments that had not been planned took place. One was the founding of MEChA, which reflected the further development of the Chicano student movement beyond the protest stage to the level of a movement with its own ideology.

The efforts at selective participation paid off. Because it brought together only the most proven student leaders throughout the state and those faculty, administrators and community leaders specifically concerned with the issues of access to higher education, the conference had not turned into mass meetings of rhetoric and polemic. A 'working' conference, it succeeded in generating substantive proceedings and dialogues that culminated in the collective writing and publication of a book-length master plan of action for Mexican Americans in higher education,[18] the first in the history of the United States. The plan was appropriately called *El Plan de Santa Barbara*. But perhaps the most important product of the conference was the spirit of unity and sense of common purpose that it generated. In a report distributed throughout the state, CCHE described the significance of the event in these terms:

> The three-day Chicano Conference of students, faculty, staff and community was an historic *encuentro*. There was *hermandad*, there was *intercambio de ideas*.... *Most* important, there was work on the issues affecting higher education and Chicanos in California.... The conference, not an end in

itself, was a strong and critical step forward.... [T]he ten workshops produced reports which will ultimately make up a *Chicano* master plan.... [I]t will be sent to Hitch, Dumke, the Regents, Reagan, et al.[19]

The plan, published six months later, was offered as a general blueprint for Chicano Studies programs; it outlined a strategy and a step-by-step process for institutionalizing programs on any given campus. The plan was designed to give the maximum control possible to Mexican American students, faculty, administrators and community leaders. The goal of institutionalization rested on the premise that the colleges and universities are strategic institutions in the struggle for Chicano liberation. The rationale underlying any request for the development of Chicano programs had to be that these were *public* institutions, and therefore had the responsibility of meeting the educational needs of *all* the public, and not just part of it. The plan stipulated:

> Secure from the institution the commitment that it will give the highest priority to the needs of the Chicano community, not because of morals or politics, but because it has the obligation as a public institution charged with serving all of society.[20]

The plan produced by the conference evolved out of the ideas and dialogue generated in its various workshops. However, its analytical framework was based to a large degree on the proposal for a Chicano Studies program at the University of California, Santa Barbara, which had been prepared by Jesús Chavarría, an assistant professor of history at that campus. He stressed the salience of racism and focused on anti-assimilationism as the point of departure for Chicano Studies. Above all, the plan placed the development of such programs within the context of a politics for change:

> Due to the racist character of American society, ... in the past only individual Mexican-Americans were able to obtain moderate status and success in a society dominated by Anglo-American values and institutions.... [T]he price of assimilation resulted ... in a turning away from the community; ... the community remained exploited, backward and static. Now Chicano university students, not unmindful of the historic price of assimilation, take change within the community as the point of departure for their social and political involvement.[21]

Clearly the plan was written to direct the development of Chicano Studies toward the goals established by the student movement. Key to that movement were pride in Mexican identity and Mexican cultural traditions and in the working-class legacy of Mexican Americans, and active involvement in struggles for social and political change. The student movement thus reflected an unequivocal break from the assimilationist, middle-class ideology of the Mexican-American Generation, as we saw in chapter 2. The generation of student activists of the 1930s had not rejected their Mexican roots, but it had emphasized their 'American' identity. The Chicano student movement rejected Americanization and argued for the importance of Chicano Studies in the quest for identity and power.

The Chavarría proposal demanded that the university 'respond to the particular needs and aspirations of the *barrio* and of the *colonia*', as it had historically responded to the needs of the dominant sectors of society.[22] It defined Chicano Studies as part of the struggle to free Chicano cultural values and lifestyle 'from the standardized criteria of Anglo-American culture'.[23] But it argued that Chicano Studies programs could serve both academic and community needs:

> In short, Chicano students are seeking an authentic freedom of expression within the university and society at large. Their call is for authentic diversification of American culture, a prospect which can only enrich the university's fulfillment of its cultural mission.[24]

The thrust of the plan was directed at the question of how to institutionalize Chicano programs on the campuses of the college and university systems. Its purpose was to provide a reference point for those currently involved in the preparation of proposals for programs, and for those who would be contemplating them in the near future. The plan also addressed the issues of the politics of negotiation with administrators, and the organization of Mexican Americans on campus. Of critical concern was how to maximize Mexican American influence in the decision-making process at each campus where programs were being developed or contemplated. In the final analysis, the plan was presented as a general analytical framework and a set of recommendations that would keep the development of programs within the perspective of the goals of the student movement.

However, the plan did not define Chicano Studies in terms substantive enough to constitute an authentically alternative curriculum. Although it did make clear that Chicano Studies should develop in the direction of an alternative ideological framework, it did not spell out a methodology for applying the ideology of *Chicanismo* to the curriculum.

The result was that Chicano Studies was broadly defined as simply curricula on 'the Chicano experience', with an overriding focus on the cultural aspects of that experience. The consensus reached by those who participated in workshops on curriculum during the conference was that Chicano Studies should not become simply another academic discipline; instead, it should also focus on developing a new relationship between students and the community. This latter focus would provide students with the opportunity to become involved in the everyday issues of their people and thus engage in practical learning experiences. This emphasis could counter the assimilationist perspective of the established university departments and existing curricula. In short, Chicano Studies was perceived as a mechanism for the inculcation of Chicano cultural values, values whose essence would counter the dominant values of US society. These new cultural values were not, however, given very explicit definition.

It was reasoned that a focus on a specifically Chicano experience would contribute to the students' discovery of Mexican cultural traditions and thereby provide a better understanding of themselves and their people. This understanding, in turn, would generate a dialectical process that would somehow join together a new identity and a new culture (one that would be expressly 'Chicano') with the political action necessary to produce change in Mexican American communities. The conference devoted little attention to how the new culture had been shaped by the dominant currents within US culture. In short, the rationale for Chicano Studies, as outlined in the plan, was predicated on an inward look at the Chicano experience and ignored external factors to find solutions to the Chicano identity crisis:

> The critical dialectics of Chicano Studies are the individual and culture which produces identity and new culture; the individual and community produces social action and change. Chicano Studies mean, in the final analysis, the re-discovery and the re-conquest of the self and of the community by Chicanos.[25]

The framers of the plan were not actually concerned with changing the university so much as they were with redirecting its resources to meet the needs of the Mexican American community. They reasoned that as more Mexican American faculty and students became visible in the university, they would generate the kind of research that could be utilized by the movement in its struggle for Chicano liberation:

> The systematic character of the racist relationship between *gabacho* society and Chicanos will not be altered unless solid research becomes the basis for Chicano political strategy and action. Rigorous analysis of conditions must be undertaken, issues identified, and priorities determined as Chicanos adopt strategies and develop tactics for the purpose of realigning our community's structural relationship to *gabacho* society.... [K]nowledge [can be] applied through university-sponsored programs, as well as by spin-off organizations, in the Chicano community.[26]

However, the plan did not spell out how the university could be compelled to produce knowledge in the interest of Mexican Americans – and in fact the plan did not go beyond the question of access to higher education. The concern of the majority of those who attended the Santa Barbara conference was undergraduate education. Chicano Studies programs were perceived as programs to address the identity crisis of Mexican American youth through the teaching of Chicano culture and history, and the development of student activists. Upon graduation these activists would return to their communities as skilled and knowledgeable leaders – able to direct movement activities at the more sophisticated levels necessary to advance the Chicano cause.

After the Santa Barbara conference a small group of young Mexican American faculty and graduate students associated with Chicano Studies programs began raising important questions as to the nature of research in their respective disciplines, and in the social sciences in particular. In a fundamental and critical way, they questioned various assumptions and perspectives within their disciplines. They became active in the organization of Chicano caucuses within the professional associations of their disciplines. Some became active in radical caucuses formed by New Left scholars.[27]

The CCHE continued to meet after the Santa Barbara conference. At a meeting held in San Diego, California, two years later, the Chicana participants called for the revision of *El Plan de Santa Barbara* to include the Chicana and her vital role in El Movimiento. In addition, they passed a resolution that underscored the need to include Chicana representation in all matters relating to CCHE policy making, the recruitment of Chicanas to faculty and administrative positions in Chicano studies, a curriculum to include the Chicana experience, and that 'the cover of *El Plan* should recognize the Chicana and her *movimiento* input'.[28]

The Quest for Paradigm

What kind of research was needed to implement the goals and objectives of Chicano Studies? What direction should it take? Were there Chicano/a scholars whose work could be emulated and built upon? Were there Mexican or Mexican American scholars doing work in areas applicable to Chicano Studies? Was there a paradigm conducive to the research called for in *El Plan de Santa Barbara* – research that could give impetus to the development of a Chicano consciousness and that would be applicable to the struggle for Chicano liberation?

At the time of the Santa Barbara conference fewer than one hundred scholars of Mexican descent held doctorates in the US.[29] At the time of the Santa Barbara conference fewer than one hundred scholars of Mexican descent held doctorates in the US.[28] The overwhelming majority were men. Of these, most held doctorates in education (EdDs), which located them in a distinctly different research network with a very different emphasis from those scholars holding a Doctor of Philosophy (PhD). Among those holding the PhD, most were teaching Spanish; few had doctorates in history or the social sciences. The Chicano Caucus in Political Science conducted a nationwide search and discovered that in 1969 only two Mexican Americans held doctorates in political science. Both were men and were teaching Latin American politics.[30]

Few of these professors identified as being of Mexican descent. Those who had begun to build a distinct Mexican American intellectual tradition did not share the ideology of the Chicano/a Generation of the 1960s, nor were they interested in helping to build Chicano Studies programs in concert with the Chicano student movement. Sánchez, Paredes and Samora were part of the Mexican-American Generation, whose ideology had been shaped by the politics of their youth during the 1930s and 1940s. As progressive as they were, they could not relate their own work to the task of building a Chicano/a consciousness in accordance with the cultural nationalist ideology of the Chicano Movement as a whole.

In Texas, however, Sánchez and Paredes influenced the leaders of the student movement. Unlike students in California, student activists in Texas had not felt the same need to engage in a quest for identity. The Mexican American Youth Organization, for example, never changed its name to Movimiento Estudiantil Chicano de Aztlán, and a Mexican American Studies Center and not a Chicano Studies Program was established at the University of Texas.

Ernesto Galarza, on the other hand, was a rarity within the Mexican-American Generation – a radical who never become part of the academy. He did not agree that it was possible to generate the kind of knowledge from university research that could result in empowerment for the Mexican American community. To him, the university was a 'cemetery of ideas' not a source of enlightenment – much less of radical or revolutionary change.[31]

There were some younger faculty members in California whose intellectual development was rooted in the Mexican-American Generation but who did become involved with the building of Chicano Studies at various levels and who in a sense became members of the Chicano Generation in the process. The most important of them were Jesús Chavarría, Rodolfo Acuña, and Octavio Romano-V.: Chavarría's father had been one of the founders of LULAC in Laredo, Texas, and he had been a member of the Junior LULAC.[32] His research on the life and ideas of Peruvian revolutionary nationalist José Carlos Mariátegui contributed to his radicalization, and he perceived a direct relationship between the ideology of Peruvian nationalism and emerging Chicano cultural nationalism. Chavarria, a recent PhD, had joined the faculty of the Department of History at the University of California, Santa Barbara, after the student walkouts of 1968.

Acuña, another recent PhD, also had deep roots in the Mexican-American Generation.[33] He was a Korean War–era veteran who had gone through college on the G.I. Bill. He had been an active member of MAPA and, as shown by the proposal he wrote for a Mexican American Studies Department at his campus, he initially represented the ideas of that generation. He too evolved into becoming a member of the Chicano/a Generation in the process of building Chicano Studies and participating in Chicano Movement politics on campus and in the community. His book *Occupied America* reflected his radicalization after the Santa Barbara conference; it was the first book on Mexican American history from a radical Chicano perspective.

Octavio Romano-V., an anthropologist, was a World War II veteran. He did not become directly involved in the building of Chicano Studies programs. But as a professor in the School of Public Health at the University of California, Berkeley, he supported the Third World Strike that took place on his campus that gave birth to Ethnic Studies and Chicano Studies in 1969.[34] Prior to the Santa Barbara conference, he founded *El Grito: A Journal of Contemporary Mexican-American Thought*. He served as one of three editors; Nick C. Vaca and Andres Ybarra, both graduate students, were the other two. Antonia Castaneda Shuyler, another graduate student, became the fourth editor two years later.

Romano-V. became first Mexican American scholar in the country to publish a critique of the role of social science in the perpetuation of negative stereotypes and myths about Mexican Americans,[35] and the first to call for a Chicano paradigm based on the following criteria:

All that is necessary at this point is an historical perspective and a paradigm by which to articulate that perspective.... [T]he eight point paradigm that follows seems most useful at present.... First, Chicanos do not view themselves as traditionally unchanging vegetables, ... but rather as creators of systems in their own right, for they have created cooperatives, mutualist societies, political blocks.... Second, Chicanos view themselves as participants in the historical process.... Third, ... This population ... constitutes a pluralistic people. Fourth, Chicanos see in their historical existence a continuous engaging in social issues.... Fifth, the concept of the illiterate Mexican-American must go.... Sixth, the Chicano must be viewed as capable of his own system of rationality.... Seventh, intellectual activity has been part and parcel of Chicano existence.... Eight, as a population whose antecedents are Mexican, the bulk of Chicano existence has been oriented to a symbiotic residence within ecosystems.[36]

El Grito became the first national Chicano literary magazine. Behind its appearance lay Romano-V.'s desire to create a magazine through which 'la gente humilde', or the common folk, could express themselves:

We needed some kind of outlet to express ourselves that would not be edited and modified. There wasn't a single farmworker's home that I went to that didn't have some books. There were volumes of history in poor homes with their walls falling apart. I dreamed of our own magazine where all this could be expressed and where we could publish our short stories, poetry, and essays.[37]

El Grito became the fulfillment of Octavio Romano-V.'s dream and with the profits from it he established Quinto Sol Publications, the first independent Mexican American publishing house. In 1971 he also created the Quinto Sol Premio, a $1000 cash award for the best book of Mexican American literature. The recipient was Tomás Rivera, at the time an unknown professor of literature at Sam Houston State University in Texas, for his book ... *y no se lo trago la tierra ... And the Earth Did Not Devour Him.* The award established Rivera as the foremost Mexican American novelist. Rivera went on to become the first Mexican American chancellor of a US research institution at the University of California, Riverside, where he served until his untimely death in 1984. Many other talented writers achieved national recognition through publication in *El Grito* and through Quinto Sol, including Rodolfo Anaya and Rolando Hinojosa Smith. Most important, Romano-V.'s magazine made a significant contribution to the development of the humanities within the field of Chicano Studies. All the founding editors of *El Grito* were men, until Antonia Castañeda Shular became a contributing editor two years after it was founded.

In 1970, the second journal of Chicano Studies, *Aztlán: Chicano Journal of the Social Sciences and the Arts,* was founded at UCLA, with the first issue appearing a year after the Santa Barbara conference. (Its subtitle was later changed to *International Journal of Chicano Studies Research.*) *Aztlán* opened with the manifesto from *El Plan Espiritual de Aztlán* that had been prepared at the 1969 National Chicano Youth Liberation Conference in Denver. The purpose of the journal was to 'promote an active quest for solutions to the problems of the barrios of America' and to 'focus scholarly discussion and analysis on Chicano matters as they related to the group and to the total American society.'[38] The articles in this first issue were prefaced with a poem about Aztlán by Alurista, one of the more prolific poets to come from the ranks of the Chicano student movement.

The initial editors of *Aztlán* were all MEChA members at UCLA. The chief editor, Juan Gómez-Quiñones, although still only a graduate student, was a part-time instructor in the Department of History at UCLA. He had been one of the prime movers of the Santa Barbara conference and a member of the editorial group that produced *El Plan de Santa Barbara.* Of the fourteen editors of the journal, only one was a woman. She was Deluvina Hernández, a graduate student in sociology at UCLA. Only five of the fourteen editors had PhDs. The articles in the first issue dealt with questions of culture and identity, Chicano history, the Chicano Movement, and a Chicano workers strike in 1933.

I became the fifteenth editor beginning with the second issue of *Aztlán*, which included a paper I had written calling for 'A Chicano Perspective of Political Analysis.'[39] The paper was a critique of political science and a call for Chicano scholars in that discipline to critically examine paradigms rooted in a 'dominant Anglo perspective which has been predicated on the cultural values and norms of the dominant society.'[40] The solution to the problems of the *barrio*, I argued, would come only from radical change based on 'radical and critical analysis' and the construction of a new paradigm for Chicano politics:

> The Chicano scholar must realize that it is not enough to write critiques pointing out the stereotypes and myths that social science has perpetuated about Chicanos. The crisis that confronts his people is too great and profound and it compels him to develop new paradigms of research and analysis that will adequately deal with the problem of poverty, alienation, and political powerlessness. He now, more than ever, must commit himself to the emancipation of his people. For he does not have the luxury of remaining in the ivory tower nor to engage in 'objective' analysis while his people are in the throes of crisis. The challenge before the Chicano scholar is to develop a Chicano perspective of political analysis. A perspective that will assure that his research will be oriented toward the needs of his community.[41]

Although I did not spell it out at the time, I envisioned that this perspective would be conducive to the development of organic Chicano/a intellectuals, not necessarily in the Gramscian traditional definition of the term, but in terms that Chicano/a scholars produced by the Chicano Movement would remain organically connected to the Mexican American community and culture, rather than maintaining only a symbolic connection.

In the fourth issue of *Aztlán*, Juan Gómez-Quiñones stressed the need for developing a new paradigm for Chicano history:

> The paradigm should reveal, historically, the inter-relations between culture and economic role, group personality configurations, mechanisms of social control, and the accumulating weight of historical experiences – all of which form the historical context. With such a paradigm one can begin to

investigate the pressures, structural characteristics and events that combine to produce the Chicano community of today.... Chicano history is, and must continue to be, innovative ... because it calls for a reconceptualization of history and the role of history in society. This means the use of new methods of inquiry and a reconstruction and reinterpretation of available sources ... a union of history as discipline and history as action on behalf of a community in its struggle for survival.... It is not the listing of 'important' names and contributions of 'Mexican Americans' to the development of 'this great country' ... but must realistically reflect the historical context of the Chicano community vis-à-vis other oppressed groups in U.S. society.... Chicano history involves more than the creation of a new discipline or area of study.... It involves the *self-definition* [Gómez-Quiñones's emphasis] of a people.[42]

The articles appearing in the early issues of *Aztlán* were largely male centered. They reflected the patriarchal nature of Chicano Studies scholarship at that time. We became more aware of the need to address gender and to publish articles dealing with gender in *Aztlán* as time went on. When I edited the special edition on 'politics and the Chicano' in 1974, I asked Adaljiza Riddell, then a graduate student in political science, to contribute an essay on Chicanas and the Chicano Movement. Her article was the first scholarly article to be published by a Chicana on the subject.[43] She addressed the roots of patriarchy in Mexican American culture, arguing that the critical issue was not the role or status of Chicanas in the movement, but the need to understand the roots of *machismo* and patriarchy. As she put it,

Machismo is a myth propagated by subjugators and colonizers who take pleasure in watching their subjects strike out vainly against them in order to prove themselves still capable of action ... exploitation of contemporary Chicanas begins in a very real sense with the Spanish conquest.... Chicanas find the women's liberation movement largely irrelevant because more often than not, it is a move for strictly women's rights ... and a share of the 'American' pie. ... The end which is desired by Chicanas is the restoration of control over a way of life, a culture, and existence. ... The concerns expressed by Chicanas for their own needs within the movement cannot be considered a threat to the unity of the *movimiento* itself. ... Including Chicanas as an integral, not subordinate, part of the group we call Chicanos, is to also diminish the ability of outside groups to manipulate and exploit us. This should be one of the goals of the Chicano *Movimiento*.[44]

Aztlán came to reflect the dialogue among the young Chicano and Chicana intellectuals of the Chicano Movement regarding the quest for a paradigm in Chicano Studies and the related quest for identity and power by the student movement and the Chicano Movement as a whole. *Aztlán* differed from *El Grito* in that *Aztlán* was more directly tied to the student movement and to those in the actual process of building programs and curriculum.

What was the new paradigm to be? There were differences of opinion among the faculty and students involved in the development of Chicano Studies. One part of the question of paradigm was the problem of where faculty could best position themselves within the college and university structure. Essentially the debate was between those who saw Chicano Studies as the development of a new discipline, and thus a separate department or program, and those who saw themselves doing research on the Chicano experience from within the established disciplines. Some junior faculty were already working in established departments and believed that research from a Chicano perspective could be done within them. This group argued that it was essential that Chicanos become faculty in established departments so as to maximize Chicano access to the resources of the university; positions in regular departments meant permanent rather than marginal status, 'hard money' rather than 'soft money'.

The other group took the position that it was essential to work within the newly formed Chicano Studies departments (or similar interdisciplinary structures). Independent and autonomous status, they argued, would be more conducive to the development of an alternative paradigm. They were concerned that faculty appointments to regular departments would be accompanied by pressure to do research in the traditional mold in order to secure tenure. They also feared that time and effort would be diverted to the teaching of traditional courses, thus hindering efforts to develop a Chicano Studies curriculum and meaningful Chicano and Chicana research.

Those committed to the development of an alternative Chicano Studies paradigm outside the traditional disciplines began to conceptualize the Mexican American experience in terms of a colonized people. They had been deeply influenced by the writings of Fanon, Memmi, and Stokeley Carmichael, the Black Panther Party's analysis of Blacks as a neo-colony in the United States, and various Latin American scholars who had developed an analysis of internal colonialism within their countries. The 'internal colony' analysis, derived from the literature on colonialism in the Third World and from the African American experience made much more sense to them than any other current interpretation of the status of people of color in the United States. The interpretations and theoretical frameworks which had been offered by social scientists and historians up to this point reflected clear racial biases.

The first reference to Mexican Americans as an internal colony was made in a paper that I delivered at a symposium on the urban crisis at UCLA.[45] The second case for the application of the internal colony model to Mexican Americans was made by Tomás Almaguer, an undergraduate student activist at the University of California, Santa Barbara, that was published in the third issue of *Aztlán*.[46] Shortly afterward, I co-authored an article with Mario Barrera and Charles Ornelas that was based on my doctoral dissertation that offered a more theoretical framework of the internal colony model. It was entitled 'The Barrio as an Internal Colony'. We defined the internal colony framework in the following terms:

> The crucial distinguishing characteristic between internal and external colonialism does not appear to be so much the existence of separate territories corresponding to metropolis and colony, but the legal status of the colonized. According to our usage, a colony can be considered 'internal' if the colonized population has the same formal legal status as any other group of citizens, and 'external' if it is placed in a separate legal category.... Chicano communities in the United States are internal colonies, since they occupy a status of formal equality, whatever the informal reality may be.... [I]nternal colonialism means that Chicanos as a cultural/racial group exist in an exploited condition which is maintained by a number of mechanisms [and] a lack of control over those institutions which affect their lives.... [It] results in the community finding its culture and social organization under constant attack from a racist society.[47]

Historian Rodolfo Acuña noted the relevance of the theory of internal colonialism in the preface to his book *Occupied America*:

> Central to the thesis of this monograph is my contention that the conquest of the Southwest created a colonial situation in the traditional sense with the Mexican land and population being controlled by an imperialistic

United States.... I contend that this colonization ... is still with us today. Thus, I refer to the colony, initially, in the traditional definition of the term and later ... as an internal colony.[48]

Guillermo Flores, a former MEChA activist and at that time a graduate student in political science at Stanford University, applied a Marxist theoretical framework to the internal colony analysis:

There is considerable overlap between monopoly capitalism and internal colonialism within the US.... [T]he utilization of the Chicano and other racial minorities as a carefully regulated colonial labor force contributed to the capital formation and accumulation processes necessary for the development of modern capitalism's monopoly stage.[49]

By 1973 the internal colony analysis had generated a significant literature. Many faculty in Chicano Studies programs throughout California, as well as elsewhere in the United States where Mexican American and Chicano Studies centers and programs had emerged, used this literature as core material for their courses. Internal colonialism became the paradigm for Chicano Studies research for many, especially those whose politics were more radical or nationalist. According to Juan Gómez-Quiñones,

A modified colonial framework allows us to relate factors that heretofore have been kept separate.... The status of the Chicano as a minority-territorial enclave is analogous to other colonial cases in different parts of the world. The aspects that this situation produces and the actions that it engenders, are important in the historical formation of the community and in its historical patterns. Some of these aspects are the caste-like social-economic relations, institutional hostility and neglect, and movements of resistance and assertion.[50]

Others, including those who had worked on the development of some aspect of the internal colony paradigm, were not satisfied. They perceived the internal colony theory as embryonic and far from viable. In 1973, two symposia were organized to discuss the status of internal colony theory. The first of the symposia was held at the University of California, Irvine, and the second at UCLA. At the Irvine symposium, there was general consensus that the internal colony paradigm was vulnerable to becoming academically rigid. Because of this, it posed the danger of redirecting Chicano research into a 'respectable' and 'legitimate' direction acceptable to the university, but not necessarily conducive to the struggle for Chicano liberation. At the UCLA symposium the participants reached a general agreement that in order to assure that the internal colony analysis remain relevant to its original objectives, it should incorporate more aspects of the Marxist analysis of colonialism.

Both symposia raised critical questions relating to the role of the institutionally based intellectual within the Chicano Movement. How would those teaching in Chicano Studies programs or doing research on the Mexican American experience prevent their work from becoming abstract? What was to be done to assure that Chicano research be directly applicable to the needs of the Mexican American community and the Chicano Movement? How could further development of the internal colony paradigm or other paradigms be assured if they were not seen as legitimate scholarship by faculty in the established disciplines and traditional departments of the university?

The Origins of the National Association for Chicana and Chicano Studies

At the annual meeting of the Southwestern Social Science Association held in March 1972, in San Antonio, Texas members of the various Chicano caucuses within the social science professions held a meeting. None was an established scholar of the Mexican-American Generation. They were all young faculty and graduate students, mostly the latter, active in or supportive of Chicano Studies programs. A consensus had emerged within those caucuses that a national Chicano association of scholar activists was needed to nurture their research. Such an organization would allow movement scholars to deal collectively with the multitude of issues confronting them in their struggle for survival and provide guidance for Chicano intellectual work within the framework of *El Plan de Santa Barbara* in the context of the Chicano Movement.

The San Antonio meeting decided to merge the various Chicano caucuses into a National Caucus of Chicano Social Scientists (NCCSS). A three-man steering committee consisted of Jaime Sena-Rivera, the chair of the La Junta de Sociólogos Chicanos in the American Sociological Association, José Cuellar, the chair of the Chicano caucus in the American Anthropological Association, and I was the chair of the Chicano Caucus in the American Political Science Association. The task of the committee was to plan a national meeting of

NCCSS to found a formal national association of Chicano scholar activists.

The meeting of the NCCSS took place 18–20 May 1973 at New Mexico Highlands University. The meeting was attended by thirty-six people, of whom twenty-one were from California, five from Colorado, seven from New Mexico, two from Texas, and one from Washington. There were twenty-eight men and eight women. Fifteen were faculty, three were staff, sixteen were graduate students, and two undergraduates. Jaime Sena-Rivera chaired the meeting, which became an intense dialogue about the nature and direction of Chicano social science research. There was consensus that social science research done along uncritical, traditional, elitist lines should be discouraged in the proposed association. There was strong support of the internal colony paradigm and Marxist class analysis; this support came mostly from the California delegation, which dominated the proceedings.[51] The role of Chicano scholars was extensively discussed. There was a general agreement that Chicano social science research should meet the following criteria:

1. Research should be 'more problem-oriented than traditional social science' and 'aim to delineate the social problems of La Raza and actively propose solutions'. Such research should 'not be abstracted or disembodied from pressing social concerns.… Scholarship cannot be justified for its own sake: It must be a committed scholarship that can contribute to Chicano liberation'.

2. That 'research projects must be interdisciplinary in nature' because 'the traditional disciplinary orientation … has served … to fragment our research in a highly artificial manner, and obscure the interconnections among variables that operate to maintain the oppression of our people'.

3. That Chicano research 'should break down the existing barriers between research and action' and be characterized by a 'dialectical relationship' between the two. For research should generate data that lead 'to more effective problem-solving action' and 'action in turn produces information that modifies and advances theoretical understanding. In order to bridge the gap between theory and practice, Chicano social scientists must develop close ties with community action groups'.

4. 'Chicano social science must be highly critical, in the double sense of rigorous analysis and a trenchant critique of American institutions. The working of

these institutions have perpetuated the unfavorable condition of the Chicano'
and liberation 'will require a radical transformation of existing institutions,
and it should be a primary task of our scholarship to prepare the ground for
such transformation.'

5. Chicano research must place 'the Chicano community ... within the context of those dominant institutional relationships that affect Chicanos' and
must be conducted at the 'local ... regional, national and international' levels
of investigation. Priority should be on the relationship between class, race, and
culture in determining the Chicano's historical experience.'[52]

The proposed association was also to set the direction for Chicano research.
It would create a communication network among Chicano scholars throughout the country and across academic disciplines, encourage the development
of new social theory and models, struggle for the recruitment of Chicanos into
all levels of the social sciences, and attempt to raise funds for research in areas
that were in line with the concerns of the association. Membership in the association was to be based on affiliation with collective research units called
focos. The *focos* were to be organized along local and regional lines, and their
work was to be interdisciplinary in scope.

The meeting of NCCSS succeeded in defining the criteria and purpose of
the national association. We decided that the new association would not be in
the mold of traditional social science professional associations. Instead of electing officers, as was the case in those associations, we elected a Coordinating
Committee to perform the task of implementing the association and planning
its first annual meeting. Those elected to the committee were Tomás Almaguer,
a graduate student in sociology at the University of California, Berkeley;
Mario Barrera, assistant professor of political science at the University of
California, San Diego; Ray Burrola, director of Chicano Studies at Colorado
State University, Fort Collins; Guillermo Lux, assistant professor of history at
New Mexico Highlands University; Teresa Aragón de Shepro, a graduate student in political science at the University of Washington; Geralda Vialpando,
an undergraduate student at the University of California, San Diego; Rodolfo
de la Garza, assistant professor of political science at the University of Texas
at El Paso; and I, then assistant professor of political science and comparative
cultures, University of California, Irvine, was elected the first chair and treasurer of the committee.

As chair, I hosted the first meeting of the committee on 17 November 1973, at my campus, the University of California, Irvine. Three members of the elected committee members were absent (de la Garza, de Shepro, and Lux). Present by invitation were Fernando Vásquez, a graduate student from UC Berkeley; Gilbert González, assistant professor of history and comparative culture at UC Irvine; Dan Moreno, a graduate student in comparative culture, UC Irvine; and Victor Baez, a graduate student in history at Colorado State University, Fort Collins. As authorized by the NCCSS at the New Mexico meeting, the committee members decided to name the association to the National Association of Chicano Social Scientists (NACSS). The members of the committee became the coordinating committee of the association and as a result I became the first chairperson of the association.

The first annual meeting of NACSS took place from 10 to 13 May 1974 at the University of California, Irvine, where I organized the conference with the assistance of one of my graduate students, Daniel Moreno. There were four panels. The first was titled 'Action Research: Community Control'. Two papers were delivered on La Raza Unida Party in Crystal City, Texas, one by Armando Navarro and the other by Hisauro Garza. Both were based on the internal colony paradigm. The other paper was co-authored by Adaljiza Sosa Riddell, an assistant professor of political science at UC Davis, and her student Robert Aguallo on political change in Parlier, California. The second panel was entitled 'Action Research: Alternative Institutions' and featured papers by Gilbert González, assistant professor of history at UC Irvine, and Tomás Atencio, the founder of La Academia de La Nueva Raza, a Chicano alternative educational institution in Dixon, New Mexico. The third panel was on the topic of 'Working Class Analysis and the Chicano' and featured papers by Ricardo Romo, assistant professor of history at UC San Diego; Victor Nelson Cisneros, a graduate student in history at UCLA; Laura Arroyo, an undergraduate in history at UCLA; and Rosalinda Gonzalez, a graduate student in comparative culture at UC Irvine. The final panel was on 'Internationalism and the Border', which featured a paper by Raul Fernandez, assistant professor of economics and comparative culture at UC Irvine.

The 1976 annual meeting of NACSS, its third, held at the University of California, Berkeley, voted to change its name from the National Association for Chicano Social Science to the National Association for Chicano Studies (NACS) in order to expand its membership and influence into the humanities. NACS thus officially became the association for Chicano Studies in the same sense that political scientists have the American Political Science Association, sociologists have the American Sociological Association, and so on. NACS has to a large degree been responsible for generating a significant body of scholarly literature on the Mexican American experience.

The 1995 annual meeting of NACS, held at Washington State University, voted to change the name once more, to the National Association for Chicana and Chicano Studies. The name change also represented the fact that a critical Chicana feminist scholarship had emerged from its embryonic stages of the 1970s. Two years prior to the name change, Chicana scholars let it be known that the period of a male-centered Chicano Studies scholarship was over and that a Chicana paradigm had emerged. As Adela de la Torre and Beatriz M. Pesquera put it, 'Chicana scholars have successfully deconstructed Chicano movement discourse that privilege the Chicano male subject and draw on male cultural symbols.'[53] In addition to the name change, the association also created Lesbian and 'Joto' (gay) caucuses in recognition of the scholarship on sexuality that had been generated by lesbian and gay scholars activists. Gloria Anzaldúa's book *Borderlands/La Frontera: The New Mestiza* was perhaps the most significant work that sparked the emergence of that scholarship.[54]

However, although some of the literature has been developed in the context of a Chicano perspective critical of US society and institutions, NACCS as an organization has not been able to accomplish many of its original objectives. It has not been able to provide the radical direction for Chicano Studies envisioned by its founders. As the membership of NACCS grew, it became a more diverse organization in ideological terms. Consequently, the internal colony model never became the dominant paradigm for Chicano Studies research – 'the entire constellation of beliefs, values, techniques, and so on shared by the members of a given community' of scholars.[55] There have been several reasons for this that are related to political, theoretical, and structural questions.

The initial basis for NACCS was the general agreement that the dominant paradigms of the social sciences had failed to meaningfully address themselves to a proper interpretation of the Chicano experience. Second, it had been the express desire of the founders of NACCS to develop an organization that could be in tune with the need to do research of import to the Chicano Movement – that is, that could contribute to a Chicano liberation process. They had anticipated the development of alternative modes of analysis that could be applied to the resolution of problems in the Chicano community.

The founding of NACCS, however, took place at a time when the student and the larger Chicano Movement were already in their decline. The internal colony paradigm had been an outgrowth of those movements and aimed at providing a substantial theoretical framework for Chicano nationalist ideology. As the movements declined, the paradigm began to lose much of its original thrust. In the minds of the young movement scholars who developed it, internal colonialization had been meaningful not only as a concept that provided an alternative interpretation of the Mexican American experience more consistent with the historical and contemporary realities of a racist society, but also with the definition of the Chicano Movement as a struggle for decolonization and anti-assimilation.

By 1973, the time of NACCS's founding, these scholars had engaged in self-criticism of their own work. Mario Barrera, for example, qualified the use of the concept. At the UCLA internal colonial symposium, held prior to the founding of NACS, Barrera said,

> I think there is truly no colonial model as such.... [w]e tend to fall into the habit of using and talking about the colonial model.... [T]here's rather a concept.... that some of us have tried to use in order to try to understand the experience of the Chicano, Puerto Rican, black and native American.... There is no one interpretation of colonialism.... [W]hen it started to be used ... to refer to the experience of national minorities here [it] was really used in a kind of polemic against liberal interpretations of the experience of these minority groups. I think the fact that it began in that kind of context influenced its direction, its central themes.... [It] still represents that kind of dialogue.[56]

By that time the concept as initially developed had become limited in its application within Chicano Studies circles. Some had come to view Marxist theory and class analysis as a major source for developing a truly alternative paradigm for Chicano Studies. They argued that the focus of the internal colony paradigm was limited to racism and ignored the class nature of Mexican American oppression in capitalist society.

Within NACCS, however, disagreement about the validity of Marxist methods and theory in the reinterpretation of the Mexican American experience were widespread. Some agreed that class analysis should be incorporated into the internal colony paradigm, while others argued for the rejection of the internal colony theory altogether. Gilbert González, who had participated in the 1969 Santa Barbara conference, rejected it because it posited a 'racial war' rather a 'correct theory' of class struggle.[57] He went on to argue that

> The theory of the internal colony model ... focuses attention upon the national question.... However, it is full of dangers and idealistic assumptions which are inherent in non-Marxist as well as anti-Marxist works. It does not place into proper perspective the questions of class and racial (and ignores sexual) exploitation. In the long run the contradictions of the theory are such that it would be of little use in the destruction of racism and exploitation. For one truly interested in the liberation of oppressed peoples (for example, whites in Appalachia) the internal colony model is an incorrect, ineffective, and ultimately counter-revolutionary theory.[58]

Another critique of the internal colony concept came from Fred Cervantes, a graduate student at the University of Southern California at the time, in a paper delivered at the annual of NACCS meeting held at the University of Texas at Austin in 1975. According to Cervantes, the concept was limited because it did not truly place 'the realities of contemporary Chicano history and politics' in proper context. According to his critique, the contemporary oppression of Chicanos was due to a 'legacy of colonialism rather than ... internal colonialism' because Mexican Americans in US society were reality a 'post-colonial minority'.[59]

The critique of the internal colony paradigm reflected an increasing lack of its acceptance within Chicano Studies circles, at least as it had initially been developed. The paradigm had been a crucial effort to radically depart from the dominant paradigms of history and the social sciences. It contributed to the development of Chicano Studies as a new field of study and research in the university. But it never achieved legitimacy in the university in its original, radical context.

The quest for a Chicano Studies paradigm had been inseparable from the quest for Chicano identity and power. The Chicano Movement had aimed at altering the status quo and changing existing power relationships. Chicano Studies, as a product of the movement, was therefore initially a struggle to challenge the paradigms that legitimized those relationships and develop an paradigm in opposition to what the established ones represented. The quest for a Chicano Studies paradigm has very much been a process of 'scientific revolutions' as defined by Thomas Kuhn:

This genetic aspect of the parallel between political and scientific development should no longer be open to doubt ... political revolutions aim to change political institutions in ways those institutions themselves prohibit.... Like the choice between competing institutions, that between competing paradigms proves to be a choice between incompatible modes of community life.[60]

It was therefore inevitable that NACCS would fail to provide the unifying school of thought to guide Chicano Studies research, as many had expected. It never developed into the association envisioned by its founders. One reason for the exceedingly broad diversity within NACCS has to do with its constituency and the enduring social relations reproduced by the structure of the university. NACCS was from the beginning dominated by graduate students immersed in the process of certification as academics. Most have chosen to comply with the dictates of the traditional disciplines of which they are a part (granted that the pressures are great) rather than explore new concepts that may be professionally risky. Chicano Studies programs have yet to initiate research-oriented Ph.D. programs that can provide training and preparation for scholar-activists that have a specific and direct focus on Chicano Studies priorities as defined by the *Plan de Santa Barbara*.

Consequently, those with a commitment to the original principles of NACCS or to conducting research in the interest of the Mexican American community found it difficult to survive in the academy. In most cases, graduate students had to work under academics who perceive Chicano Studies in pejorative terms rather than as a legitimate discipline. Graduate students had to undergo the pressures of complying with the traditional criteria of academic work in order to successfully complete their PhD program. Very few found supportive faculty in established departments when they attempted to focus their research on other than the traditional projects. In the process, some succumbed to traditional scholarship in order to enhance their career prospects. Others stayed in their departmental programs as teaching assistants, research assistants, or part-time faculty, or dropped out of the university to become community organizers or pursue careers outside academia. Chicano Studies programs have served supportive roles for many students – a fact that is not always sufficiently acknowledged. Faculty in Chicano Studies programs by contrast have had to conform to the 'publish-or-perish' dictate of the universities. Consequently, there are few who conform to the 'scholar-activist' ideal that the original NACCS founders had envisioned. Most have broken virtually all their ties with community politics, and immersed themselves totally in traditional academic life.

NACCS continues to exist, but has become much like any other academic professional association, albeit with a distinctive Mexican American cultural ambiance. Regular annual meetings are held and academic papers are presented. The political ambiance that had originally permeated the association has lessened. The priorities of NACCS lie in graduate student survival and faculty development. Its concern has shifted to the need to legitimize Chicano scholarship within established traditional disciplines, and away from ideological challenges to the dominant paradigms. An analysis of the current state of affairs within NACCS – most notably the drift away from its original objectives, and the change in its priorities – is directly related to the diverse directions taken by Chicano Studies programs since their inception. Such an analysis requires taking into account the larger context and politics (external and internal) that have plagued Chicano Studies programs from their beginning. Special attention would have to be given to (1) the external forces that have impinged on the development of the programs and, (2) the exact nature of the ideological differences within the programs as they have developed and as new faculty staff have been selected. Such an analysis would shed light on why the programs are so vulnerable to the dictates of the university, and why the quest for paradigm became a quest for numerous paradigms within Chicano Studies.

Although NACCS has never been able to accomplish its original, radical objectives, it nevertheless continues to grow in membership. Its more pronounced academic orientation has not precluded it from serving as a forum for critical discourse on issues facing Mexican Americans and other Latino/as. Within the ranks of NACCS there are still those who identify as movement scholars and activists, and they have contributed to the development of a left-oriented scholarship.[61] A vibrant Chicana feminist and a lesbian/gay scholarship has also emerged from the ranks of NACCS.[62] Several leading feminists created a journal, *The Third Woman*.[63] Others founded Mujeres Activas en Letras y Cambios Sociales (MALCS).[64] Artists and poets active in NACCS have achieved national and international recognition for their works,[65] and have significantly contributed to an increasingly visible Mexican American art and literature that continues to grow in importance.

The Mainstreaming of Chicano Studies

After the Santa Barbara conference, Chicano Studies programs were established in one form or another on every campus of the University of California and the state college and university systems, as well as those community colleges where a significant number of Chicano students were enrolled. A few others were established outside California. Many of the proposals for these programs had been developed prior to the conference, but the proceedings of the conference and the plan, published six months later, were extremely useful in implementing programs where none had existed or were in the planning stage before the conference. Of particular importance were those sections of the plan dealing with tactics, strategy, curriculum, and above all, ideological content; these provided the direction that many students and faculty were seeking to help them confront campus administrators.

The spirit of unity that marked the conference did not last long. Division over goals, ideology, and the role of students in the governance of programs began to develop soon after the conference. Internal dissent was further aggravated by the politics of administrators and faculty who opposed the whole concept of ethnic studies. The same issues that came to plague the student movement also affected the Chicano Studies programs.

The organization CCHE, which had changed its name from Chicano Coordinating Committee on Higher Education to Chicano Council on Higher Education, provided the first example of the divisions that were beginning to surface. CCHE had been responsible for organizing the Santa Barbara conference, and that body had first developed the idea of a Chicano Studies master plan. As noted elsewhere, the members of CCHE were primarily students, faculty, administrators, and community activists interested in the organization of a statewide network of people involved in the development of Chicano programs. Most of the members were from the campuses of the University of California and the state college and university system. Before the conference some concern had been expressed within CCHE about differences in priorities between those in the UC system and those in the state college system. Because of the nature of California's three-tier higher education system, those at the UC level were criticized for their 'elitist' perspectives.

Chicano Studies advocates in the state colleges and two-year institutions saw themselves as more community oriented. These differences were put aside at the conference because of the urgency of initiating programs, but later manifested themselves as soon as the spirit of unity and urgency subsided.

The consequence was that those in the UC system opted to focus almost exclusively on the University of California and politics peculiar to that level of the state's three-tier higher education system. Those in the state college system also began to focus on their own system. The community college people felt their interests were ignored – or at least considered secondary to those of the four-year institutions. Most either dropped out of CCHE or became indirect participants, since they perceived both the UC and state college CCHE members as elitists. Built-in internal differences that were never adequately addressed thus made it impossible to bring about statewide and national coordination of Chicano programs.

The failure of CCHE to become a statewide coordinating body meant that local campus and community politics took precedence in the development of Chicano Studies programs. The ideals of *El Plan de Santa Barbara* could not be realized on a statewide level. Students within MEChA as well as Mexican American faculty and administrators disagreed over the varying emphases and priorities of the different programs. Those eventually hired for faculty and administrative positions usually did not share the objectives or ideological orientation outlined in the plan; some were not even aware of its existence.

At most campuses the programs fell into the control of people who did not support the development of Chicanos Studies as a radical alternative or with a community focus. The lack of Chicanos with doctoral degrees led to the hiring of individuals without adequate preparation or appropriate credentials. Thus positions went to those previously involved in War on Poverty programs, high school and junior college teachers, administrators in government agencies – and, in a few cases, to community activists. Others were graduate students in the process of earning their PhD's. Some of these graduate students had been in the Chicano student movement and therefore carried with them some commitment to the ideals of *El Plan de Santa Barbara*. Most, however, simply aspired to particular career goals in established departments. The isolated few who held PhD's and had been faculty members in existing departments took over programs and administered them within the mold of existing academic units.

By 1972, the MEChA leadership in California had begun public criticism of Chicano Studies faculty for lacking commitment to the goals of the student movement. They argued that faculty concern for professionalism (and upward mobility) came at the expense of student and community needs. MEChA concluded that the faculty had excluded students from meaningful participation in the governance of Chicano Studies programs.

In reality, student participation in the decision-making process of Chicano Studies programs had been dealt a severe blow by university administrators. For example, the Third World College proposed by Mexican American and other students of color at UC Berkeley met strong opposition during the Third World student strike in 1969. Police and university repression and the negative propaganda from the Chancellor, Academic Senate faculty, and Governor Reagan had blocked student efforts to establish a power base. Student activists had been compelled to compromise in their demand for a Third World College. Instead of a college they got a Department of Ethnic Studies with programs in Chicano, Black, Asian, and Native-American Studies.

On 9 September 1970, the president of Fresno State College canceled the La Raza Studies Program, which was headed by Eliezer Risco-Lozada, a participant in the Santa Barbara conference and one of the Los Angeles 13. Risco-Lozada and the other faculty members teaching Chicano Studies were fired because they were perceived as radicals by the president and by Mexican American faculty members in traditional departments.[66] The president offered two public reasons for canceling the program. First, the college was unable to recruit 'qualified' faculty. Second, the Mexican American community did not agree with him about what model the program should follow.[67] The program was reinstituted with a new faculty later in the year as a result of intense community pressure.

In 1971 the administration of the University of California, San Diego, where students had proposed a Third College named after Patrice Lumumba and Emiliano Zapata, made it unequivocally clear they would not tolerate any academic unit under the control of militant Third World students concerned with 'political' rather than academic issues. The Third College was not given the name requested by students, and was placed under the administration of a African American professor who made it clear that he would pursue the goals prescribed by the university. In spite of the administration's actions, students continued their opposition to Mexican American faculty who they perceived as unresponsive to student and community needs. One of the most intense struggles occurred at the UCLA campus, where the director of the Chicano Studies Center, sociologist Rodolfo Alvarez, was asked to resign by MEChA:

The Center is not now, nor will it be in the future if it continues as it is, sensitive to the needs of the Chicano students or community. It has become a bureaucratic institution, helping only those programs which advance its own ambitious self-interests. But it is the Chicano students and Chicano community that justify the existence of the ... Center, not vice versa, and the power is still with the people. It is up to us Chicanos to change the situation in our Center as soon as possible, or we may as well not have one at all.[68]

Alvarez was replaced by Juan Gómez-Quiñones, one of the leading figures of the Santa Barbara conference and editors of *El Plan de Santa Barbara*. Ironically, years later Gomez-Quiñones was himself forced to resign as director of the Chicano Studies Center when essentially the same criticism was leveled at him.

At California State University at San Diego, Chicano Studies faculty tried to develop a program with a Marxist orientation, emphasizing class struggle as opposed to an overbearing focus on culture. They were attacked by both cultural nationalists and by Trotskyists in the Socialist Workers Party:

Chicano Studies Faculty leadership ... has tried to force its 'class struggleists' [sic] ideology upon all the students.... has used the study group concept as a shabby substitute for democratic decision-making in MEChA.... has substituted paper-work, constant long inept meetings and bureaucracy for authentic political action.... has attempted to eliminate ideologically and physically our cultural and revolutionary nationalists concepts.[69]

This conflict resulted in the ouster of the faculty group in control of the Chicano Studies program and caused irreparable internal divisions.

At the California State University at Northridge the issue of sexism emerged when the Chicano Studies Department on that campus fired Ana Nieto-Gómez, one of the first Chicana feminists to emerge from the ranks of the student movement. She was one of the first to criticize the Chicano Movement for its sexism and Chicano Studies for its lack of analysis of gender issues.[70] Her firing became a divisive issue within many Chicano Studies programs. Women supporting her case saw the issue as a manifestation of Chicano reaction to 'Chicana feminism':

It had to happen – sooner or later, it was inevitable that the question of feminism in the movement would come to a clash.... Chicanos ... have been putting down the liberation of women as either a 'white trip', a cop out, a bourgeois trip, etc.... [T]he liberation of women has always been shoved aside.... Sexism is well-embedded within the Chicano movement.... [I]f one ignores the struggle of women, then one is guilty of sexism.[71]

The Nieto-Gómez case accelerated demands by some feminists within the student movement for the establishment of Chicana Studies programs.

At other campuses internal differences were not always couched in political terms but instead manifested themselves in personality clashes. In theory, interdisciplinary work and curricula were seen as necessary to Chicano Studies programs, but in practice the hiring and promotion of faculty were based on the traditional criteria of the established disciplines. At the University of California, Berkeley, for example, this led to internal ideological conflict between faculty trained in the humanities and those trained in the social sciences. Those in the humanities argued for an emphasis on Chicano culture, while those in the social sciences stressed class analysis and community studies.

The internal conflicts that have plagued Chicano Studies programs since their inception have been exacerbated by external forces and pressures brought to bear by the university itself. As academic units, the programs have had to conform to university regulations. This has placed them in a precarious political position. Originally envisioned as alternative or parallel structures within the university – with a genuine degree of autonomy – the programs have encountered difficulties from the beginning. Administrators have not tolerated any program that has developed in a direction that they see as antithetical to the stability of the university. Conflicts at various campuses throughout California have shown how harshly administrators have acted against programs they see in this light. Those administering the programs have thus had to pursue a course of action that attempts to legitimate their academic program in order to avert drastic cutbacks in funding and resources or to protect their own power to control the programs. In some cases young faculty members who have persisted in trying to carry out *El Plan de Santa Barbara*, or who advocated a departure from traditional academic criteria in the interest of community research and activity, were not granted tenure.

One such case occurred at California State University, Los Angeles, when Richard Santillán was denied recommendation for tenure by the tenured faculty in the Chicano Studies Department on the grounds that he lacked fluency in Spanish, that his work consisted of 'political pamphleteering with little or no solidly based scholarly research', and finally that 'his contributions to the university' suffered 'severely'.[72] Santillán had been a founding member of UMAS and MEChA as an undergraduate and had been one of La Raza Unida's leading organizers in Los Angeles. It's interesting to note that Santillán was later awarded tenure at the California State Polytechnic University at Pomona.

The push for legitimacy by most faculty in Chicano Studies programs resulted in harsh criticism from the student movement:

> The Chicano Studies departments were established in the late 1960's as a reaction against racism and for the development of the right of self-determination.... In their development ... the departments have tended to become the oppressor, or sub-oppressor, instead of striving for self-determination.... With rare exceptions, Chicano Studies do not address themselves to the material or economic foundations of racism, cultural chauvinism and the forms of separation, exclusion, and subordination which we, as a people, experience.... [A]s the strategy of repression unfolds, so does the process of cooptation.[73]

Chicano Studies programs also came under attack from Mexican American faculty in established departments, some of whom had always perceived the movement for Chicano Studies as a fad, generated by demagogues who could not land a job in legitimate academic departments and who therefore needed to create such programs for employment. For example, Manuel Machado Jr., criticized Chicano Studies:

> Separate Chicano Studies programs fail to take up valid historical questions.... [T]hey are dedicated to the proposition that a rip-off has been perpetrated against all Mexican-Americans and that today's Anglos should ... atone for the sins of the past. Some institutions in California ... have burgeoning academic empires ... staffed by untrained and incompetent teachers, preach[ing] a gospel of separatism and boondoggle programs aimed not at furthering knowledge but at using the lecture hall and seminar room as centers for political agitation.[74]

Opposition like Machado's has existed among faculty of Mexican descent who have sided with university administrators and white faculty in efforts to undermine the programs. They successfully mobilized bias against Chicano

Studies programs on the grounds that the programs have a political orientation rather than academic substance. This type of ideological assault was a factor in the decline in student enrollment in Chicano Studies courses. Lower enrollments, in turn, have made the programs vulnerable to budget cutbacks and
perhaps even elimination. Efforts have been under way at several campuses to
place the programs under the control of traditional academic departments. At
the University of California, Irvine, the Program in Comparative Culture was
at one time moving toward the status of a separate school with departments of
Chicano, Black, Asian, and Native American studies. The program was then
brought under the School of Social Sciences, and its curriculum was revised
to conform to traditional guidelines.

Still other programs were pressured to redefine their objectives in terms of
'American Multi-Cultural Studies' – an objective that de-emphasizes Chicano
content in favor of comparative ethnic approaches deemed more legitimate by
the university. Sonoma State College provides an example; there the program
was asked to plan for integration into more 'rationally sound and economically
feasible academic units.'[75] An internal review of that program was conducted,
aimed at expressing administration concerns:

[W]e should like to know the rationale for maintaining that Mexican-
American Studies is a bona fide discipline in itself, with academic and
intellectual integrity and uniqueness.... [W]e should like for you to
specify the structure and methodology that will make that discipline both
educationally feasible and deliverable, as contrasted with a mere hope or
an ideological objective.... [W]e should like to be advised on the meaning
and value of and the needs for a separate degree program.... [W]e are
requesting that your faculty reassess their course offerings in terms of the
explicit objectives of the ... program, concentrate their efforts in those areas
that are defensibly multi-racial, and utilize other departments/disciplines
for courses which are not.[76]

At the University of California, Berkeley, there was constant pressure on
faculty in ethnic studies programs to conform to traditional academic criteria.
In 1972 all Afro-American Studies faculty members, most of whom had com-
munity- and student-interest orientations, were fired by the chancellor and replaced with faculty who had 'legitimate' academic credentials. Afro-American
Studies was then moved out of the Department of Ethnic Studies into the

College of Letters and Sciences as a bona fide department of its own.

This move served to undermine development of a Third World College. Faculty in Chicano, Asian, and Native American studies resisted efforts to be moved into the College of Letters and Sciences, but were compelled to 'legitimize' their programs while maintaining a symbolic commitment to the goals of the proposed Third World College of 1969. They have complied with university pressures to exclude direct participation of students in decision-making, opting for complete faculty control of the programs. Despite their efforts to achieve academic respectability, Chicano Studies and other ethnic studies curricula have essentially not achieved this goal. After all, 'legitimacy' and 'academic respectability' ultimately translate into academic *power*, something that established faculty, established disciplines, and established departments do not share or give up easily. The Committee on Educational Policy of the Academic Senate, for example, in response to requests for the certification of ethnic studies courses as meeting the university-wide American History and Institutions requirements, denied these requests on the following basis:

> [T]he history of Native Americans (like the comparable course in Chicano History), although clearly taught in an historical context, remains too narrow in focus and content to satisfy the requirement that every student at the University of California demonstrate a proficiency in the history of the United States.... The criterion is not which ethnic group provides a relevant perspective, but rather which courses provide a student with the broadest view of the history and formal institutions of this country.[77]

Chicano Studies programs on other campuses have not been so directly threatened. Some have been able to maintain legitimacy within the university because of joint faculty appointments with established departments. Programs with such arrangements seem to pose less of a threat, and therefore criticism from university administrators has been minimal. Other programs, although they may not have to share faculty appointment power with established departments, are in relatively strong positions due to good working relationships with faculty in other departments. And of course some campuses simply have more sympathetic chancellors, presidents, and other high-level administrators. Chicano Studies at the University of California, Santa Barbara, has been the only one able to develop its own PhD program, inaugurated in the fall of 2005, thirty-seven years after the first Chicano Studies department in the nation was created in the fall of 1968 at California State University at Los Angeles.

Overall, however, it is clear that the position of Chicano Studies programs has remained tenuous. The decline of the student movement and the difficulties of movement scholar-activists in surviving tenure struggles, coupled with university budget cuts, has left the programs vulnerable to extreme cutbacks, redirection, or a phase-out. Chicano Studies programs that enjoy high student enrollments and a significant number of tenured faculty have survived, but those that don't may not.

The future of Chicano Studies cannot be predicted without considering current economic and political trends in the United States. The intense political activity of the 1960s is over – and has apparently been forgotten by many who lived through the turbulence of that decade. The war in Iraq has not had the same response as generated by the Vietnam War. And although millions marched in the immigrant rights protests in 2006, there are no manifestations of discontent similar in magnitude to the upheavals that occurred with dramatic consistency in the *barrios* and ghettos throughout the country in the late 1960s.

Local, state and national politics have shifted from the center to the right, from liberal social-welfare accommodation to fiscal conservatism. Liberal politicians, who in the past had been vocal dissidents and strong advocates for the poor and 'economically disadvantaged', have acquiesced in rigid austerity measures affecting health, education and welfare programs. The move to the right has corresponded to a growing intolerance for the affirmative action programs that were a result of the political pressures of the 1960s.

The US Supreme Court decision on the Bakke case reinforced opposition to Chicano and ethnic studies in institutions of higher education. It was the first blow against affirmative action. The Bakke decision has made it unconstitutional for universities to support equal opportunity based on quotas designed to increase the Mexican American presence in higher education. Proposition 209 was the final blow and ended affirmative action in California. Other anti-affirmative action court rulings and electoral propositions have also succeeded in ending affirmation action programs in other States. Most schools have thus seen a general decline in efforts to recruit Chicano students. Chicano Studies programs have been perceived as part of the university's affirmative action effort, and in a very real sense they have also been one of the university's War on Poverty programs. But new times have made them seem expendable.

The Future of Chicano Studies

How Chicano Studies programs will fare in the future remains to be seen. Based on the events and trends of the past ten years, their future might not seem very promising. Internal conflicts and external pressures to conform to traditional academic criteria have made it extremely difficult for those in the quest for a Chicano Studies paradigm to devote themselves to this crucial task. A critical look at the nature and structure of the university and, in particular, its role as perhaps the most important institution in the shaping of dominant societal values and ideology (the kind of ideology needed by those who rule) would have provided evidence that the opposition met by Chicano Studies, and similar programs, was inevitable, for in the final analysis the university has been created and shaped by those with the same general economic, political, and cultural affinities as those who rule. Their roles and tasks have been defined by the particular structure of the society of which they are a part. They have functioned as legitimizers of the dominant values of US society which are centered in a capitalist political economy. As Edward Shils has put it, intellectuals

> through their provision of models and standards, by the presentation of symbols to be appreciated, ... elicit, guide, and form the expressive dispositions within a society.... Members of every society, and above all those who exercise authority in it, need to have ... some sense of the stability, coherence, and orderliness of their society.... By means of preaching, teaching, and writing, intellectuals infuse into sections of the population which are intellectual neither by vocation nor by social role, a perceptiveness and an imagery which they would otherwise lack.[78]

The founders of the Chicano Studies programs did not ostensibly seek to radically restructure the university, but simply to gain access to its resources with the purpose of applying them to the needs of the Mexican American community. The programs were not conceived as revolutionary in nature. But their objectives, as outlined in *El Plan de Santa Barbara*, reinforced such a perception on the part of the opposition and, in particular, by those who governed the university. Thus the goals of Chicano Studies programs were seen as antithetical to the academic enterprise. The emphasis of the programs on service to the Chicano community and on the development of a critical Chicano consciousness and identity was sufficient to justify the mobilization of bias against the programs by university administrators and the faculty in established departments.

What has saved Chicano Sudies is the demographics of a growing Mexican Latino/a population. Mexican Americans are the largest Latino group in the United States, and this growth may result in larger numbers of students of Mexican descent attending college, especially in the Southwest. On the other hand, greater numbers of Mexican American students will not necessarily materialize into larger enrollments for Chicano Studies programs. The times have changed and there is no Chicano Movement that compels the average student to become an activist or study Mexican American culture.

The fact that Chicano Studies remains a fledgling discipline, with a still tenuous hold on university resources, ought not to divert our attention from the important contributions it has made thus far. It has made possible the hiring of Chicano/a faculty in traditional departments and the rise of Mexican Americans to important administrative positions. In the University of California system, faculty from Chicano Studies departments significantly contributed to the appointment of the first Chicano chancellor in the system, Tomás Rivera, one of the first nationally recognized scholars of Chicano literature, at the UC Riverside campus. Other Chicano and Chicana faculty have been appointed to other high-level administration positions such as deanships and vice chancellorships. Apart from helping to maximize the Mexican American presence in the colleges and universities, Chicano Studies has made other contributions that may not be as obvious, but in the long run are much more significant. It has produced thousands of students since 1968 who have gone on to graduate and professional schools and become professionals who are playing important roles in local, state, and national politics. It is yet too early to assess their impact on the political and economic institutions (which, it must be remembered, previously pursued policies of systematic exclusion and, at the very least, could not empathize with Mexican American needs). Most important, it has made possible the development of community activists and grassroots leaders who continue to engage in the politics of social change. For example, many of the leaders in immigrant rights organizations are products of Chicano Studies, something true of civil and human rights organizations as well.

Chicano Studies has also made possible the development of Mexican American academic intellectuals. Prior to the inception of the programs, little was known about Mexican American intellectual tradition and history. The work of the Mexican-American Generation had gone largely unnoticed and unappreciated before the 1960s. Despite their accommodationist and assimilationist ideology, individuals like George Sánchez, Julián Samora and Américo Paredes received the recognition they had long deserved through Chicano Studies programs, as did the work of radical scholar–activist Ernesto Galarza. Their work has been linked to that produced by contemporary Chicano/a scholar-activists. Even though Chicano Studies programs and the National Association for Chicana and Chicano Studies have not been able to develop as envisioned by their founders, significant research on the Mexican American experience continues to be produced by the scholar–activists who came out of the 1960s and who have survived in the university. There are no longer many scholar-activists, but younger scholars in Chicano/a Studies have emerged who are producing important books that expand the knowledge of the Mexican American experience. This is particularly true in the case of Chicana feminist scholarship as well as in the case of lesbian/gay scholarship. Much of this research departs from traditional academic concerns and in the process has exposed the bias of many of the dominant paradigms in the social sciences. Much has also been done toward developing more theoretical perspectives. Chicano Studies must be placed in the context of a larger historical process: the political and intellectual development of an oppressed working class. This process does not originate in a vacuum but is directly related to the larger societal context that influences the political consciousness of all intellectuals. It is a dialectical process that always results both in opposition to cultural and ideological hegemony and in the legitimization of that hegemony. The quest for paradigm continues in the twenty-first century.

Notes

1 Richard E. Lopez and Julián Samora, 'George Sánchez and Testing', in Américo Paredes, ed., *Humanidad: Essays in Honor of George I. Sánchez*, Los Angeles 1977, pp. 107–15.

2 George I. Sánchez, *The Forgotten People*, Albuquerque 1940, p. viii.

3 Ibid.

4 Américo Paredes, *With His Pistol in His Hand*, Austin 1958.

5 Julián Samora and James Watson, 'Subordinate Leadership in a Bicultural Community: An Analysis', *American Sociological Review*, August 1954, pp. 413–21.

6 Ernesto Galarza, *Merchants of Labor*, Santa Barbara 1964, p. 259.

7 'Proposal for Raza Studies', 1968, proposal by students at San Francisco State College, author's files.

8 'BSC–MAYA Demands', unpublished pamphlet, author's files.

9 Mexican American Student Confederation,'A Third World College', mimeo, n.d., p. 2.

10 Ralph C. Guzmán, 'Proposal for the Creation of a Mexican American Studies Program', 1968, author's files.

11 I was asked by both Professor Guzmán and the UMAS leadership to serve as the facilitator in efforts to resolve the conflicts between the two sides. I had been president of UMAS, and at that time I was serving as Guzmán's research assistant; unfortunately, this attempt to bring the two sides together was unsuccessful.

12 'Proposal for the Establishment of a Mexican American Cultural and Research Center, 1968, author's files.

13 'Bachelor of Arts Program: The San Fernando Model'. This proposal was published in *El Plan de Santa Barbara*, pp. 104–15.

14 'A Proposal for a Chicano Studies Program: The Santa Barbara Model', published in *El Plan de Santa Barbara*, pp. 92–102.

15 René Nuñez, interview, 3 January 1979.

16 CCHE letter, 12 March 1969; in author's files.

17 *El Plan de Santa Barbara*, p. 10.

18 The document was edited by Jesús Chavarría, Fernando de Necochea, Juan Gómez-Quiñones, Paul Sanchez and Armando Valdez – all prominent members of the CCHE Steering Committee. Chavarría did most of the editing work and wrote the manifesto that became the document's preface. Jesús Chavarría, interview, 27 May 1980.

19 Jesús Genera, letter to conference participants, n.d., in author's files.

20 *Plan de Santa Barbara*, p. 15.

21 Ibid., p. 92.

22 Ibid.

23 Ibid., p. 93.

24 Ibid.

25 Ibid., p. 40.

26 Ibid., p. 78.

27 For example, I became a member of the Left Caucus for a New Political Science. I was also a cofounder of the Chicano Caucus of the Political Science Association and ran for vice president of the American Political Science Association in 1970 as the candidate of the Left and Chicano caucuses. Chicano caucuses were also formed in the anthropology, sociology, and history professional associations as well as the Southwestern Social Science Association.

28 See *Hijas de Cuahtemoc*, no. 1, April 1971, p. 8.

29 Ron Lopez et al., *Chicanos in Higher Education: Status and Issues*, Los Angeles 1976.

30 Report issued by the Chicano Caucus in Political Science; in author's files.

31 Ernesto Galarza, interview, 10 June 1979.

32 Jesús Chavarría, interview, 27 May 1980.

33 Rodolfo Acuña, interview, 3 January 1979.

34 Octavio Romano-V., interview, 28 March 1979.

35 'The Anthropology and Sociology of the Mexican American: The Distortion of Mexican American History', *El Grito*, vol. 2, no. 1, Fall 1968, pp. 13–26.

36 'Social Science, Objectivity and the Chicanos', *El Grito*, vol. 4, no. 1, Fall 1970, pp. 4–16.

37 Octavaio Romano-V., interview.

38 *Aztlán*, vol. 1, no. 1, Summer 1970, p. vi.

39 Carlos Muñoz Jr., 'A Chicano Perspective of Political Analysis', *Aztlan*, vol. 1, no. 2, Fall 1970, pp. 15–26.

40 Ibid., p. 21.

41 Ibid., p. 24.

42 Juan Gómez-Quiñones, 'Toward a Perspective on Chicano History', *Aztlán*, vol. 2, no. 2, Fall 1971, pp. 2, 39.

43 When she subsequently completed her PhD, she became the first Chicana political scientist in the nation.

44 Adaljiza Sosa Riddell, 'Chicanas and El Movimiento', *Aztlán*, vol. 5, no.1 and 2, Spring and Fall 1974, pp. 155–65.

45 Carlos Muñoz Jr., 'On the Nature and Cause of Tension in the Chicano Community: A Critical Analysis', published in summary form in *Aztlán*, vol. 1, no. 2, Fall 1970, pp. 99–100.

46 Tomás Almaguer, 'Toward the Study of Chicano Colonialism', *Aztlán*, vol. 2, no. 1, Spring 1971, pp. 7–20.

47 Mario Barrera et al., 'The Barrio as Internal Colony', in Harlan Hahn, ed., *People and Politics in Urban Society*, Beverly Hills 1972, pp. 465–98.

48 Rodolfo Acuña, *Occupied America: The Chicano's Struggle Toward Liberation*, San Francisco 1972, p. 3.

49 Guillermo Flores, 'Race and Culture in the Internal Colony: Keeping the Chicano in His Place', in Frank Bonilla, ed., *Structures of Dependency*, Stanford, Calif. 1973, p. 190.

50 Gómez-Quiñones, 'Toward a Perspective', pp. 5, 6.

51 The proceedings of the meeting were summarized in the first NCCSS newsletter, which Mario Barrera and I prepared. It was subsequently published as an appendix in Reynaldo Flores Macias, ed., *Perspectivas en Chicano Studies: Papers Presented at the Third Annual Meeting of the NACSS*, Los Angeles 1977, pp. 214–20.

52 Ibid., pp. 215, 216.

53 Adela de la Torre and Beatriz M. Pesquera, eds, *Building with Our Hands: New Directions in Chicana Studies*, Berkeley 1993, p. 2.

54 Gloria Anzaldua, *Borderlands: La Frontera: The New Mestiza*, San Francisco 1987.

55 Thomas Kuhn, *The Structure of Scientific Revolutions*, Chicago 1959, p. 175.

56 Unpublished proceedings, Symposium on Chicano Studies, UCLA, 1973; author's files. See also Mario García, 'Inside the Beast: Internal Colonialism and the Chicano', *La Luz*, November 1974, pp. 27–28, for an excellent account of the symposium.

57 Gilbert González, 'A Critique of the Internal Colonial Model', *Latin American Perspectives*, Spring 1974, pp. 154–61.

58 Ibid., pp. 160–61.

59 Fred Cervantes, 'Chicanos as a Post-Colonial Minority', in Macias, *Perspectivas*, p. 16.

60 Kuhn, *Scientific Revolutions*, pp. 93–94.

61 See Estevan T. Flores, 'The Mexican-Origin People in the United States and Marxist

Thought in Chicano Studies', in Bertell Ollman and Edward Vernoff, eds, *The Left Academy: Marxist Scholarship on American Campuses*, vol. 3, New York 1986.

62 NACS, *Chicana Voices: Intersections of Class, Race, and Gender*, Austin 1986.

63 The editors were Norma Alarcón, Ana Castillo, and Cherríe Moraga.

64 MALCS is a women's collective that developed from a Berkeley-based group called Mujeres en Marcha and from the ranks of NACS. Its founding director was Adaljiza Sosa Riddell.

65 See Shifra M. Goldman and Tomás Ybarra-Frausto, eds, *Arte Chicano: A Comprehensive Annotated Bibliography of Chicano Art, 1965–1981*, Berkeley 1985.

66 Letter to the editor, *La Gente*, 27 February 1973.

67 Chicano Affairs Governing Board, 'Position Paper', n.d., p. 1; author's files.

68 Eliezer Risco-Lozada, interview, 26 January 1979.

69 Kenneth A. Seib, *The Slow Death of Fresno State: A California Campus Under Reagan and Brown*, Palo Alto 1979, p. 120.

70 Ana Nieto-Gómez, 'La Femenista', *Encuentro Femenil*, vol. 1, no. 2, pp. 34–37.

71 Editorial, *La Gente*, March 1976, p. 2.

72 As reported in University *Times*, 13 February 1979, pp. 3, 5.

73 Editorial, *La Gente*, February 1975, p. 19.

74 Manuel A. Machado Jr., *Listen Chicano! An Informal History of the Mexican American*, Chicago 1978, pp. 143–50.

75 Memo from Dr. Procter, vice president of academic affairs, to Professor Neves, director of Mexican American Studies, 10 April 1978; in author's files.

76 Ibid.

77 'Ethnic Studies Does Not Meet Standards', *Daily Californian*, 15 June 1978, p. 7.

78 Edward Shils, *The Intellectuals and the Powers and Other Essays*, Chicago 1972, pp. 4, 5.

6

From *Chicano* to *Hispanic*: The Politics of a New Generation

The Chicano student movement and the larger Chicano Movement of which it was a major part exemplified the politics of a decade unique in the history of the United States. The politics of mass protest that emerged during the 1960s had a profound impact on students across the nation. Mexican American youth, like other Americans, were able to witness the struggles against racism and against the Vietnam War as the mass media daily focused attention on those movements. Almost despite themselves, the mass media, particularly television, made it easier for youth from all walks of life to see the contradictions between US government actions and US democratic and constitutional ideals. As a result, many young people were compelled to question what they had been taught in school about US democracy.

But times changed. The movements of the sixties that had been sources of inspiration for Mexican American youth disappeared into the pages of history by the mid-1970s. Most of the leaders of those movements did not play a central role in the political struggles of the late 1970s and 1980s. César Chávez, for example, no longer commanded the mass media attention he had received in the 1960s and early 1970s as the political impact of the farmworker movement faded. Tijerina's land grants movement in New Mexico was virtually dead by 1970. By 1974 the Chicano Movement had suffered a sharp decline as a result of both internal division and repression.

The 1972 La Raza Unida Party national convention held in El Paso, Texas was both the first and last time Chicano Movement activists came together in an attempt to unify all ideological sectors of the movement. The effort failed despite public gestures by movement leaders to promote an image of solidarity. Behind the scenes, José Angel Gutiérrez (elected the national chairman of the party at the convention), Corky Gonzáles and Reies López Tijerina did not resolve their personal and ideological differences. Gonzáles bitterly complained about the take over of the party by the 'intellectuals'.[1] Tijerina aired his antagonism toward Gonzáles by calling him a 'frustrated leader', and Gonzáles remained critical of Gutiérrez's pragmatism.[2]

These conflicts within the movement took place in a climate of government harassment, spying, and use of provocateurs. FBI documents that I have obtained reveal that Chicano student movement organizations and other groups within the Chicano Movement were indeed targets of political surveillance and infiltration by FBI agents and other undercover local and state police intelligence personnel that were part of FBI Director J. Edgar Hoover's COINTELPRO program.[3] Even before the 1968 student walkouts in Los Angeles and the subsequent emergence of the Chicano Movement, meetings between Mexican American, African American, and white radical activist youth were closely monitored.

In testimony before a subcommittee of the US Senate Committee on the Judiciary chaired by Senator Thomas J. Dodd, Sgt. Robert J. Thoms, a member of the Los Angeles Police Department's Intelligence Division, made clear the extent of political surveillance conducted on individual leaders and their organizations in California and other parts of the Southwest in 1967–68:[4] 220 individuals and 199 organizations were identified in his testimony.[5] José Angel Gutiérrez and MAYO, Corky Gonzáles and the Crusade for Justice, and Reies López Tijerina and the Alianza de Pueblos Libres were included along with leaders of SNCC, US (a Black nationalist organization headed by Ron Karenga), the Black Panther Party, and Students for a Democratic Society.

After the 1968 Los Angeles high school strike, FBI Director Hoover issued orders to infiltrate chapters of the United Mexican American Students:

There has been a recent rise in the formation of various Mexican-American organizations mostly throughout the Southwestern part of the United States. While they all originate with the purpose of bettering the educational, economic, and general stature of the Mexican-Americans ... experience has shown that these organizations do become more militant and aggressive as time goes on. Certain ... organizations are coming under communist influence and are holding classes in Marxist-Leninist ideology. Others ... are arming themselves and holding classes in weaponry. Others have tried to align themselves or cooperate in activities of the Black Panther Party. ... Your investigation of the UMAS should be penetrative and receive aggressive attention.[6]

The internal divisions that occurred within organizations of the Chicano Movement were indeed attributable to ideological conflict, personality clashes between leaders, and sexist attitudes toward women. But there is no doubt that those divisions were also attributable to agents of the FBI and other intelligence agencies, their paid informants, and provocateurs. The case of Frank Martinez is a good example. In a public confession, Martinez admitted to having been an undercover agent for the Alcohol, Tobacco, and Firearms Division of the US Treasury Department between 1969 and 1971.[7] During that time he infiltrated the MAYO organization in Texas and the Brown Berets and other organizations in California. He also took on leadership responsibilities as cochair of the Chicano Moratorium Against the War in Vietnam.

Martinez admitted committing various acts designed to undermine the Chicano Movement.[8] He disrupted a march in Alicia, Texas. He set up a 'gun buy' at Texas A & M University with the local MAYO chapter, created dissension within the ranks of the Brown Berets and MAYO, burned a cross in front of a VISTA worker's home, and created antagonism between the Brown Berets and the Chicano Moratorium in Los Angeles that resulted in conflicts between the two cochairs of the latter organization. The rumors he spread resulted in the ouster of one of them, Rosalio Muñoz, and in Martinez's appointment as cochair replacing Muñoz. He later provoked a police raid of the Moratorium office by carrying a .410 caliber shotgun in front of the office. Finally, Martinez provoked and led an attack on US Senator John Tunney of California when the senator was visiting the East Los Angeles Community College campus in which Tunney was kicked and his assistant beaten.

Political surveillance, infiltration of movement organizations, conspiracy indictments of leaders, and mass arrests of movement activists were forms of ideological repression that played a major role in the decline of the Chicano Movement. Violent repression on the part of police agencies was also a contributing factor. The Crusade for Justice was a primary target of all these forms of repressionm,[9] including the police violence that resulted in the kill-

ing of one of its young leaders, Luis Martinez. Two members of the Black
Berets organization in New Mexico, Antonio Cordova and Rito Canales,
were killed by police on 29 January 1972. The Chicano Moratorium antiwar
rally of 20,000 people in East Los Angeles on 29 August 1970 resulted in
the death of three Mexican Americans; Mark Ward, a fifteen-year-old Brown
Beret, and noted *Los Angeles Times* journalist Ruben Salazar were two of the
three. Hundreds of others present at the rally were injured by attacking police.
Six members of UMAS at the University of Colorado, Boulder, were blown
to bits in cars in two separate incidents. Killed on 27 May 1974 were Neva
Romero, Reyes Martinez and Una Jaakola, and on 29 May UMAS President
Florencio Granados, Heriberto Teran and Francisco Dougherty. A seventh
UMAS member, Antonio Alcantar, was seriously injured but survived. These
cases were never solved, though police concluded that the victims 'accidentally
triggered both blasts while making bombs.'[10] Movement activists, however, believed that their comrades had been targets of police or FBI COINTELPRO
hit squads. Acts of violent repression such as these initially generated mass
student and community support for the movement, but in the long run they
contributed to the movement's demise.

By the 1980s Mexican American students at both the high school and college levels were generally unaware of the Chicano Movement or the history of
the sixties, except for the few who took courses in Chicano Studies. However,
enrollment in Chicano Studies declined sharply on most campuses during
the late 1970s and 1980s. Although MEChA continued to exist, the level of
Mexican American student activism declined along with Chicano Studies enrollments. Student activism in the tradition of the 1960s did emerge briefly
during the 1980s over issues of apartheid in South Africa, US intervention
in Central America, racism on campus, and defense of affirmative action, but
those issues did not have the same level of impact on Chicano student activists
as had the issues of the 1960s. Jesse Jackson's presidential campaigns of 1984
and 1988 also contributed to the brief re-emergence of sixties-style student
activism. But relatively few Mexican American student activists participated
in the Jackson campaigns, and few became active in the Rainbow Coalition.

Those campaigns were to some extent an extension of the civil rights movement. The rhetoric of Jackson's Rainbow Coalition reflects ideas rooted in the
Black and Chicano Movements of the 1960s. But those campaigns, especially
that of 1988, differed significantly in ideological terms from the 1960s movements. Jackson articulated demands for the political empowerment of people

of color through participation in the mainstream of US electoral politics. Mobilization of the African American and Mexican American vote replaced demands for self-determination and creation of alternative political institutions, as called for by Black and Chicano nationalism.

In the 1980s Mexican American students, like other youth in the United States, were exposed to political ideas that for the most part were not conducive to their radicalization. Compared with the 1960s, the politics of the 1980s resembled the super-patriotism and anticommunism of the 1940s and 1950s. The Reagan 'revolution' reinforced the conservative trend that had begun in the 1970s. The politics of the 1970s and 1980s thus contributed to the return to prominence of the old guard pro-assimilationist and liberal reformist Mexican American organizations. LULAC in particular resurfaced as the leading national Mexican American political organization. LULAC and the Mexican American Legal Defense Fund (MALDEF) have been the principal Mexican American lobbies in the corridors of ruling-class power.

At the same time and for similar reasons, neoliberal politicians like Henry Cisneros, the mayor of San Antonio, Texas who was a serious contender for the 1984 Democratic Party vice-presidential nomination; Federico Peña, the mayor of Denver, Colorado; and Toney Anaya, former governor of New Mexico, have emerged as the new voices of Mexican American political leadership. They replaced César Chávez, Delores Huerta, Reies Tijerina, and Corky Gonzáles as the heroes and role models for the new generation of Mexican American political activists. These new heroes have promoted 'Hispanic' identity for Mexican Americans and represent a renewal of the Mexican-American middle-class political tradition that was shaped by the generation of the 1930s.

The political tradition of the Mexican-American Generation was never completely disrupted by the Chicano Movement or the politics of the 1960s. In fact, Mexican American youth militancy and protest actually created more opportunities for middle-class elites to participate in the higher circles of the Democratic Party. Initially turned off by the politics of mass confrontation, they soon learned to use those politics for their own ends. Politicians from the Mexican-American Generation initially spoke out harshly against the tactics and ideology of the Chicano Generation. Congressman Henry B. Gonzalez, for example, denounced Chicano militants as racists-in-reverse and spreaders of hatred. Other, more liberal politicians were moved by the Chicano Movement to become more aggressive in the quest for Mexican American equality and representation in the politial process. For example, the late US Senator Joseph M. Montoya expressed more progressive liberal sentiments. As a keynote speaker at a 1971 national conference of 'Hispanic' organizations held in Washington, D.C., he echoed many of the central concerns of the Chicano Power Movement:

> We have come to belabor the conscience of America, ... to awaken it to injustices. ... Our people are victims of a series of evils. ... We come to remind America of our presence and plight. ... Nor do we come as supplicants, with hats in hand and eyes cast down, as did our forebears. Rather, we are here as equals, unafraid [sic] of no man; determined to settle for full equality and nothing less. ... The Hispano, Chicano, and Boricua now possesses an aggressive identity. He is spiritually armed with La Causa. He wants action, progress, self-determination, true equality. ... We shall do this without giving up our heritage, customs, culture or language. ... We seek our own leaders, our own professionals. ... For too long we have been the 'Silent People', quietly enduring a second-class role. ... ¡Ya Basta![11]

The language was somewhat different from the speeches of most Chicano Movement leaders although the message was essentially the same. The key difference was that the speech reflected the middle-class elite commitment to the capitalist ideology of the state. In Montoya's words, 'We assemble because we retain faith in this country, its ideas and institutions ... in spite of what we have suffered at its hands. ...'[12] As the militant and radical organizations comprising the Chicano Movement began to decline, the Democratic Party politicians and the leadership of liberal reformist organizations picked up the momentum the movement had generated.

By the mid-1970s, many former activists in the Chicano Movement had become involved in mainstream electoral politics. For example, William Velasquez, one of the founders of MAYO in Texas and an early Raza Unida Party activist, founded the Southwest Voter Registration and Education Project. Others joined MALDEF after graduation from law school. Their efforts have contributed to opening up the electoral process through litigation and the implementation of procedures made possible by the Voting Rights Act. The result was increased Mexican American participation in political campaigns at the local, state, and national levels and in the struggle for reapportionment. In California, for example, some former leaders of La Raza

Unida Party spearheaded the successful effort to create new state and congressional districts conducive to the election of Mexican Americans.

Mexican American congressional representation increased from four prior to 1980 to nine by 1984. Two Mexican Americans have served as governor of New Mexico, Jerry Apodaca in 1975–79 and Toney Anaya in 1983–87. Significant increases have taken place in the number of elected Mexican American officials in the Southwest at the local and state government levels. By 1988, there were 3360 Latino elected officials in the US, 75 percent of them in Texas, California and Colorado, where the Chicano Movement was strongest in the 1960s.[13]

In 1984, Mexican Americans for the first time played an important role in both the Democratic and Republican conventions. A Democrat from California, Richard Alatorre, served as chair of the important Convention Credentials Committee, the first Mexican American to serve in that capacity. The vice-chair of the Democratic National Committee, State Senator Polly Baca from Colorado, proudly proclaimed that the 1984 convention featured the largest number of 'Hispanic' delegates in the history of the party – 271 delegates and 92 alternates. As she put it prior to the convention, 'We will be visible on the floor, in the caucuses, with the candidates, and on the air. It's no longer a question of inclusion, we're there, and we're making the most of it.'[14] At the 1984 Republican convention, Katherine Ortega, treasurer of the United States, was the first Mexican American and first woman to be the keynote speaker of a major political party convention. The 1988 Democratic and Republican conventions also reflected a high degree of Mexican American participation.

Mexican Americans have thus come a long way from their days of invisibility in national electoral politics. But the politics of accommodation have yet to result in significant gains in political representation. Mexican Americans remain under-represented at all levels of government and far from achieving political power. And the visibility of Mexican Americans in the 1984 and 1988 conventions and the relative upswing in Latino electoral victories, when measured against the realities of Reaganism and neoliberalism, add up to little in the way of improved conditions for the Mexican and Mexican American working class. The middle class has grown significantly and has even prospered as a result of the federal government's support for small business and some incentives from Reaganomics. But Mexican American workers, like the working class as a whole, lost ground after Reagan became president. They suffered as a result of the Reagan administration's attack on unions and they lost most of the strikes organized during the 1980s. Union busting contributed to keeping most Mexican American workers in the unorganized sector of the labor force. Cutbacks in social welfare and educational programs had a profoundly negative impact on the working-class poor. Poverty and unemployment increased, especially among Mexican American youth.

Reaganomics also had an impact on the politics of the liberal reformist and accommodationist Mexican American organizations. The lack of federal funding to support their programs and organizations resulted in a shift to the private sector as a new source of funding. MALDEF, for example, lost the federal grants it relied on during the Carter administration. As a result, MALDEF has been compelled to form partnerships with the same corporate sector that contributed to the support and legitimacy of the Reagan administration. MALDEF's ideology remains liberal-reformist since it continues to engage in legal struggle for Mexican American civil rights in the courts, but it must be careful not to challenge the status quo directly lest it lose its new source of funding. Another example is the National Council of La Raza, founded in 1968 to promote community organization and mobilization. It moved into the field of economic development and now works closely with the corporate sector.

LULAC, the largest national Mexican American political organization, has also shifted political direction, and now has a stance reminiscent of its original conservative roots. Liberal attorney Mario Obledo was replaced by Reagan Democrat Oscar Moran, an insurance executive, as president in 1985. Under Obledo's leadership the organization had become an outspoken liberal critic of the Reagan administration and had been particularly vocal on the issue of immigration during the congressional debates over the proposed Simpson-Mazzoli legislation. Obledo had also taken leadership in protesting United States intervention in Central America.

Upon assuming office Moran made clear what the new LULAC policies would be. First, he signed an agreement with Adolph Coors Co., pledging support for the controversial plan of that anti-union brewery for aid to the Latino community. He hailed the agreement as 'another bridge for the Hispanic community with corporate America'. Previously, LULAC had boycotted Coors beer in support of the national boycott of Coors organized by the labor movement. Moran announced that LULAC would not criticize US foreign policy in Central America until it completed a new two-year study. He also made it clear that LULAC would not take a militant stand against efforts by the Reagan administration to curtail bilingual education. Moran announced LULAC's new ideological direction for the 1980s in these terms: 'It's time for Hispanics to make the system work for us instead of trying to go against the system.'[15]

The shift in LULAC reflected a nationwide conservative trend among Mexican Americans and other Latinos. The fact that Reagan received from 33 percent to 52 percent of the Latino vote in his bid for re-election in 1984 speaks directly to the point.[16] The ranks of Mexican Americans in the Republican Party are increasing as a result of the party's aggressive recruitment of young middle-class leaders and its all-out effort to get the Latino vote in 1984 and 1988. In 1984 the Democrats spent approximately $120,000 to promote the Mondale-Ferraro ticket among Latino voters whereas the Republicans spent $6 million to promote Reagan and Bush among Latinos.[17]

A few ambitious Mexican American Democratic politicians or aspiring ones switched to the Republican Party in response to enticements of future elective or appointive office. Support for the Republican Party among Mexican Americans is not as strong as it is among Cuban Americans, but it is nonetheless growing.[18] This trend will no doubt continue, since President Bush appointed two Mexican Americans to cabinet positions in his administration: former New Mexico congressman Manuel Lujan as secretary of the interior, and Texas educator and scientist Lauro Cavazos as secretary of education. They were the first Mexican Americans to serve in the cabinet. The fact that they were appointed by a Republican president was not lost on Mexican American politicians and Mexican American voters. In addition, Reagan's super-patriotic propaganda themes, sure to be continued by his successors, strike a chord with many Mexican Americans.

Mexican American youth are of course not exempt from the anticommunism endemic in US society. This ideological hegemony has resulted in a deep-rooted distrust of left politics among Mexican Americans. The Communist and Socialist parties established some legitimacy in the working class between the 1920s and 1940s, but this influence was eroded during the McCarthy era. This political orientation has made it difficult for Mexican American leftists to gain a foothold in their own communities. The Chicano Movement produced two Mexican American Marxist organizations: the August Twenty-ninth Movement, which emerged out of the La Raza Unida Party Labor Committee, and the Centro de Acción Social Autónoma, or Center for Autonomous Social

Action (CASA). ATM was the first Mexican American Marxist-Leninist organization ever to develop independently of the white left. Prior to its emergence, Mexican American leftists had historically participated in the old left communist and socialist parties, albeit minimally since there were never many of them. ATM's basic objective was to create a multinational communist party and replace the old-guard Communist Party USA. ATM underwent various phases of ideological fragmentation and those members who survived eventually contributed to the creation of the League for Revolutionary Struggle.

CASA has disappeared altogether as the result of internal power struggles. Originally founded by Bert Corona to defend the rights of undocumented Mexican workers, it was taken over by more radical youth elements. The new leadership aimed to steer the Chicano Movement in the ideological direction of a revolutionary nationalism rooted in the concept of *sin fronteras,* 'without borders'. This concept defined Mexican Americans as *Mexicanos,* part of Mexico's working class. CASA pushed the issue of immigration as the focal point of political activism, but its goal of uniting Mexican American and Mexican workers never came close to realization. The efforts of its former members and other political activists to generate support for the undocumented among the majority of Mexican Americans were also unsuccessful. Divisions continue to exist among Mexican Americans over the issue of immigration and, given the high Mexican American unemployment rate, immigrants are vulnerable to the charge that the undocumented take jobs away from US workers. The support that does exist for undocumented Mexican workers has come from the more liberal Mexican American political activists and from those who fear their own loss of civil rights and job opportunities as a result of repressive anti-immigrant legislation.

The Reagan administration profited from Mexican American anticommunism in pursuing its policy of intervention in Nicaragua and El Salvador. Mexican Americans have been scarce in the ranks of the thousands who have protested against the war in Central America and against aid to the *contras*. The 'Rambo' mentality of Reagan and his foreign policy and military advisors took hold, especially among Mexican American youth. Latino soldiers, including Mexican Americans, served as advisors in El Salvador and to the *contras* in Honduras. At one point during US maneuvers in Honduras in 1985 most of the US forces were Mexican Americans from the Texas National Guard. In 1986 Governor Deukmejian approved the sending of two military police units made up of Mexican Americans and other Latinos from the California

National Guard to Honduras. A spokesman for the Guard rationalized this action, claiming that 'our people will be able to communicate with the locals.'[19]

Mexican American elected officials especially reflect this anticommunist impulse. The Hispanic Caucus in Congress, for example, never spoke out strongly against the Reagan administration on the issue of Central America. One chair of the caucus, New Mexico Rep. Bill Richardson, actually voted in favor of the $27 million in 'humanitarian aid' to the *contras* in 1985, as did two other caucus members, Manuel Lujan and Albert Bustamante. None of the Hispanic Caucus members who traveled to Nicaragua to meet with President Ortega prior to the 1985 *contra* aid debates returned with any praise for the Sandinistas. On the whole, the Hispanic Caucus continued to form part of the progressive wing in Congress, but it did not play the same role as the Black Caucus in aggressively challenging the Reagan administration on foreign policy issues. Nor did it challenge President George H. W. Bush directly. Whereas the Black Caucus spearheaded attacks on apartheid in South Africa and some of its members were actually arrested for their participation in anti-apartheid protests, no member of the Hispanic Caucus acted similarly with respect to Central America. African Americans have historically identified with other African peoples, whereas Mexican Americans and other Latinos have not had a similar tradition of solidarity with the peoples of Latin America. Immigration is the only foreign policy–related issue on which the Hispanic Caucus has opposed the Reagan administration and congressional conservatives.

Henry Cisneros, then the leading Mexican American politician in the nation, did not take any strong stand against US foreign policy in Central America. On the contrary, he was appointed by Reagan to the Kissinger Commission on Central America. As a member of that commission, he politely challenged the commission's recommendations supporting Reagan's search for a military solution. Thus, Cisneros effectively personified the dominant trends in Mexican American politics. He was a centrist in the Democratic Party and a neoliberal in ideological orientation. At the same time, he was pragmatic about the need to maintain a degree of ethnic identity to sustain his base in the Mexican American community.[20]

The conservative trend in Mexican American politics does not, however, necessarily translate into right-wing politics across the board. The shift among moderate reformist organizations such as LULAC and MALDEF from demanding federal aid to bargaining for corporate funding is nevertheless significant. These organizations have not become right-wing per se in consequence.

But they have moved to a more clearly defined centrist position. Similarly, it is not probable that Mexican Americans will shift en masse from the Democratic Party to the Republican Party. But there is little doubt that Mexican American politicians in the Democratic Party will continue to support the party's traditional centrist leadership. This was evident during the 1988 presidential primaries. Only one prominent Mexican American legislator in the California Assembly endorsed Jesse Jackson; the rest supported Dukakis. Jackson did not receive the endorsement of any other prominent Mexican American elected official in any of the southwestern states.

The fact that there was no significant visible Mexican American opposition to US foreign policy in Central America did not translate into complete support for the Reagan administration. In certain parts of the country the Sanctuary movement has received support among Mexican Americans, particularly as a result of the strong support for that movement from the more progressive sectors of the Catholic Church. As governor of New Mexico in 1986 Toney Anaya proclaimed the entire state a sanctuary for Central American refugees. Mexican American political activists in some of the Texas and Arizona border towns and in the Bay Area of Northern California also became more visible in the movement.

Despite the pro-white *Hispanic* identity-label, Mexican Americans have increasingly become victims of racism. Racist sentiments against both Mexicans and Mexican Americans over the issue of 'illegal aliens' are a reality. The Ku Klux Klan has been engaged in a racist harassment campaign against them in the recent past, and white politicians sometimes echo those attitudes. In Dallas, Texas, for example, the deputy mayor pro tem, in taking a strong stand against Mexican immigration, put forth these arguments in letters to state legislators and congressmen:

> Neighborhoods are totally being destroyed by the invasion ... your mother, grandmother, or elderly aunt, etc., who has worked hard over the years to maintain and upkeep her property ... all of a sudden her security is threatened because illegals with no moral values have moved next door to her. As a result, daily her health begins to deteriorate because she gets little or no sleep for fear of being robbed, raped, or killed.[21]

The 1984 campaign for US Senate in Texas provided yet another example of the way in which racism is directed toward Mexican Americans. Kent

Hance, one of the Democratic candidates in the primary, campaigned on the issue that Texas was threatened by the invasion of 'illegal aliens'. While ostensibly the right wing's target is the undocumented, racists in practice do not bother to distinguish between Mexican Americans and Mexican immigrants; darker-skinned Mexican Americans are especially affected by attacks on the undocumented. Such racial harassment results in a progressive political response from sectors of the Mexican American community. In Dallas, for example, the chair of the Coalition of Hispanic Organizations and the president of the Mexican American Bar Association angrily responded to the racist remarks by the deputy mayor quoted above.

These racial attacks stimulate support among Mexican Americans for coalition politics with African Americans and other people of color. Jesse Jackson received 15 percent of the Mexican American vote in California during the presidential primaries of 1984. That support increased to 36 percent of the vote in the 1988 primary. Jackson's Rainbow Coalition made attempts to increase the Mexican American and Latino presence in its ranks, and named Mario Obledo chair of the Rainbow's Board of Directors. But the Coalition remained a Black-run organization, headquartered in Chicago and far away from the political realities of the southwestern United States where most Mexican Americans reside.

The emergence of a well-defined Mexican American left politics is more problematic. Like the US left as a whole, the Mexican American left is fragmented and diffused. Anticommunism and other conservative trends in Mexican American politics obviously hinder the building of a strong left sector. The prospects for a united ideological Mexican American left are poor, but those for a popular left based in nonsectarian organizations or groups are more promising. In the San Francisco Bay Area, for example, progressive Mexican American and Latino activists are involved in coalition politics with labor, the church, gay and lesbian groups, the anti-apartheid movement, the anti-nuclear movement, the Central American solidarity movement, and the progressive sector of the Democratic Party as well as in several traditional socialist and communist parties and groups engaged in building a mass movement for peace, jobs, and justice. Mexican American activists contributed to a march and rally of 50,000 people in San Francisco in April of 1985 and 100,000 in 1986 to protest US intervention in Central America, apartheid in Africa, attacks on labor, and racial, gender, and class injustice.

The State of the Chicano Student Movement

What are the prospects for re-emergence of the Chicano student movement and of MEChA in particular as strong political forces? MEChA is all that remains of the Chicano Movement and is the only student organization visible on some campuses in the US that has direct links with the politics of the 1960s. Students for a Democratic Society, for example, ceased to exist by 1970. Progressive white and African American student organizations do exist but under new names and with no direct connection to the ideological frameworks or programmatic orientations of their predecessors. The dramatic student protests that took place in 1984 over the issue of university divestment in South Africa marked the first time that African American and white student activists engaged in political activity resembling the politics of the 1960s.

MEChA continues to promote the quest for a Chicano identity and political power for people of Mexican descent, but for the most part it has done so at a symbolic level as opposed to the practice of struggle that characterized the movement's politics in the late sixties and early seventies. Most significantly, MEChA has confined its politics to the campus, and particularly to issues related to affirmative action. Few MEChistas participate in community politics on a day-to-day basis. The Chicano Generation of the sixties has meanwhile moved on to work in a variety of political struggles, and many have dropped out of politics altogether – as has been the case with other activists of the 1960s. The term *Chicano* is not as popular among activist youth as it once was. The neo-separatist, nationalist thrust of the movement no longer rings true to the vast majority of them. As noted earlier, the politics of the 1980s, as epitomized by politicians like Cisneros, Peña, and Anaya, have forged a new political identity for the present generation of student activists. The term *Hispanic*, which has replaced *Chicano* and *Mexican American*, reflects a new political consciousness more akin to the politics of the 1930s and 1940s than to the politics of the 1960s.

Two of the most important intellectuals of the Chicano Generation, Luis Valdez and Jesús Chavarría, now argue that Mexican Americans should think of themselves as Hispanic. Chavarría, the key mover of the Santa Barbara conference and principal editor of *El Plan de Santa Barbara*, dropped out of academic life after he was denied tenure at the University of California, Santa Barbara. He later founded the magazine *Hispanic Business* and serves as its publisher. In its tenth anniversary issue, he noted with pride that *Hispanic Business* has created an entirely new, national Hispanic media audience; high-end, educated, bilingual, sophisticated about the national culture, and less and less sensitive to national origin and more and more conscious of being or becoming *Hispanic* [Chavarría's emphasis] American.[22]

Chavarría also noted that his magazine significantly contributed to the building of a US Hispanic Chamber of Commerce and through creating awareness of the 'growing clout' represented by Hispanic firms his magazine 'serves the most influential class in its market segment.'[23]

Luis Valdez has also departed from his earlier ideological framework to embrace Hispanic identity, but in somewhat different terms than Chavarría. Valdez considers his contemporary work 'assimilationist on terms that are mutually acceptable' – that is, not the terms given by the dominant white culture.[24] He sees it in positive terms as a confrontation between white European and Latin American 'melting pots'. To him, the term *Hispanic* is thus not a rejection of Mexican culture, but on the contrary legitimizes 'mestizo-ness' and 'mulatto-ness', or the multiracial and multicultural realities of Mexican Americans and other Latinos. Hispanic identity, therefore, represents in his thinking the making of a new dominant culture which is no longer based solely on Anglo-Saxon Protestant European culture.

Valdez still heads the Teatro Campesino, which he founded in the 1960s, but he has in addition recently become a successful Hollywood director. *La Bamba*, the story of rock singer Richie Valens, was a box office success. Because it was the first successful major motion picture about Mexican Americans in the history of the film industry, Valdez has opened doors in Hollywood for other Latino filmmakers. *La Bamba* has been criticized by some because it does not address the legacy of the Chicano Movement, but it did introduce the Mexican American experience in a meaningful way to the US and international public. Valdez's success and that of his Teatro, however, have forced him to accommodate the realities of working within US capitalism:

When you have an organization, and the evolution of the Teatro is an example, you must exist economically, you become involved in budgeting, in cash flow, in profit and loss, in paying wages, pensions, workmen's compensation, social security, in the very inner workings of business in America. We're a unionized theatre company. It's hard to pay union wages, and yet it's just. So it becomes a business. Even though you're not necessarily motivated by a profit motive, the business of the country forces you to concentrate on those realities.[25]

Mexican American student activism, even within MEChA, generally reflects a thrust toward assimilation and integration in the context of a mainstream politics of accommodation and the reformism of liberal capitalism. This trend was made clear at the seventh annual National Chicano Student Conference held at the University of California, Berkeley in the spring of 1986. The conference was plagued with ideological struggle between two factions of MEChA activists advocating, on the one hand, a return to the ideology of Chicano cultural nationalism as defined by *El Plan de Santa Barbara*, and on the other, an internationalist politics as espoused particularly by the League for Revolutionary Struggle (LRS). The conference was disrupted by the nationalist faction and ended on a divisive note. The overwhelming number of student activists attending the conference were not attracted by either ideological alternative. Many of them identified as Hispanics, and a few were Republicans representing Ivy League schools.

MEChA in California continued to be plagued by internal divisions exacerbated by the LRS faction's attempt to give the organization political direction. Opponents of LRS accused it of working in MEChA in order to build the party rather than to strengthen MEChA in accordance with the original nationalist ideological framework of *El Plan de Santa Barbara*. The LRS leadership denied this accusation and promoted a nationalism of its own in the pages of its newspaper, *Unity*. LRS was effective in mobilizing MEChA to participate in demonstrations around strikes by Mexican workers and issues of educational inequality. Members of the MEChA chapter at the University of California, Santa Cruz, for example, participated in the 1985–87 Watsonville Canning strike and many were arrested.[26] LRS was also instrumental in mobilizing MEChA support statewide for annual 'Spring Action' marches and rallies at the state capitol in Sacramento to demand educational equality for students of color. These marches were successful efforts at building coalitions with the Asian Pacific Student Union, the African/Black Student Statewide Alliance, and progressive white student organizations. Finally, LRS was one of the major left groups within Jesse Jackson's Rainbow Coalition and consequently was able to exert influence on MEChA's more radical members.

The influence of LRS notwithstanding, the 1989 conference commemorating the twentieth anniversary of MEChA indicated that the organization is moving towards the mainstream rather than towards radical politics. The key-note speaker and conference 'guest of honor' was Texas congressman Kika de la Garza – ironically one of the Mexican American politicians who opposed MAYO and La Raza Unida in Texas in the 1960s. An equally revealing mea-sure of MEChA's new politics was the list of sources of funding for the con-ference. Included on the list on conference benefactors were Apple Computer Corporation, MCA Corporation, Bank of America and Honda. Public agen-cies listed included the California Highway Patrol and the California Youth Authority.[27]

MEChA's dilemma is, of course, that the current political atmosphere has not been conducive to the tactics and strategies of the sixties. As long as racism remains a problem for Mexican Americans, however, some will attempt to re-vive the Chicano Movement, and the quest for a Chicano identity will remain a top priority for some in the Chicano student movement. But the complex regional nature of the Mexican American experience and their multicultural and multiracial character make it highly unlikely they will succeed in recreat-ing the Chicano Movement of the sixties.

The legacy of that movement, however, remains important to the devel-opment of future counter-hegemonic Mexican American social and political movements. Although MEChA is not today the organization it was in the 1960s and early 1970s, it symbolizes the fact that the quest for identity and power is part of a historical process of political struggle. As long as racism ex-ists, MEChA will not completely disappear. In the words of Gina Hernandez, the keynote speaker at the 1986 MEChA California conference,

> Chicanos today are not much better off than we were 30 years ago. Racist immigration policy still keeps our Mexicano brothers and sisters locked at the border; locked out from creating a better life for themselves, and for their children in a land that was once their own. ... Chicano and Mexicano workers face severe working conditions with few benefits. In the high schools Chicano youth fight against a 50% drop-out rate ... affirmative action is under attack. ... These are realities we all have to deal with, whether we call ourselves Chicano, Mexican-American, Hispanic, Latino, or whatever. ... The struggle for our educational rights is part of our struggle as a people for justice, equality, and self-determination. ... Anti-communism will not scare us away ... from standing up for what we believe in. It will not blind us and cause us to lose sight of the goals of MEChA and the struggles of

our Raza. ... The movement is not like it was in the 60s or 70s. This does not mean we will not fight as hard or aren't as committed to the struggle, but it does mean that we must go forward and not be held to the attitudes and methods of the past.[28]

Notes

1 Conversation between Gonzáles and the author at the La Raza Unida Party convention.

2 The author brought the leaders together in Tijerina's hotel room during the convention.

3 Much has been published recently about political surveillance and repression of social and political movements prior to the 1960s and during that decade and afterwards. See Robert Justin Goldstein, *Political Repression in Modern America: 1870 to the Present*, Cambridge 1978, and David J. Garrow, *The FBI and Martin Luther King, Jr.: From 'Solo' to Memphis*, New York 1981. See also Alan Theoharis, *Spying on Americans: Political Surveillance from Hoover to the Huston Plan*, Philadelphia 1978.

4 Subcommittee to Investigate the Administration of the Internal Security Act and Other Internal Security Laws, 'Extent of Subversion in the "New Left": Testimony of Robert J. Thoms', 91st Congress, Second Session, 20 January 1970.

5 Corky Gonzáles, Reies López Tijerina, Bert Corona, members of the Brown Berets and UMAS, and other Mexican American activists were included. Luis Valdez's Teatro Campesino was identified as 'a propaganda arm uniting the black and brown movement', 'Testimony of Robert J. Thoms', p. 31. See also José Angel Gutiérrez, 'Chicanos under Surveillance: 1940 to 1980', in Renato Rosaldo, ed., *Lecture Series Monograph*, vol. 2, Spring 1986, pp. 29–58.

6 Director, FBI, (100-451531) to SAC, Seattle (100-29518), 'United Mexican American Students (IS-Spanish American) July 3, 1969'.

7 Counter-intelligence work was not restricted to the FBI and other police agencies. It was an extensive network that included other federal and state agencies, the Secret Service and all branches of the US military.

8 'Chicano Informer Confesses', *El Grito Del Norte*, vol. 5, no. 2, 10 April 1972.

9 Ernesto B. Vigil, *The Crusade for Justice: Chicano Militancy and the Government's War on Dissent*, Madison, Wis. 1999.

10 Frank Gay, 'Debate About Chicano Activists' Fiery Deaths Continues', *Colorado Daily News*, 5–7 May 1989.

11 *Congressional Record*, 29 October 1971.

12 Ibid.

13 National Association of Latino Elected and Appointed Officials, *1988 National Roster of Hispanic Elected Officials*, Washington, D.C. 1989.

14 'Con Su Voto: With Your Vote', Democratic National Committee Newsletter, Summer 1984, p. 3.

15 *Wall Street Journal*, 19 March 1986, p. 54.

16 Reports of the Latino vote in the 1984 election vary. The *New York Times* estimated 33 percent vote for Reagan, while the Republican Party National Committee estimated 52 percent.

17 Federico A. Subervi-Valez, et al., 'Capturing the Hispanic Vote: Republican Political Advertising Efforts in the 1984 Presidential Elections', unpublished paper, 1985.

18 Richard Santillán, *Latinos in US Politics: 1960 to 1984*, forthcoming.

19 *Oakland Tribune*, 11 April 1986.

20 Carlos Muñoz Jr. and Charles Henry, 'Coalition Politics in San Antonio and Denver: The Cisneros and Peña Mayoral Campaigns', in Rufus Browning et al., eds, *Racial Politics in American Cities: Blacks and Latinos in the United States*, New York 1989.

21 *Dallas Morning News*, 11 February 1985.

22 Editorial, *Hispanic Business*, April 1989, p. 4.

23 Ibid.

24 Interview, Luis Valdez, 11 August 1982.

25 Ibid.

26 See Frank Bardacke, 'Watsonville: A Mexican Community on Strike', in Mike Davis and Michael Sprinker, eds, *Reshaping the US Left: Popular Struggles in the 1980s: The Year Left 3*, London 1988, for the best critical analysis of the strike.

27 MEChA, 'Celebrating Our Past: To Win Our Future', 20th Anniversary Conference, 21–22 April 1989, Los Angeles, California.

28 Proceedings, Statewide MEChA Conference, 14–15 November 1986, pp. 1–4.

Epilogue: From *Chicanismo* to Multiracial Democracy

Much has changed in the twenty years since this book was first published, and in the forty years since the Chicano Movement was born. The Chicano Movement was a product of the political and social turbulence that marked the 1960s and early 1970s, a period that saw mass civil rights struggles of people of color in conjunction with revolutions against colonialism and imperialism across Asia, Africa, and Latin America. In the US, we were initially inspired by Dr. Martin Luther King Jr, Malcolm X, Rosa Parks, César Chávez, Dolores Huerta, Corky Gonzalez, and Reies Lopez Tijerina. Third World revolutions contributed to the further development of our critical consciousness: leaders like Che, Fidel Castro, Ho Chi Minh, and Mao Zedong were influences in addition to the more immediate experiences and political traditions of Mexican American communities.

That era of revolutionary upheaval gave way to a conservative counter-revolution, built on the market-centered neoliberal restructuring that ended the postwar boom in the mid 1970s and fueled by a backlash against the gains of people of color, women, and gays and lesbians. In the post–Cold War era following the collapse of the Soviet bloc in 1989–91 the US emerged as the sole world superpower, with (officially) 737 military bases around the world. Ironically, the US military has in the process become, in effect, one of the few remaining affirmative action programs. Latino/as continue to be over-represented on the battlefield: a Latino immigrant from Guatemala, Lance

Corporal José Antonio Gutierrez, was the first casualty in the war in Iraq. In this empire's global reach, Bill Clinton, who pushed NAFTA through the US Congress, and his successor, George W. Bush, have surpassed the ambitions of the Founding Fathers, whose original goal was to build an empire in the Western Hemisphere extending from the arctic coast of North America to the tip of South America.

Globalization, with its attendant economic and social restructuring, has had profound impacts on people of Mexican decent and other Latino/as in the United States. In the 1960s there were just three visible Latino/a population groups: Mexicans, Puerto Ricans, and Cubans, with Mexicans being much the largest of the three. Today there are seventeen distinct groups within the US Latina/o populations, with new waves of immigration being driven by war (for example, US interventions in Chile, Nicaragua, El Salvador, Panama, and other countries) and economic upheaval (the result of failed 'Washington Consensus' free market economic policies throughout much of the Third World). The 1960 US Census reported that Latino/as were 3.5 percent of the US population. In 2006, the Bureau of the Census reported Latino/as had become 14.8 percent of the total U.S. population, bypassing African Americans and thus becoming the largest people-of-color population. Mexican Americans remain the majority of the 17 Latino/a population groups. The political demographics of the US have thus become much more diverse and complex.

As communities of color have grown relative to the white/Anglo population, conservative movements have emerged to preserve the structure of racial/ethnic/class/patriarchal privilege that has traditionally marked US society. These movements have mounted powerful attacks on affirmative action, multiculturalism, and immigration and undocumented immigrants. Conservatives have, for example, been able to redefine affirmative action as racism-in-reverse against whites. In 1996 in California, the state's voters – who are wealthier and whiter than the state's population as a whole – passed Proposition 209, which outlawed affirmative action in higher education and employment, leading to a drastic decline in the African American and Latino enrollment in the state's college and university systems. A year after its passage, admissions of these underrepresented groups at UC Berkeley declined by 55 percent. The school admitted 66 percent fewer blacks, 54 percent fewer Latino/as, and 61 percent fewer Native Americans. As a result of their success in California, conservatives have mounted campaigns to pass similar legislation in other states. In

Texas, the state Supreme Court in *Hopwood v. Texas* terminated affirmative action in higher education.[1] In Michigan, the courts decided in favor of a watered down higher education affirmative action that allowed for race as one of many criteria for admission. What is never acknowledged by either the liberal defenders of affirmative action or by its opponents is the historical reality that affirmative action was in fact a direct response to longstanding white racial preferences reflecting a structure of white racial privilege that has marked US society from the beginning.[2]

Even Republican President Gerald Ford defended affirmative action in an op-ed piece in the *New York Times* during debates on *Grutter v. Bollinger*, a Supreme Court case from Michigan in which the plaintiffs sought a decision similar to *Hopwood*: "Times of change are times of challenge ... already the global economy requires an unprecedented grasp of diverse viewpoints and cultural traditions. America remains a nation with have-nots as well as haves. Its government is obligated to provide for hope no less than for the common defense ... at its core, affirmative action should try to offset past injustices by fashioning a campus population more truly reflective of modern America and our hopes for the future."[3]

Meanwhile, multiculturalism and diversity have for conservatives become the new communism, to be attacked as anti-American, subversive, and divisive in nature. Latino/as have been made the central target of those who oppose diversity and the new immigrants. Samuel P. Huntington, a political scientist at Harvard, has argued in his books *The Clash of Civilizations* and *Who Are We?: The Challenges to America's National Identity* that Latino/as are the most serious threat to Eurocentric US national identity and culture.[4] In his words, "The single most immediate and most serious challenge to America's traditional identity and border security comes from the immense and continuing immigration from Latin America, especially from Mexico."[5] Anti-immigrant racial politics have resulted in a war against immigrants, especially Latino/a immigrants with Mexicans being the main targets because they are the vast majority of the undocumented.

The war is being waged by the Department of Homeland Security that was created after 9/11 by President Bush. The new department took over the responsibilities of the Immigration and Naturalization Service (INS). The enforcement duties of the INS were assigned to a division in Homeland Security called Immigration Customs Enforcement (ICE), and it has become the terrorist arm of Homeland Security. It regularly conducts raids in workplaces where immigrants are visible in the workforce, in communities where they live, and often breaks into their homes to arrest at will those they suspect are undocumented immigrants. Even immigrants with legal status in the US are often harassed, arrested, and sometimes deported without any trial. The raids have resulted in the breakup of hundreds of families. Undocumented parents have been imprisoned and deported without recourse to legal protection. Their US-born children have been left behind to fend for themselves. Many have been taken in by relatives or neighbors, but in some cases they are left homeless. In effect, it is a terrorist war against people whose only crime is trying to make an honest living by working hard for low wages.

The US–Mexico border has been a war zone since long before 9/11. Prior to the war in Iraq, the American Friends Service Committee, a Quaker human-rights organization, issued a report that documented upward of 4,600 soldiers engaged in day-to-day 'counter-drug operations' along the US–Mexico border. The Pentagon was spending $800 million a year on low-intensity warfare. Special Forces troops provided year-round training to local and state police agencies. It was President Bill Clinton who started the militarization of the border—not George W. Bush—underscoring the fact that both Democrats and Republicans have supported the building of the monstrous wall that now exists on the border. The wall has forced immigrants to attempt their entry into the United States through dangerous desert areas where walls have not yet been built, with many more hundreds of them now dying in the process from dehydration and exposure to the desert's intense heat. It has also resulted in many more Latinas becoming the victims of rape and other sexual molestations.

These 'culture wars' began as an ideological counter-offensive against more inclusive accounts of US history in schools and have expanded to include a range of issues that have served to divide the electorate and keep conservatives in power. Typical examples include the 'US English' state campaigns to promote English as the official language (and to prohibit the official use of other languages—and especially Spanish), and California's Proposition 227, passed by voters in 1998, which outlawed bilingual education in favor of the forced-assimilation policies used to absorb immigrants in the early twentieth century. In higher education, attacks on diversity have taken the form of attempts to marginalize ethnic studies programs and departments throughout the nation.

Economic globalization, failed neoliberal economic policies, and the passage of the North American Free Trade Agreement in 1993 in particular, have led to displacement of workers and farmers in Mexico and other Latin American countries. The result has been a surge of immigrants, both documented and undocumented, into the United States, and at the same time increased off shoring of factory jobs and outsourcing of other jobs. Conservatives have played on plant closures and increased immigration to whip up anti-immigrant campaigns—even as they take full advantage of immigrant labor. For example, a right-wing group calling itself the 'Save Our State' organization has embarked upon a vulgar xenophobic attack on Latino/a immigrants to 'save' California. The governor of New Mexico, Bill Richardson, a Mexican American and a 2008 presidential candidate for the Democratic Party, declared the presence of undocumented immigrants a crisis requiring emergency response. So did the governor of Arizona, Janet Napolitano, another Democrat. They both requested that President Bush send National Guard troops to protect their state's borders. California governor Arnold Schwarzenegger, a Republican, publicly expressed support for the Minute Men, a predominantly white vigilante group that patrols the US–Mexico border.

In 2006, the Republican-controlled US House of Representatives passed the Sensenbrenner bill making illegal entry into the United States a felony. This attempt to criminalize undocumented immigrants compelled millions of them to come out of the shadows throughout the nation to protest the injustice of the Sensenbrenner legislation. On 24 March, during the same month that the East Los Angeles walkouts took place in 1968, I was one of the estimated one million people who marched to protest that legislation in the largest of the numerous other marches that took place that spring that collectively totaled 5 million people. The vast majority who marched were Latino/a immigrants, and the majority of them were undocumented. Those who marched made it clear to the US Congress and the nation as a whole that they were hard-working men and women, not criminals or terrorists bent on endangering the security of the United States.

The massive protests ended with a national economic boycott on May Day (1 May) aimed at making the nation aware of the importance of undocumented immigrants to the economy of the United States. The US Senate did not attempt to pass similar Sensenbrenner legislation. Most important, the protests generated a passion for social justice throughout the nation that has not happened since the 1960s. Many of the organizers of the boycott and the protest marches were veterans of the 1960s Chicano Movement and the Farm Workers Movement.

Mexican Americans have made considerable gains in the forty years since the student 'blow-outs' in Los Angeles in 1968. The Chicano Movement opened doors of equal opportunity in higher education and employment. The Chicano student movement in particular made possible the creation of Chicano and Chicana Studies in institutions of higher education, leading to the emergence of a critical mass of Mexican American and other Latino intellectuals in the academy. They have produced hundreds of scholarly books on every aspect of the Mexican American experience. Chicano Studies, as is true of all the other ethnic studies curricula, has made the learning experience meaningful to undergraduates of all races and ethnicities and has helped prepare them to understand the realities and complexities of our multiracial and multicultural nation.

The movement also produced artists, poets, dramatic artists, fiction writers, and filmmakers. Mexican Americans in the professional sector dramatically increased – for example, among public school teachers, social workers, health workers, and in business and corporations. The movement also increased Latino participation in the Democratic and Republican parties. The fact that there are more Mexican Americans serving in local governments, state legislatures, and in the US Congress can be directly attributed to the Chicano Movement because it awakened the leadership of the Democratic and Republic parties to the need to recruit Mexican Americans. Mexican American women have dramatically emerged to become visible leaders at the national, state, and local levels. Most importantly, they are now at the forefront with men in the struggles for social justice and peace. Mexican Americans, as is the case with all Latino/as, have indeed come a long way since the 1960s. But they still have a long way to go as they remain underrepresented in the dominant political, social, and economic institutions of our nation.

The Chicano Movement was a product of the turbulent political times that characterized the late twentieth century. As was the case for the other civil rights movements created and organized by people of color, the Chicano Movement emerged to challenge white supremacy and racial oppression, evolving from a politics of integration into the mainstream of society to a politics of racial and ethnic nationalism centered on rediscovery of and reconnection to their respective ancestral roots in the America's and the Third World.

The Chicano Movement evolved into a quest for identity centered on the Mexican indigenous roots of Mexican culture. It was a movement to decolonize the Mexican American mind from the baggage of assimilation and the inferiority complex that had resulted from centuries of European colonization in Mexico and the US. The politics of Chicano identity, notwithstanding its patriarchal character, were progressive for their time: they generated self-esteem and ethnic pride and helped create a sense of empowerment never before felt by Mexican Americans, especially the youth.

But Chicano cultural nationalism, as was also the case for Black nationalism, Asian, and American Indian nationalism, did not result in a revolutionary politics that gripped the masses of people of color. The Chicano Movement, for example, reached a large portion of Mexican American youth, primarily the college student sector. The movement developed mass support for its civil rights agenda, but Chicano identity and its cultural nationalist ideology was never adopted by the majority of Mexican Americans. This was especially true for Mexican immigrants because immigrants don't come to the United States in search of identity. They know they are Mexican, and they come only to find work. Research on ethnic identification conducted over the years since the 1960s indicates that the majority have identified and continue to identify as Mexican Americans or Mexicans, with Hispanic becoming prominent in the 1980s. According to the Latino National Survey, *Latino* has more recently emerged along side of *Hispanic* as the ethnic identity preferred by the majority of Mexican Americans in a pan-ethnic context.[6]

Chicano nationalism thus not only failed to unite all Mexican Americans, but it was also not conducive to the development of a united front of progressive people of color. Although many symbolic alliances took place, especially between African Americans and Mexican Americans, such alliances seldom led to the development of effective and viable coalitions. For the most part, Black and Chicano nationalism fostered antagonisms and tensions between the two communities. The major reason for this was that each of the movements remained focused on their own constituencies. One of the popular slogans of the Chicano Movement, for example, was 'mi raza primero', or 'my people first'. On college campuses and in communities across the country Blacks and Chicano/as were often pitted against each other over 'limited' resources – fighting over the crumbs made available by white power structures.

The politics of identity ironically have become extremely useful for those who rule. President Bush claims that he is committed to diversity—and in fact he has learned to play the racial and ethnic identity game extremely well. He has appointed Blacks, Latinos, and Asians to his administration, and some of them have become powerful members of his inner circle. African American Condoleeza Rice and Mexican American Alberto Gonzalez became key parts of the Bush imperial machinery. Gonzalez, whose origins are rooted in the poor working immigrant class of south Texas, was one of the leading architects of the Patriot Act and the lawyer who advised Bush that he could order the torturing of suspected terrorists in Iraq and elsewhere.

Diversity has become a profit-making tool for corporations as well. More people of color are featured in television commercials and newspaper ads selling their products. Latino and other entrepreneurs of color often use diversity to maximize their economic opportunities in the capitalist framework as opposed to directly contributing to reducing poverty in communities. The most vulgar example is Cinco de Mayo, when Mexican beer and liquor, primarily tequila, commercials are constantly aired on radio and television and such ads appear prominently in the printed media. They contribute to the perpetuation of alchoholism among Latinos, one of the major health problems in Latino communities.

The civil rights movements of the 1960s contributed to the growth of the Black and Latino middle class, but they were not able to reduce the gap between the rich and the poor. That gap is wider today that it was in the 1960s. The rich have gotten richer and the poor poorer – a trend apparent among whites as well. In the case of Mexican Americans, the politics of identity have not resulted in the fundamental restructuring of dominant social, political, and economic institutions. Nor have they resulted in racial and ethnic equality for Mexican Americans. To the contrary, identity politics have been used to maintain the political and economic status quo and to perpetuate the dominant social order. Those politics have bred ethnic interest group politics that hinder the development of viable and effective people of color coalitions that can promote the collective good of those communities.

As long as white supremacy continues to define their fortunes, Mexican Americans and other people of color must continue to maintain the uniqueness of their respective identities and cultures. The struggle for the decolonization of the mind started by the Chicano Movement must continue to be waged. But radical racial and ethnic nationalism or mainstream interest group ethnic politics must not be the major focus of the present day struggles for civil and human rights.

The challenge for the twenty-first century is to develop political strategies that can lead to the unification of not only a large sector of the Latino population, but other people of color and progressive whites, on the common ground of commitment to social justice and peace here and abroad. Those strategies cannot be implemented within the existing Democratic Party. As those of us who created La Raza Unida Party learned, there is no real difference between the Democrats and the Republicans. They are equally committed to corporate power and promoting domestic and international policies that have enabled US multinational corporatons to dominate the global economy. They are both instruments of those who own the means production and an economic system geared to maximizing profits at the expense of human needs. We need a new movement that can lead the nation toward the building of an authentic multiracial democracy committed to meeting the human needs of the society. This new movement, however, must be based on new ideas that correspond to the realities of the twenty-first century. It cannot be based on the ideas of nineteenth-century Marxism. The polemical language and slogans emanating from those ideas will not take root among our communities today – and in fact haven't since the class struggles of the 1930s.

As the largest population of color in the nation, Latino/as must play a central role in the development of the new movement. The lessons of the Chicano Movement must be learned well so that the mistakes made by my generation of activists will not be repeated. The first lesson is that the struggle against racial and ethnic oppression cannot be the only goal of the new movement as it was for the Chicano Movement and the other civil rights movements of the 1960s. That struggle must be connected to struggles against class, gender, and sexuality oppression as well.

Although the majority of the leaders and the rank and file of the Chicano Movement were from the working class, we did not have a collective class-consciousness that allowed us to understand the historical role of capitalism in the colonization and oppression of Mexican Americans and other people of color. The new movement for multiracial democracy must have a focus on the poor and working class, including immigrant workers. It must be part and parcel of the trade union movement. It must lead the war against poverty and corporate power. And it must lead the struggle And it must lead the struggle against the millitary-industrial complex that is responsible for the militarization of our society.

In addition to race and class, the new movement must also incorporate gender. The Chicano Movement was patriarchal, as was the case with all the movements of the 1960s, inasmuch as it was the product of young men and

women who were products of the patriarchy inherent in Mexican culture and
the dominant US eurocentric culture. The leadership of the new movement
must have both male and female leadership. Mexican American women and
other Latinas have emerged as visible leaders in academia, electoral politics,
and in community organizations and have become a powerful voice for social
justice and peace in the US and throughout the Americas.

And last but not least, an acceptance of diversity in sexuality must also be
incorporated by the new movement. It is difficult to know how many Chicano
gays and Chicana lesbians were involved in the Chicano Movement. Like sexism, homophobia also permeated the movement, and no doubt it kept gays
and lesbians who were in the movement in the closet for fear of the consequences of coming out. Historian Deena J. Gonzalez points out that even
among Chicana academic feminists, coming out had serious consequences.[7]

The struggle for an authentic multiracial democracy across the nation must
include all progressive people of color and whites who remain outside the corridors of power. But the fact that Latino/as are the majority of people of color
in California and have become the majority community of color in other states
of the nation does not mean they will automatically become the leading force
in the building of that democracy.

Diversity is also a reality within the Latino/a population. We may share
some cultural traditions and histories, but each of the seventeen distinct
Latino/a groups within the Latino population has its own unique cultural
identity. There is also diversity, as there is among all racial and ethnic groups,
in political ideologies and values. There are conservatives and liberals, and,
thank God, there are some revolutionaries as well.

A new Latino/a leadership must emerge to take on the responsibility
of forging a new politics that goes beyond the indigenous identity that the
Chicano Movement promoted. Latino/as have historically been multicultural,
multiethnic, and multiracial peoples throughout the Americas, including the
United States. Mexicans, for example, in addition to being a *mestizo* people
of Spanish and indigenous roots, have also had other roots; African, Asian,
Middle Eastern, and other European roots beyond Spanish. The African root
was planted by the thousands of African slaves who were taken to Mexico
by the Spaniards. There were more Africans in Mexico in the 1500s than
there were Europeans. The first slave rebellion in the Americas took place in
Veracruz, Mexico. A slave by the name of Yanga organized a guerrilla army
that defeated the Spanish forces sent to capture them. African Mexicans

(Afro-Mestizos) played important roles in the 1810 revolutionary war for Mexican Independence from Spain. One of the generals of the Mexican revolutionary army was an Afro-Mestizo by the name of Vincente Guerrero, who became president of Mexico after the revolution and whose first major official act was to outlaw slavery. Mexico thus became the first nation in the Americas to do so.[8]

The Asian root of Mexican culture was planted by the Pilipino slaves taken to Mexico by the Spanish. That root was expanded by the Chinese and other Asians who fled the United States as a result of the Asian exclusion acts passed by the US Congress in the 1920s. The Middle Eastern roots were planted by the Arabs and Jews who came with the Spanish conquistadores and later as postcolonial immigrants. The European root was expanded when Irish, Italians, Germans, and others emigrated to Mexico during the late 1800s and 1900s.

Latinos in the United States thus represent a complex identity as a people of color. In a very real sense, they represent all the racial and ethnic groups in the nation. As part of the largest and fastest growing racial/ethnic population in the US, Latino/a activists committed to social justice and peace have a major responsibility to play a central role in the struggle for the building of an authentic multiracial democracy – in particular, a central leadership role in the building of bridges between the different racial and ethnic groups in the nation. Especially important is the building of "Black and Brown" unity because African Americans and Latino/a Americans are the two largest populations of color in the United States and because Latino/as are also part of the African Diaspora in the Americas.

The task will require a new vision of democracy that must include people of all colors. We are not islands unto ourselves. Latino/a liberation is not possible without making possible the liberation of people of all colors, including the millions of whites who are not part of the structure of power. Whatever new vision emerges, it must be revolutionary in nature. It must radically deviate from the limited democracy that prevails today and make possible the transformation of our nation into one that promotes social and economic justice and peace and not war and destruction throughout the world. This vision cannot take root overnight. But it must be planted. The most important lesson I have learned in the forty years that I have been marching for freedom and peace is that life is struggle, and struggle is life. What's most important, however, is to always know that victory is in the struggle!

Notes

1 In 2003 the US Supreme Court overturned the *Hopwood* decision in *Grutter v. Bollinger.*

2 For an account of the recent history of white racial privilege, see Ira Katznelson, *When Affirmative Action Was White: A History of Racial Inequality in Twentieth-Century America,* New York 2005.

3 *New York Times,* 8 August 1999.

4 Samuel P. Huntington, *The Clash of Civilizations,* New York 1996; a second edition targeting Muslims appeared in 2002; *Who Are We? Challenges to America's National Identity,* New York 2004.

5 Samuel P. Huntington, 'The Hispanic Challenge', *Foreign Policy,* March/April 2004, p. 30.

6 More information on the Latino National Survey is available at http://depts.washington.edu/uwiser/LNS.shtml.

7 See her article 'Speaking Secrets: Living Chicana Theory' in Carla Trujillo, ed., *Living Chicana Theory,* Berkeley 1998.

8 See Theodore G. Vincent, *The Legacy of Vicente Guerrero, Mexico's First Black Indian President,* Gainesville, Fl. 2001.

Appendix: El Plan de Santa Barbara

Manifesto

For all peoples, as with individuals, the time comes when they must reckon with their history. For the Chicano the present is a time of renaissance, of *renacimiento*. Our people and our community, *el Barrio* and *la colonia*, are expressing a new consciousness and a new resolve. Recognizing the historical tasks confronting our people and fully aware of the cost of human progress, we pledge our will to move. We will move forward toward our destiny as a people. We will move against those forces which have denied us freedom of expression and human dignity. Throughout history the quest for cultural expression and freedom has taken the form of a struggle. Our struggle, tempered by the lessons of the American past, is an historical reality.

For decades Mexican people in the United States struggled to realize the 'American Dream'. And some – a few – have. But the cost, the ultimate cost of assimilation, required turning away from *el Barrio* and *la colonia*. In the meantime, due to the racist structure of this society, to our essentially different life style, and to the socio-economic functions assigned to our community by Anglo-American society – as suppliers of cheap labor and a dumping ground for the small-time capitalist entrepreneur – the *Barrio* and *colonia* remained exploited, impoverished, and marginal.

As a result, the self-determination of our community is now the only acceptable mandate for social and political action; it is the essence of Chicano commitment. Culturally, the word *Chicano*, in the past a pejorative and class-bound adjective, has now become the root idea of a new cultural identity for our people. It also reveals a growing solidarity and the development of a common social praxis. The widespread use of the term *Chicano* today signals a rebirth of pride and confidence. *Chicanismo* simply embodies an ancient truth: that man is never closer to his true self as when he is close to his community.

Chicanismo draws its faith and strength from two main sources: from the just struggle of our people and from an objective analysis of our community's strategic needs. We recognize that without a strategic use of education, an education that places value on what we value, we will not realize our destiny. Chicanos recognize the central importance of institutions of higher learning to modern progress, in this case, to

the development of our community. But we go further: we believe that higher education must contribute to the information of a complete man who truly values life and
freedom.

The destiny of our people will be fulfilled. To that end, we pledge our efforts and
take as our credo what José Vasconcelos once said at a time of crisis and hope: 'At this
moment we do not come to work for the university, but to demand that the university
work for our people.'

Political Action

Introduction

For the Movement, political action essentially means influencing the decision-making process of those institutions which affect Chicanos, the university, community
organizations, and non-community institutions. Political action encompasses three
elements which function in a progression: political consciousness, political mobilization, and tactics. Each part breaks down into further subdivisions. Before continuing
with specific discussions of these three categories, a brief historical analysis must be
formulated.

Historical Perspective

The political activity of the Chicano Movement at colleges and universities to date has
been specifically directed toward establishing Chicano student organizations (UMAS,
MAYA, MASC, MEChA, etc.) and institutionalizing Chicano Studies programs. A
variety of organizational forms and tactics have characterized these student organizations.

One of the major factors which led to political awareness in the 60s was the clash
between Anglo-American educational institutions and Chicanos who maintained
their cultural identity. Another factor was the increasing number of Chicano students
who became aware of the extent to which colonial conditions characterized their communities. The result of this domestic colonialism is that the *barrios* and *colonias* are
dependent communities with no institutional power base of their own. Historically,
Chicanos have been prevented from establishing a power base and significantly influencing decision-making. Within the last decade, a limited degree of progress has
taken place in securing a base of power within educational institutions.

Other factors which affected the political awareness of the Chicano youth were:
the heritage of Chicano youth movements of the 30s and 40s; the failures of Chicano
political efforts of the 40s and 50s; the bankruptcy of Mexican-American pseudo-
political associations, and the disillusionment of Chicano participants in the Kennedy
campaigns. Among the strongest influences on Chicano youth today have been the
National Farm Workers Association, the Crusade for Justice, and the Alianza Federal

de Pueblos Libres. The Civil Rights, the Black Power, and the Anti-war movements were other influences.

As political consciousness increased, there occurred simultaneously a renewed cultural awareness which, along with social and economic factors, led to the proliferation of Chicano youth organizations. By the mid 1960s, MASC, MAYA, UMAS, La Vida Nueva, and MEChA appeared on campus, while the Brown Berets, Black Berets, ALMA, and La Junta organized in the *barrios* and *colonias*. These groups differed from one another depending on local conditions, and their varying state of political development. Despite differences in name and organizational experience, a basic unity evolved.

These groups have had a significant impact on the awareness of large numbers of people, both Chicano and non-Chicano. Within the communities, some public agencies have been sensitized, and others have been exposed. On campuses, articulation of demands and related political efforts have dramatized NUESTRA CAUSA. Concrete results are visible in both the increased number of Chicano students on campuses and the establishment of corresponding supportive services. The institutionalization of Chicano Studies marks the present stage of activity; the next stage will involve the strategic application of university and college resources to the community. One immediate result will be the elimination of the artificial distinctions which exist between the students and the community. Rather than being its victims, the community will benefit from the resources of the institutions of higher learning.

Political Consciousness
Commitment to the struggle for Chicano liberation is the operative definition of the ideology used here. *Chicanismo* involves a crucial distinction in political consciousness between a Mexican American and a Chicano mentality. The Mexican American is a person who lacks respect for his cultural and ethnic heritage. Unsure of himself, he seeks assimilation as a way out of his 'degraded' social status. Consequently, he remains politically ineffective. In contrast, *Chicanismo* reflects self-respect and pride in one's ethnic and cultural background. Thus, the Chicano acts with confidence and with a range of alternatives in the political world. He is capable of developing an effective ideology through action.

Mexican Americans must be viewed as potential Chicanos. *Chicanismo* is flexible enough to relate to the varying levels of consciousness within La Raza. Regional variations must always be kept in mind as well as the different levels of development, composition, maturity, achievement, and experience in political action. Cultural nationalism is a means of total Chicano liberation.

There are definite advantages to cultural nationalism, but no inherent limitations. A Chicano ideology, especially as it involves cultural nationalism, should be positively phrased in the form of propositions to the Movement. *Chicanismo* is a concept that integrates self-awareness with cultural identity, a necessary step in developing political consciousness. As such, it serves as a basis for political action, flexible enough to include the possibility of coalitions. The related concept of La Raza provides an internationalist scope of *Chicanismo*, and La Raza Cósmica furnishes a philosophical precedent. Within this framework, the Third World Concept merits consideration.

Political Mobilization

Political mobilization is directly dependent on political consciousness. As political consciousness develops, the potential for political action increases.

The Chicano student organization in institutions of higher learning is central to all effective political mobilization. Effective mobilization presupposes precise definition of political goals and of the tactical interrelationships of roles. Political goals in any given situation must encompass the totality of Chicano interests in higher education. The differentiation of roles required by a given situation must be defined on the basis of mutual accountability and equal sharing of responsibility. Furthermore, the mobilization of community support not only legitimizes the activities of Chicano student organizations but also maximizes political power. The principle of solidarity is axiomatic in all aspects of political action.

Since the movement is definitely of national significance and scope, all student organizations should adopt one identical name throughout the state and eventually the nation to characterize the common struggle of La Raza de Aztlán. The net gain is a step toward greater national unity which enhances the power in mobilizing local campus organizations.

When advantageous, political coalitions and alliances with non-Chicano groups may be considered. A careful analysis must precede the decision to enter into a coalition. One significant factor is the community's attitude towards coalitions. Another factor is the formulation of a mechanism for the distribution of power that ensures maximum participation in decision making: i.e., formulation of demands and planning of tactics. When no longer politically advantageous, Chicano participation in the coalition ends.

Campus Organizing: Notes on MEChA

Introduction

MEChA is a first step to tying the student groups throughout the Southwest into a vibrant and responsive network of activists who will respond as a unit to oppression and racism and will work in harmony when initiating and carrying out campaigns of liberation for our people.

As of present, wherever one travels throughout the Southwest, one finds that there are different levels of awareness on different campuses. The student movement is to a large degree a political movement and as such must not elicit from our people the negative responses that we have experienced so often in the past in relation to politics, and often with good reason. To this end, then, we must re-define politics for our people to be a means of liberation. The political sophistication of our Raza must be raised so that they do not fall prey to apologists and *vendidos* whose whole interest is their personal career or fortune. In addition, the student movement is more than a political movement, it is cultural and social as well. The spirit of MEChA must be one of 'hermandad' and cultural awareness. The ethic of profit and competition, of greed and intolerance, which the Anglo society offers must be replaced by our ancestral communalism and love for beauty and justice. MEChA must bring to the mind of every young Chicano that the liberation of his people from prejudice and oppression is in his hands and this responsibility is greater than personal achievement and more meaningful than degrees, especially if they are earned at the expense of his identity and cultural integrity.

MEChA, then, is more than a name; it is a spirit of unity, of brotherhood, and a resolve to undertake a struggle for liberation in a society where justice is but a word. MEChA is a means to an end.

Function of MEChA – To the Student

To socialize and politicize Chicano students on their particular campus to the ideals of the movement. It is important that every Chicano student on campus be made to feel that he has a place on that campus and that he has a feeling of *familia* with his Chicano brothers. Therefore, the organization in its flurry of activities and projects must not forget or overlook the human factors of friendship, understanding, trust, etc. As well as stimulating *hermandad*, this approach can also be looked at in more pragmatic terms. If enough trust, friendship, and understanding are generated, then loyalty and support can be relied upon when a crisis faces the group or community. This attitude must not merely provide a social club atmosphere but the strengths, weaknesses, and talents of each member should be known so that they may be utilized to the greatest advantage. Know one another. Part of the reason that students will come to the organization is in search of self-fulfillment. Give that individual the opportunity to show what he can do. Although the Movement stresses collective behavior, it is important that the individual be recognized and given credit for his efforts. When people who work in close association know one another well, it is more conducive to self-criticism and re-evaluation, and this every MEChA person must be willing to submit to. Periodic self-criticism often eliminates static cycles of unproductive behavior. It is an opportunity for fresh approaches to old problems to be surfaced and aired; it gives new leadership a chance to emerge; and this must be recognized as a vital part of MEChA. MEChA can be considered a training ground for leadership, and as such no one member or group of members should dominate the leadership positions for long periods of time. This tends to take care of itself considering the transitory nature of students.

Recruitment and Education

Action is the best organizer. During and immediately following direct action of any type – demonstrations, marches, rallies, or even symposiums and speeches – new faces will often surface and this is where much of the recruiting should be done. New members should be made to feel that they are part of the group immediately and not that they have to go through a period of warming up to the old membership. Each new member must be given a responsibility as soon as possible and fitted into the scheme of things according to his or her best talents and interests.

Since the college student is constantly faced with the responsibility of raising funds for the movement, whether it be for legal defense, the grape boycott, or whatever reason, this is an excellent opportunity for internal education. Fund-raising events should always be educational. If the event is a symposium or speech or debate, it is usually an excellent opportunity to spread the Chicano Liberation Movement philosophy. If the event is a *pachanga* or *tardeada* or *baile*, this provides an opportunity to practice and teach the culture in all its facets. In addition, each MEChA chapter should establish and maintain an extensive library of Chicano materials so that the membership has ready access to material which will help them understand their people and their problems. General meetings should be educational. The last segment of each regular meeting can be used to discuss ideological or philosophical differences, or some event in the Chicano's history. It should be kept in mind that there will always be different levels of awareness within the group due to the individual's background or exposure to the movement. This must be taken into consideration so as not to alienate members before they have had a chance to listen to the arguments for liberation.

The best educational device is being in the *Barrio* as often as possible. More often than not the members of MEChA will be products of the *Barrio*; but many have lost contact with their former surroundings, and this tie must be re-established if MEChA is to organize and work for La Raza.

The following things should be kept in mind in order to develop group cohesiveness: 1) know the talents and abilities of each member; 2) every member must be given a responsibility, and recognition should be given to their efforts; 3) if mistakes are made, they should become learning experiences for the whole group and not merely excuses for ostracizing individual members; 4) since many people come to MEChA seeking self-fulfillment, they must be given the opportunity to develop a positive self-image as a Chicano; 5) every opportunity must be seized to educate the student to the Chicano philosophy, culture, and history; 6) of great importance is that a personal and human interaction exist between members of the organization so that such things as personality clashes, competition, ego-trips, subterfuge, infiltration, provocateurs, cliques, and mistrust do not impede the cohesion and effectiveness of the group. Above all the feeling of *hermandad* must prevail so that the organization is more to the members than just a club or clique. MEChA must be a learning and fulfilling experience that develops dedication and commitment.

A delicate but essential question is discipline. Discipline is important to an organization such as MEChA because many may suffer from the indiscretion of a few. Because of the reaction of the general population to the demands of the Chicano, one can always expect some retribution or retaliation for gains made by the Chicano, be it in the form of legal action or merely economic sanction on the campus. Therefore, it becomes essential that each member pull his load and that no one be allowed to be dead weight. *Carga floja* is dangerous, and if not brought up to par, must be cut loose. The best discipline comes from mutual respect, and, therefore, the leaders of the group must enjoy and give this respect. The manner of enforcing discipline, however, should be left up to the group and the particular situation.

Planning and Strategy

Actions of the group must be coordinate in such a way that everyone knows exactly what he is supposed to do. This requires that at least rudimentary organizational methods and strategy be taught to the group. Confusion is avoided if the plans and strategies are clearly stated to all. The objective must be clear to the group at all times, especially during confrontations and negotiations. There should be alternate plans for reaching the objectives, and these should also be explained to the group so that it is not felt that a reversal of position or capitulation has been carried out without their approval. The short, as well as the long, range value and effects of all actions should be considered before action is taken. This assumes that there is sufficient time to plan and carefully map out actions, which brings up another point: don't be caught off guard, don't be forced to act out of haste; choose your own battleground and your own time schedule when possible. Know your power base and develop it. A student group is more effective if it can claim the support of the community and support on the campus itself from other sectors than the student population.

The Function of MEChA – To the Campus Community

Other students can be important to MEChA in supportive roles; hence, the question of coalitions. Although it is understood and quite obvious that the viability and amenability of coalition varies from campus to campus, some guidelines might be kept in mind. These questions should be asked before entering into any binding agreement. Is it beneficial to tie oneself to another group in coalition which will carry one into conflicts for which one is ill-prepared or involve one with issues on which one is ill-advised? Can one safely go into a coalition where one group is markedly stronger than another? Does MEChA have an equal voice in leadership and planning in the coalition group? Is it perhaps better to enter into a loose alliance for a given issue? How does the leadership of each group view coalitions? How does the membership? Can MEChA hold up its end of the bargain? Will MEChA carry dead weight in a coalition? All of these and many more questions must be asked and answered before one can safely say that he will benefit from and contribute to a strong coalition effort.

Supportive groups. When moving on campus it is often well-advised to have groups who are willing to act in supportive roles. For example, there are usually any number of faculty members who are sympathetic, but limited as to the number of activities they will engage in. These faculty members often serve on academic councils and senates and can be instrumental in academic policy. They also provide another channel to the academic power structure and can be used as leverage in negotiation. However, these groups are only as responsive as the ties with them are nurtured. This does not mean, compromise MEChA's integrity; it merely means laying good groundwork before an issue is brought up, touching bases with your allies before hand.

Sympathetic administrators. This is a delicate area since administrators are most interested in not jeopardizing their positions and often will try to act as buffers or liaison between the administration and the student group. In the case of Chicano administrators, it should not a priori be assumed that because he is Raza he is to be blindly trusted. If he is not known to the membership, he must be given a chance to prove his allegiance to La Causa. As such, he should be the Chicano's man in the power structure instead of the administration's Mexican-American. It is from the administrator that information can be obtained as to the actual feasibility of demands or programs to go beyond the platitudes and pleas of unreasonableness with which the administration usually answers proposals and demands. The words of the administrator should never be the deciding factor in students' actions. The students must at all times make their own decisions. It is very human for people to establish self-interest. Therefore, students must constantly remind the Chicano administrators and faculty where their loyalty and allegiance lie. It is very easy for administrators to begin looking for promotions just as it is very natural for faculty members to seek positions of academic prominence.

In short, it is the students who must keep after Chicano and non-Chicano administrators and faculty to see that they do not compromise the position of the student and the community. By the same token, it is the student who must come to the support of these individuals if they are threatened for their support of the students. Students must be careful not to become a political lever for others.

Function of MEChA – Education

It is a fact that the Chicano has not often enough written his own history, his own anthropology, his own sociology, his own literature. He must do this if he is to survive as a cultural entity in this melting pot society which seeks to dilute varied cultures into a grey upon grey pseudo-culture of technology and materialism. The Chicano student is doing most of the work in the establishment of study programs, centers, curriculum development, entrance programs to get more Chicanos into college. This is good and must continue, but students must be careful not to be co-opted in their fervor for establishing relevance on the campus. Much of what is being offered by college systems and administrators is too little too late. MEChA must not compromise programs and curriculum which are essential for the total education of the Chicano for the sake of expediency. The students must not become so engrossed in programs and centers created along established academic guidelines that they forget the needs of the people which these institutions are meant to serve. To this end, *Barrio* input must always be given full and open hearing when designing these programs, when creating them and in running them. The jobs created by these projects must be filled by competent Chicanos, not only the Chicano who has the traditional credentials required for the position, but one who has the credentials of the Raza. Too often in the past the dedicated pushed for a program only to have a *vendido* sharp-talker come in and take over and start working for his Anglo administrator. Therefore, students must demand a say in the recruitment and selections of all directors and assistant directors of student-initiated programs. To further insure strong if not complete control of the direction and running of programs, all advisory and steering committees should have both student and community components as well as sympathetic Chicano faculty as members.

Tying the campus to the *Barrio*. The colleges and universities in the past have existed in an aura of omnipotence and infallibility. It is time that they be made responsible and responsive to the communities in which they are located or whose members they serve. As has already been mentioned, community members should serve on all programs related to Chicano interests. In addition to this, all attempts must be made to take the college and university to the *Barrio*, whether it be in form of classes giving college credit or community centers financed by the school for the use of community organizations and groups. Also, the *Barrio* must be brought to the campus, whether it be for special programs or ongoing services which the school provides for the people of the *Barrio*. The idea must be made clear to the people of the *Barrio* that they own the schools and the schools and all their resources are at their disposal. The student group must utilize the resources open to the school for the benefit of the *Barrio* at every opportunity. This can be done by hiring more Chicanos to work as academic and non-academic personnel on the campus; this often requires exposure of racist hiring practices now in operation in many college and universities. When functions, social or otherwise, are held in the *Barrio* under the sponsorship of the college and university, monies should be spent in the *Barrio*. This applies to hiring Chicano contractors to build on campus, etc. Many colleges and universities have publishing operations which could be forced to accept *Barrio* works for publication. Many other things could be considered in using the resources of the school to the *Barrio*. There are possibilities for using the physical plant and facilities not mentioned here, but this is an area which has great potential.

MEChA in the *Barrio*

Most colleges in the Southwest are located near or in the same town as a *Barrio*. Therefore, it is the responsibility of MEChA members to establish close working relationships with organizations in that *Barrio*. The MEChA people must be able to take the pulse of the *Barrio* and be able to respond to it. However, MEChA must be careful not to overstep its authority or duplicate the efforts of another organization already in the *Barrio*. MEChA must be able to relate to all segments of the *Barrio*, from the middle-class assimilationists to the batos locos.

Obviously, every *Barrio* has its particular needs, and MEChA people must determine with the help of those in the *Barrio* where they can be most effective. There are, however, some general areas which MEChA can involve itself. Some of these are: 1) policing social and governmental agencies to make them more responsive in a humane and dignified way to the people of the *Barrio*; 2) carrying out research on the economic and credit policies of merchants in the *Barrio* and exposing fraudulent and exorbitant establishments; 3) speaking and communicating with junior high and other high school students, helping with their projects, teaching them organizational techniques, supporting their actions; 4) spreading the message of the movement by any media available – this means speaking, radio, television, local newspaper, underground papers, posters, art, theatres; in short, spreading propaganda of the Movement; 5) exposing discrimination in hiring and renting practices and many other areas which the student because of his mobility, his articulation, and his vigor should take as his responsibility. It may mean at times having to work in conjunction with other organizations. If this is the case and the project is one begun by the other organization, realize that MEChA is there as a supporter and should accept the direction of the group involved. Do not let loyalty to an organization cloud responsibility to a greater force – *la Causa*.

Working in the *Barrio* is an honor, but is also a right because we come from these people, and, as such, mutual respect between the *Barrio* and the college group should be the rule. Understand at the same time, however, that there will initially be mistrust and often envy on the part of some in the *Barrio* for the college student. This mistrust must be broken down by a demonstration of affection for the *Barrio* and La Raza through hard work and dedication. If the approach is one of a dilettante or of a Peace Corps volunteer, the people will know it and react accordingly. If it is merely a cathartic experience to work among the unfortunate in the *Barrio* – stay out.

Of the community, for the community. *Por la Raza habla el espiritú.*

Rebecca Muñoz of Arizona and Félix Gutiérrez, editor of *The Mexican Voice*, Los Angeles, 1941.

March 1968: striking Mexican American students in Los Angeles meet with presidential candidate Robert F. Kennedy at Kennedy's request.

YMCA Older Mexican Boys Camp, Camp Arbolado, California, summer 1941. The names of leaders and some of the boys were inked in by Félix Gutiérrez, who labeled himself 'Yahoodi' (center, second row).

The Los Angeles student 'blowouts', March 1968: striking Mexican American students rally outside Lincoln High School.
Photo by Raúl Ruiz

The Los Angeles high school strike: students from Lincoln High School march on the Board of Education offices.

Striking students outside Lincoln High School.

Photograph by Raúl Ruiz

Striking students at Belmont High School.

Photograph by Raúl Ruiz

UMAS activist Monte Perez speaking to striking students across the street from Roosevelt High School..

The Los Angeles 'blow-outs', March 1968: students demonstrate in front of the Board of Education.

VIVA
LA
RAZA

EDUCATION
NOT
CONCENTRATION
CAMPS

UMAS activist Francisco Martinez speaks to striking Los Angeles students across the street from Garfield High School.

Corky Gonzáles leads a protest march through downtown Denver during the 1969 Chicano Youth Liberation Conference.

Brown Beret contingent marching at the Chicano Moratorium Against the War in Vietnam, 29 August 1970.

MEChA contingent at the Chicano Moratorium.

The Chicano Moratorium marches through East Los Angeles..

Photograph by Gilbert Cárdenas

Brown Berets stand at attention at a protest march in Los Angeles, 1970.

Photograph courtesy The Larry Trujillo Collection

José Angel Gutiérrez, Reies López Tijerina, and Corky Gonzáles in a rare display of unity at the 1972 La Raza Unida Party national convention.

Police confront students in front of Sather Gate during the Third World Strike at the University of California, Berkeley, 1969.

Index

Printed in the United States
By Bookmasters